HERMENEUTIC PHENOMENOLOGY IN EDUCATION

PRACTICE OF RESEARCH METHOD
Volume 4

Series Editor
Wolff-Michael Roth, *University of Victoria, Canada*

Scope

Research methods and research methodology are at the heart of the human endeavors that produce knowledge. Research methods and research methodology are central aspects of the distinction between folk knowledge and the disciplined way in which disciplinary forms of knowledge are produced. However, in the teaching of research methods and methodology, there traditionally has been an abyss between descriptions of how to do research, descriptions of research practices, and the actual lived research praxis.

The purpose of this series is to encourage the publication of books that take a very practical and pragmatic approach to research methods. For any action in research, there are potentially many different alternative ways of how to go about *enacting* it. Experienced practitioners bring to these decisions a sort of scientific *feel for the game* that allows them to do what they do all the while expressing expertise. To transmit such a feel for the game requires teaching methods that are more like those in high-level sports or the arts. Teaching occurs not through first principles and general precepts but by means of practical suggestions in actual cases. The teacher of method thereby looks more like a coach. This series aims at publishing contributions that teach methods much in the way a coach would tell an athlete what to do next. That is, the books in this series aim at *praxis of method*, that is, teaching the feel of the game of social science research.

Hermeneutic Phenomenology in Education

Method and Practice

Edited by

Norm Friesen
Thompson Rivers University, Kamloops, Canada

Carina Henriksson
School of Education, Psychology and Sport Science,
Linnaeus University, Växjö, Sweden

and

Tone Saevi
NLA University College, School of Education, Bergen, Norway

SENSE PUBLISHERS
ROTTERDAM / BOSTON / TAIPEI

A C.I.P. record for this book is available from the Library of Congress.

ISBN 978-94-6091-832-2 (paperback)
ISBN 978-94-6091-833-9 (hardback)
ISBN 978-94-6091-834-6 (e-book)

Published by: Sense Publishers,
P.O. Box 21858, 3001 AW Rotterdam, The Netherlands
https://www.sensepublishers.com/

Note that with three exceptions (Chapters 3, 5, and 7), the contributions collected in this text appeared in their original form in the peer-reviewed open-access journal *Phenomenology & Practice*, http://www.phandpr.org.

Printed on acid-free paper

TABLE OF CONTENTS

TABLE OF CONTENTS

CARINA HENRIKSSON AND NORM FRIESEN

1. INTRODUCTION

HERMENEUTIC PHENOMENOLOGY

Understanding hermeneutic phenomenology as a research method requires the definition and discussion of terms that may initially appear daunting – beginning with the phrase "hermeneutic phenomenology" itself. *Phenomenology* is the study of experience, particularly as it is lived and as it is structured through consciousness. "Experience" in this context refers not so much to accumulated evidence or knowledge as something that we "undergo." It is something that happens *to* us, and not something accumulated and mastered *by* us. Phenomenology asks that we be open to experience in this sense. *Hermeneutics*, for its part, is the art and science of interpretation and thus also of meaning. Meaning in this context is not a thing that is final and stable, but something that is continuously open to new insight and interpretation. Hermeneutic phenomenology is consequently the study of *experience* together with its *meanings*. Like hermeneutics, this type of phenomenology is open to revision and reinterpretation: it is about an openness to meaning and to possible experiences. Hermeneutic phenomenology, in short, is as much a disposition and attitude as it is a distinct method or program for inquiry. As Max van Manen, one of the principle proponents of hermeneutic phenomenology as a research method, puts it: This approach represents an "attitude or disposition of sensitivity and openness: it is a matter of openness to everyday, experienced meanings as opposed to theoretical ones" (2002a, n.p.).

As it is considered in this collection, namely as a qualitative research method in educational (and related) research, hermeneutic phenomenology is clearly distinct from other qualitative research methods, and also from other phenomenological approaches. It rejects the claim of some phenomenological methods that ideal "essences" of experience or consciousness can be isolated outside of the researcher's cultural and historical location. In its emphasis on the interpretation and reinterpretation of meaning, it rejects any "transcendental" claim to meaning or any research conclusions that are fixed once and for all. It does not study objects or phenomena as (potentially) objective, but as necessarily meaningful. As Emmanuel Levinas says, it does not seek to "understand the object, but its *meaning*" (1987, p. 110, *italics added*). Also, unlike many other phenomenological and qualitative research approaches, hermeneutic phenomenology is particularly open to literary and poetic qualities of language, and encourages aesthetically sensitized writing as both a *process* and *product* of research.

* * *

In this introduction, we describe these and other characteristics of hermeneutic phenomenology as a research method primarily in education and secondarily, in

N. Friesen et al. (eds.), Hermeneutic Phenomenology in Education, 1–14.

related fields such as healthcare and social work. We show how these qualities are both discussed explicitly and illustrated implicitly in the various chapters of this collection. We begin with an overview of the history and philosophy associated with hermeneutic phenomenology, and we describe some of the presuppositions underlying it. We then provide an overview of the chapters gathered together in this collection, and subsequently, we conclude by drawing out a number of themes prevalent in these individual texts.

Phenomenology has its origins in the work of Edmund Husserl, who framed it primarily in philosophical terms – specifically as study of "essences," of transcendental, ideal structures of consciousness. Since Husserl's time, phenomenology as both a philosophy and method of inquiry has developed in a number of different directions, often reflecting distinct philosophical orientations. One of the key occurrences in this history is its movement from the idealist or "transcendental" realm of essences to the "immanent" world of everyday objects and concerns. This development, as well as others in the history of hermeneutic phenomenology, is marked through the contributions of key philosophical figures. Some of the most celebrated are Martin Heidegger, Maurice Merleau-Ponty, Emmanual Levinas, and Jean-Paul Sartre, who have both widened and deepened its philosophical features. Heidegger, a student of Husserl, played a particularly important (and at times problematic) role in emphasizing the phenomenology's concern with "immanence," and in connecting it with hermeneutics. Heidegger articulated these emphases or shifts in the program of phenomenology by placing priority on the study of "being," on how we find ourselves or simply "are" in the world. This is a type of study otherwise known as "ontology."

In *Being and Time* (1962), Heidegger explains that our ontology or being in the world, presents us with a fundamentally "hermeneutical Situation" (sic; p. 275). This is a situation, as he describes it, in which we are compelled to ask questions about ourselves, about the nature of the (hermeneutic) situation itself, and about who we should be and become in it. As Nelson (2001) puts it, this situation is one "in which I always find myself ... to be a question for me and [which] places me into question." Heidegger, for his part, puts this somewhat more abstractly:

> such an Interpretation obliges us first to give a phenomenal characterization of the entity we have taken as our theme, and thus to bring it into the scope of our fore-having [*Vorhaben*; plan/intention], with which all the subsequent steps of our analysis are to conform. (p. 275)

Hermeneutics as the art and science of interpretation is understood here as necessitated by our ontology; it is required by our situation in the world. This situation places us in question and is a question for us. And the phenomenal characterization of these themes forms the basis "with which all the subsequent steps of our analysis are to conform."

Hermeneutician Paul Ricoeur (1991) explains the relationship between phenomenology and hermeneutics as follows:

> beyond the simple opposition there exists, between phenomenology and hermeneutics, a mutual belonging which it is important to make explicit ... On the one hand,

hermeneutics is erected on the basis of phenomenology and thus preserves something of the philosophy from which it nevertheless differs: *phenomenology remains the unsurpassable presupposition of hermeneutics.* On the other hand, phenomenology cannot constitute itself without a *hermeneutical presupposition.* (pp. 25-26)

In other words, it is impossible to study experience without simultaneously inquiring into its meaning, and it is impossible to study meaning without experiential grounding. Ricoeur goes further by explaining that language is also inextricably involved in this mutual dependency of meaning and experience:

> Experience [not only] *can* be said, it *demands* to be said. To bring it to language is not to change it into something else but, in articulating and developing it, to make it become itself. (p. 39)

Experience and language, for both Ricoeur and for the hermeneutic phenomenology he is describing, are co-emergent, with language having not merely a descriptive function, but one that is expressive, and "co-constitutive" of experience. As Lye (1996, n.p.) explains, "Our symbolic world is not separate from our beings, especially in regard to language: we 'are' language." Experience becomes what it is when it is put into language, particularly when this language has figurative, rhythmic, alliterative or related qualities that connect it with sounds, rhythms, and figures as they are (or can be) experienced. It is in this sense or for this reason that phenomenology encourages aesthetically sensitized writing as both part of the research process and in the completed research product.

In the last few decades of the 20th century, research in education has seen an increasing interest in qualitative methods like hermeneutic phenomenology. This has been accompanied by a shift from exclusively deductive research and explanation to an acknowledgement of the value of inductive research and understanding – approaches that derive their findings by beginning with concrete particulars. The awakening of interest in phenomenology can be explained by an accompanying emphasis on everyday concerns in the domain of public and professional practices like education. Phenomenological research in these fields is frequently undertaken by scholars who have strong roots in their own disciplines. As a result, phenomenology can be said to have evolved into a relatively mature empirical science, capable of being attuned to the methodological needs associated with each specific discipline in question. These individual disciplinary domains provide fertile soil for methodological variations associated with phenomenology and hermeneutics – methods sometimes collectively known as the "human sciences."

Seen as a research method, phenomenology in general (rather than hermeneutic phenomenology in particular) has in the last thirty of forty years been developed as a method for undertaking research in fields such as education, nursing, psychology, and social work. A wide range of phenomenological methods or pathways have developed, and these can be described briefly by characterizing scholars and methodological innovators as falling into two generations. The first might start with van Kaam (1966) in psychology, whose broadly descriptive approach was developed further in the context of what has come to be known as the Duquesne school of phenomenological psychology. Amedeo Giorgi (1970, 1985), one of the most prominent members of this school, formalized descriptive phenomenology into what is known as an "empirical-structural" method – an approach characterized as "classically Husserlian." (Langdridge, 2007, p. 55). Also coming from psychology, Donald Polkinghorne (1983) has developed an approach that gives particular emphasis to the role of narrative. Colaizzi (1973) and Moustakas (1990, 1994) have made contributions that underscore dialogue, as well as the researcher's own of self-discovery, in the research process. In this context, van Manen (1990) stands out as having developed a type of phenomenology that is explicitly and emphatically hermeneutic, and also as having a focus which is primarily educational.

A second generation of practice-oriented phenomenological scholars have continued this tradition of intradisciplinary and transdisciplinary methodological experimentation and innovation. These phenomenological researchers, who have written on phenomenology as method is a more or less closely knit group, and have published on their own or together in various constellations – with some having contributions in this collection. Some of the orientations build on Husserl's transcendental phenomenology, but also include significant reference to subsequent developments in the phenomenological tradition. At Bournemouth University, Les Todres (2007) has developed a phenomenology, building on the works of Giorgi, which shows how poetic dimensions help researchers in health and social care and in psychology flesh out and understand lived experiences. Closely linked to the work of Todres is the Swedish researcher Karin Dahlberg (2008), whose reflective lifeworld method is widely used even outside Sweden. Writing from the disciplinary perspective of psychology, and from the UK, are Finlay (2011; see also in this volume) and Langridge (2007), who have published extensively on phenomenology as method. Among the UK based researchers, Smith, Flowers, and Larkin (2009) stand out with their Interpretative Phenomenological Analysis (IPA). The orientation is described as hermeneutic, but the theoretical foundation seems to rely more on the works of contemporary colleagues than on the philosophical works of Heidegger, Gadamer, or Ricoeur. At Seattle University, Steen Halling (2008) has developed what he calls "Dialogical Phenomenology," which puts emphasis on the researchers' participation and their dialectical co-operation, like the methods of Colaizzi and Moustakas before him. Like Todres, Halling appreciates and sees literature and poetry as important features of description and understanding.

This book provides an overview, or perhaps more accurately, a sampling of hermeneutic phenomenological research and methods from some of the many perspectives identified briefly here. Whether these methods are considered "pure" and methodologically "rigorous," or whether they are viewed as hybrids giving the researcher freedom to improvise, the focus in this volume is to show how and why phenomenological research can promote different knowledge and deeper understanding of pedagogical practice.

PART I: INTRODUCING HERMENEUTIC PHENOMENOLOGY

The first perspective from which this method is explored is the methodological and philosophical: How does hermeneutic phenomenology differ methodologically from other phenomenological orientations in research? What is the epistemology and ontology underpinning hermeneutic phenomenology? How widely do these methodological foundational understandings of method converge or diverge in the literature and in practice? Questions of these kinds form the focus of the first part of the book, "Introducing Hermeneutic Phenomenology," which explores the method in terms of the metaphorical aspects of sound, voice and aurality. The vocabulary of the "ear" is perhaps better suited to a discussion of presence, disposition and ontology, than in the terms of vision and the eye. This visual vocabulary, with its emphasis on distance, observation and analysis – rather than the rhythm, feeling and ambience associated with the ear – is all too familiar from positivistic philosophical and natural-scientific traditions.

There are today a number of phenomenological research methods, towards which educational researchers can lean; hermeneutic phenomenology is only one. But what counts as phenomenology overall or in general? Are there certain boundaries which we need to keep within in order to claim that we are doing phenomenological research? If so, who decides on and guards these boundaries?

In Chapter 2, *Debating phenomenological methods*, Linda Finlay goes much further in inquiring into and differentiating between different types of orientations in phenomenological research than we have been able in this introduction. She asks: What counts as phenomenology? How do the various orientations differ from one another and what might they have in common? In a personal manner, Finlay offers a mapping of some of the most widely used methods today. Six particular questions are raised and contested: (1) How tightly or loosely should we define what counts as phenomenology? (2) Should we always aim to produce a general (normative) description of the phenomenon or is idiographic analysis a legitimate aim? (3) To what extent should interpretation be involved in our descriptions? (4) Should we attempt to set aside or to foreground researcher subjectivity? (5) Should phenomenology be more science than art? (6) Is phenomenology a modernist or post-modernist project or is it neither? Finlay discusses these six questions by referring to some of the most knowledgeable contemporary phenomenological researchers, tracing their standpoints back to their respective philosophical roots. Finlay also expresses her own position on the question: What counts as phenomenology? Phenomenological research, she insists, needs to involve rich descriptions of the life-world or lived experience. Finlay emphasizes that the researcher needs to adopt a phenomenological attitude in which judgements about the phenomenon in question are suspended. Finlay's chapter offers an excellent starting point for beginners in the field of phenomenological research. For more experienced researchers, Finlay's text serves as a reminder of the importance of methodical and methodological awareness.

In Chapter 3, *The phenomenological voice: It, I, we and you*, Norm Friesen provides an approach that is similarly amenable to the needs of beginners and the expectations of more advanced researchers. He explores the relation between lived experience, its voice, and ethics. By identifying and describing four different voices or perspectives – "I," "you," "it," and "we" – Friesen shows the interconnection of different kinds of knowledge, whether natural scientific, subjective, intersubjective or ethical. Lived experiences are initially figured by Friesen as constitutive of subjective knowledge, which only be described by an "I," but this "I" is not just a unique person: the "I" is first and foremost a human being among other human beings. The "I," Friesen goes on to show, is always already defined in terms of the "we," which he identifies as the perspective of intersubjectivity.

The "we," however, presents a challenge, since it is "sometimes associated with the suppression of difference and even with acts of hate." By showing how lived time, space, body and relation are intimately interconnected and how our life-world is expressed through language, Friesen arrives at the conclusion that the pronoun "we," in phenomenological writing, invites the reader to affirm or differ with what is being said. Phenomenological texts could be described as "open conversations into the future" (Cooley, 1902, p. 9). Or as Friesen puts it perhaps more phenomenologically: "[a text] invites the reader to breathe his or her own life into its descriptions and meanings." This, in itself, is an ethical act, involving practices and knowledge that are normative, or can be judged – at least to some degree – in terms of "right" or wrong" Friesen holds.

The theme of language and ethics continues in Chapter 4, *"An event in sound" – Considerations on the ethical-aesthetic traits of the hermeneutic phenomenological text*, but is treated from a slightly different angle. Bringing up a variation on what will become a familiar theme in this collection, Henriksson and Saevi's focus is the voice of the text and its aesthetic-ethical dimensions. How can a text remain true to descriptions and interpretations of any lived experience, given that they contain possibilities which are prereflective, and in this sense, also prelinguistic? This challenge can be illustrated by citing a work of fiction:

> In ancient times, in certain dry areas, there lived a feline called largodil with long neck and short legs. It is said that the scribes of a certain tribe, who passed through the Sinai desert, used the shape of the animal as a basis for a sign, which in course of time and through the Phoenicians, became the letter L. Barely had they started to scribble the sign on the first cave walls before the largodil disappeared from the face of the earth. (Kjaerstad, 2002, p. 17)

Intrigued by Kjaerstad's text and challenged by van Manen's (2002b) postulate that "every word kills and becomes the death of the object it tries to represent" (p. 244). Henriksson and Saevi undertake a careful examination of the relationship between poetry, poetic writing, literature, traditional academic writing, and lived experiences. The authors hold that lived experiences can be understood metaphorically, as "events in sound" which have the ethical and aesthetic virtues of both truth and beauty. Henriksson and Saevi argue that, as hermeneutic phenomenological writers, we dwell in the borderland between a "poetic attitude" and a utilitarian writing style.

In Chapter 5, *Cognitive Phenomenology: Tracking the microtonality in/of learning*, education research methodologist and science education researcher, Wolff-Michael Roth undertakes what he refers to as "cognitive phenomenological" investigation. Phenomenological research, Roth implies, is the study of "micro-tonality" and "micro-emotionality" of experiences of a "fraction of a second" in an attempt to uncover the "pre-noetic," experience as it arises before interpretation or reflection. Roth emphasizes that the study of this pre-reflective experience must begin with a recognition of *passivity* in human engagements. Such a passivity, Roth explains, that is "not the counterpart of will"; it is not voluntary, but rather, is part of a way of engaging, an orientation or attitude. With his focus on the pre-intentional, prereflective and passive, Roth puts his finger on a tension that underlies hermeneutic-phenomenological investigation: Namely, its attempt to use reflection and description – which are both active and guided by intention – to get closer to that which is prereflective and not intentional and in this sense, sometimes passive. Van Manen (2007) refers to this as the "pathic," Waldenfels (2006) uses the phrase "that which is not willed," and Roth characterizes it enigmatically as "passibility" – a term he defines elsewhere simply as "our capacity to be affected" (2011, p. 18).

As Friesen does in Chapter 3, Roth refers to both "first" and "third person perspectives" to identify ways of looking at the world that are relevant to phenomenological research. However, Roth's intended meaning is markedly different: It is phenomenological descriptions in Roth's chapter that are told from the perspectives of the first and third person, in a literal, grammatical sense, as either the author's own experience or as that of someone else. These "perspectives" do not correspond to knowledge that is either singularly subjective, or that makes the claim to an impersonal objectivity, as Friesen discusses. After taking the reader through a series of descriptions and examples, in both the first and third person grammatical perspectives, Roth comes to a conclusion that highlights the affinity of his approach with hermeneutic phenomenology as it is represented in much of the rest of this book: Both are concerned with the avoidance of "the third" – of laws, rules and order, whether theoretical or methodological in origin – which "interferes with and contaminates the foreign or strange." All hermeneutic phenomenology is concerned with avoiding the labels and "laws" of theory, which – as Henriksson and Saevi have pointed out – can all too easily "kill" the phenomenon under investigation. Attempts to negotiate this difficult and in some ways impossible avoidance of the orders of theory and of methodological prescription are, in different ways, discussed and demonstrated in the papers that follow these three introductory chapters.

PART II: HERMENEUTIC PHENOMENOLOGY: REFLECTION AND PRACTICE

The second part of the book follows by sounding out the relationship between method, theory, reflection and practice, showing these interrelationships to be both intricate and integral. Hermeneutic phenomenology uses concrete examples and descriptive, reflective writing to take scholarly discourse out of the realm of explicit, theoretical generality and bring it closer to the particularities of engaged practice. It does this in the hope of fostering a kind of pathic, non-cognitive forms of awareness – the attitude or disposition that is fundamental to hermeneutic phenomenological investigation itself. The language of theory and generality, and the competencies and capabilities associated with it, can draw researchers and practitioners away from this type of awareness.

Chapter 6, *The creativity of 'unspecialization': A contemplative direction for integrative scholarly practice*, by Kate Galvin and Les Todres starts with an exploration into forms of knowledge that since the beginning of the modern era, have guided scholarship in relation to practice. What was once seen as modernity's great dignity – the differentiation of science, art, and morality – has become postmodernity's great disaster, the dis-integration of knowing, valuing and doing.

Drawing on Aristotle and his concept of *phronesis* in which knowing, doing and valuing are inseparably intertwined, Galvin and Todres connect it to Heidegger on *Denken* and Gendlin on the "entry into the implicit." Based on this, the authors promote ways of knowing and acting that are "unspecialized," since they involve ways of integrating the knowledge of head, heart and hand. Such an integrated form of knowledge would see scholarship as a "seamless" way of being. But what is this way of being?

Galvin and Todres identify this as essentially an *embodied* way of being, and they offer an experiential account of an artist who is struggling to find an expression for "more than words can say." The meaning at the core of this experiential account is easily translatable to other professional practices such as nursing, counselling, and pedagogy. Teachers, nurses, and psychologists are often in a position in which they struggle to find ways of seeing their pupils, patients, and clients holistically through their lived experiences.

Throughout the chapter, Galvin and Todres show how forms of applied knowledge, which integrate knowing and being, and include the ethical dimension of the 'good,' are constitutive of the creativity of "unspecialization." In this way, the authors point us to a different view on what scholarship can be, in its integration with practice, and how integrated, applied knowledge can present a path to a more profound and reflective involvement in human existence.

In Chapter 7, *Hermeneutic phenomenology and pedagogical practice*, Carina Henriksson explores the connection between educational research and pedagogical practice. In doing so, she takes as a starting point Merleau-Ponty's suggestion that phenomenology "has given a number of present-day readers the impression, on reading Husserl or Heidegger, not so much of encountering a new philosophy as of recognizing what they had been waiting for" (Merleau-Ponty, 1962, p. viii). But: What is it that teachers have been waiting for? In answering this question Henriksson shows us how pedagogical practice is often at odds with research and theory, since the latter do not address questions in their concrete situatedness: What do I say to my class at *this* moment? What can I do for *this* child? Through lived-experience descriptions and narratives, Henriksson illuminates some of the aspects of pedagogical practice which are often overlooked in research, but deeply felt by teachers. The experiential accounts and Henriksson's understanding of them shows how hermeneutic phenomenology can give teachers a different knowledge and deeper understanding of what goes on in classrooms – and this knowledge, she avers, represents "what they had been waiting for."

With its strong focus on the lifeworld and lived experiences, hermeneutic phenomenology bridges the gap between what theory and educational documents say *should* take place in the classroom and what *actually* takes place in every-day pedagogical practice. As such, this method, approach, attitude or disposition could be described as a "reality check." Hermeneutic phenomenology is, according to Galvin and Todres (Chapter 6), also a relatively seamless way of seeing pedagogy. Framed by ethical considerations, it involves hand (acting), heart (feeling), and head (thinking). As discussed above, hermeneutic phenomenology embraces the thought that language and our world view are intertwined: language shapes our world and our world is shaped by language. Hermeneutic phenomenology writes and talks in a language, which as Henriksson argues, makes the world of pedagogical practice recognizable for teachers.

PART III: A "SCIENCE OF EXAMPLES": ILLUSTRATIONS AND ADAPTATIONS

Phenomenology has been famously described as "a science of examples" (van den Berg, 1955, p. 54) and the book concludes with a small number of examples of the application of hermeneutic phenomenology to research in education. These feature adaptations and modifications to the method that include its combination with photography and narrative, and drawing and interviewing techniques. Van Manen uses the phrases "methodical reduction" and "flexible narrative rationality" to characterize these and other types of adaptations of the method to the subject matter being investigated. Like the more general phenomenological reduction, its methodological counterpart entails the "bracketing" of established answers and approaches to what is being researched. But whereas the phenomenological reduction involves the exclusion of conventional theoretical explanations that may get in the way of the lived experience, the methodological reduction requires the exclusion of methodological convention:

> Bracket all established investigative methods or techniques, and seek or invent an approach that seems to fit most appropriately the phenomenological topic under study. … One must experiment with a methodologically informed inventiveness that fuses the reflective and the prereflective life of consciousness. One needs to invent a flexible narrative rationality, a method for investigating and representing the phenomenon in question. (2002, n.p.)

In both the methodological and the general phenomenological reductions – as well as in van Manen's characterization of "flexible narrative rationality," Roth's earlier statements concerning the exclusion of "the third" take clear, practical form: Although it can never be accessed in "unfalsified" or purely pre-noetic terms, phenomenology has as its goal the exclusion of the third, of theoretical or methodological "answers" that would come between the researcher and the experience under investigation.

In Chapter 8, the focus of Anna Kirova and Michael Emme's methodological experimentation is to be found in the genre of the Fotonovela. This is a genre that presents a method which bridges hermeneutic phenomenology and arts-based research by combining photography with basic verbal and pictorial elements. The method was originally developed as a means to let immigrant children express their lived experiences of the first school day in their new country. The main question is, "What methods of inquiry can be used to access 'embodied understanding' more directly, and, in particular, the lifeworlds of immigrant children as they leave the familiar 'home world' and enter the 'alien world' of a new school?" Besides the emphasis on the photonovella, this question is explored with the help of three theoretical notions: Gadamer's notion of understanding as a linguistic "happening," the constantly renewed enactment of tradition; Heidegger's understanding of the relationship between language and being; and Gendlin's belief that our relational and bodily understandings exceed any precisely formulated "languaged," or otherwise patterned, ways of describing it. In conclusion, Kirova and Emme argue that the fotonovela, as a collage method, that may offer a deeper understanding of embodied experiences and the complex relationships between body, language, and image.

The relationship between body, movement, and language is further explored in Chapter 9, Charlotte Svendler Nielsen's *Children's embodied voices: Approaching children's experiences through multi-modal interviewing*. Building on Merleau-Ponty, Gendlin, and Mindell, Svendler Nielsen develops a multi-modal interview method, which enables explorations of how children experience their bodies in movement and how these experiences can be expressed through language, drawings, music, and movement itself. Step by step, and through examples from her research, Svendler Nielsen explains the different phases of the multi-modal interviewing approach. She also describes how she has created narratives from interviews and children's log books and drawings, and how these narratives were analyzed and interpreted. Svendler Nielsen closes her chapter with an insightful discussion on how her multi-modal approach could be used as a pedagogical tool, and how teachers' awareness of children's experience bodily movement can ultimately affect the child's well-being, relationships, and quality of life.

Chapter 10, *Seeking pedagogical places* by Andrew Foran and Margaret Olson, is not *about* reflection in an overt sense; rather it is an appeal for us to reflect on pedagogical practice. Where does teaching take place and what is the meaning of pedagogical places? When does a space become a place where education unfolds? School rules often set the limit for when teaching is supposed to take place and school buildings often set the physical limits for where teaching and learning are appropriate: teaching and learning take place during the daytime in classrooms. By means of evocative anecdotes, all written by teachers, Foran and Olson show that a pedagogical place actually has little to do with the physical surroundings. Rather, any place that draws teacher and students together, any place where teachers and students are absorbed and drawn into an educative experience is a pedagogical place. One of the conclusions that Foran and Olson formulate is that "the importance a place can have in a person's being can border on spiritual sanctity ... This is a full-body experience, the intentional awareness of being-in-the-world that encourages the body, beyond the desk, the classroom, or the school."

Educative experiences, as Foran and Olson points out, can happen anywhere and anytime. Not just for the student but for the teacher too. Consider this poem from the Swedish author, Sven Nyberg:

After all my years
at university
I was assigned
to check the boys' toilet
before morning assembly.

One bleak winter morning,
in my zealousness,
I caught a thirteen-year old
special-ed student,
who somewhat helplessly
sucked on a cigarette.

"And who is this, then?"
my stern voice echoed.

The boy looked me
 straight into my eyes
 "A human being," he
solemnly said.

It would take a very uncaring teacher not to have pause for thought when reading an account of this kind. Poems and other types of literature can be powerful and transformative, as they *situate* our embodied being in concrete particularities – which abound in Nyberg's brief and relatively terse poem: "after years of university," "the bleak morning" before the assembly, and the helplessness of the thirteen year-old. In this way, literature is able to connect us in significant ways to the world and to ourselves.

In Chapter 11, *How literature works: Poetry and the phenomenology of reader response*, Patrick Howard investigates some of these special powers of literature. Building on Rosenblatt's notion of a mutual *transaction* occurring between reader and text, Howard employs hermeneutic phenomenology to further explore how the text can be lived and felt. The first few pages of the chapter lets us be a part of a lesson in which a grade 9 class, together with their teacher, reads and comments on poems written by local poets. Howard, a very talented writer himself, shows, through his writing about the lesson, how literature is educative or formative because it is an aesthetic experience which can have lived meaning for the student.

One student's written response to a poem becomes the backdrop for Howard's further exploration into literary engagement, texts as "situations," and embodied language. In the hands of Howard, this student's comment on the poem vividly illustrates Bachelard's (1958/1994) observation of how

> The image offered us by reading the poem now becomes really our own. It takes root in us ... It becomes a new being in our language, expressing us by making us what it expresses; in other words, it is at once a becoming of expression, and a becoming of our being. Here expression creates being. (p. xxiii)

As a scholar of both literature and phenomenology, Bachelard helps teachers – and students – see what can be possible by cultivating a deeper understanding of reader and text.

* * *

As the reader will see, each chapter in this collection has its own unique way of describing, understanding and engaging with hermeneutic phenomenology. The reader will also notice that none of the chapters offers a ready-made manual for doing hermeneutic phenomenological research. Instead, this book should be seen as offering different pathways within a common methodological landscape. This certainly makes hermeneutic phenomenology more difficult and elusive than other methods, but as both Gadamer (1975) and Rorty (1979) maintain, the method of phenomenology is that there is no method.

The fact that there is "no" method might leave us with a feeling of abandonment, of being left in the middle of nowhere with nothing more than a burning desire to undertake an experientially meaningful research study. So, to whom do we turn for guidance?

In phenomenological philosophy and methodology we find the tools we need to design a method for our research question; the phenomenological scholars provide us with theoretical knowledge. But in the process of understanding this knowledge, there is an obvious danger that literature confuses more than it clarifies. When we find that there is a plethora of perspectives within phenomenology, our open mind might turn into the antithesis – a closed mind.

If there is no method and if the philosophers we turn to do not challenge us, there is just one salvation on the road to method: the research question. Moustakas (1990) puts it well when he says:

> The heuristic researcher is not only intimately and autobiographically related to the question but learns to love the question. It becomes a kind of song into which the researcher breathes life not... because the question leads to an answer, but also because the question itself is infused in the researcher's being. It creates a thirst to discover, to clarify, and to understand crucial dimensions of knowledge. (p. 43)

Anyone who has undertaken hermeneutic-phenomenological research knows how a research question, at the beginning, is difficult to put into words. It is there, but more as an extra-linguistic feeling or sensing or empathy; waiting to play, to challenge, to tease us, even to command us – but finally to also liberate us. This thirst to discover, clarify and understand the research question is ultimately an attentive, unchained wandering into the soul of the question. Through reflection, we may find that what we actively have been searching for was already there, passively waiting for our acknowledgment.

* * *

Finally, in introducing this collection, we are grateful to acknowledge the indispensible role that the online, open access journal, *Phenomenology & Practice* has played both in providing the vast majority of the chapters presented in this collection, and in developing, since its inauguration in 2006, a communal forum for hermeneutic phenomenological writing. With the exception of chapters 3, 5, and 7 (and this introductory chapter), all of the contributions to this collection originally appeared in *Phenomenology & Practice*, and four of these chapters originally appeared in a special issue on methodology published in 2009. Chapter 3, Norm Friesen's *Experiential evidence: I, we and you* has been adapted from his 2011 monograph, *The Place of the Classroom and the Space of the Screen: Relational Pedagogy and Internet Technology* (New York: Peter Lang). Chapter 5, Wolff-Michael Roth's *Hermeneutic phenomenology and congnition: Tracking the microtonality in/of learning* and Chapter 7, Carina Henriksson's *Hermeneutic phenomenology and pedagogical practice* have not previously been published.

REFERENCES

Bachelard, G. (1958/1994). *The poetics of space. The classic look at how we experience intimate places.* Boston, MA: Beacon Press.

Colaizzi, P.F. (1973). *Reflection and research in psychology: A phenomenological study of learning.* Dubuque: Kindall/Hunt.

Cooley, C.H. (1902/1981). *Samhället och individen.* Göteborg: Korpen.

Dahlberg, K., Dahlberg, H., & Nyström, M. (2008). *Reflective lifeworld research.* Lund: Studentlitteratur.

Finlay, L. (2011). *Phenomenology for therapists: Researching the lived world.* Oxford: John Wiley.

Gadamer, H-G. (1975). *Truth and method.* New York: Seabury.

Giorgi, A. (1970). *Psychology as a human science: A phenomenologically based approach.* New York: Harper and Row.

Giorgi, A. (Ed.). (1985). *Phenomenology and psychological research.* Pittsburgh: Duquesne University Press.

Halling, S. (2008). *Intimacy, transcendence, and psychology: Closeness and openness in everyday life.* New York: Palgrave Macmillan.

Heidegger, M. (1962). *Being and time.* New York: Harper & Row.

Kjaerstad, J. (2003). *Tecken till kärlek.* Stockholm: Månpocket.

Langdridge, D. (2007). *Phenomenological psychology: Theory, research and method.* Harlow: Pearson Education.

Levinas, E. (1987). *Language and proximity. Collected philosophical papers.* Dordrecht: Martinus Nijhoff.

Lye, J. (1996). Some principles of phenomenological hermeneutics. http://www.brocku.ca/english/courses/4F70/ph.php.

Merleau-Ponty, M. (1962). *Phenomenology of perception.* London: Routledge.

Moustakas, C. (1990). *Heuristic research: Design, methodology, and applications.* Newbury Park, CA: Sage.

Moustakas, C. (1994). *Phenomenological research methods.* London: Sage.

Nelson, E. S. (2001). Questioning practice: Heidegger, historicity, and the hermeneutics of facticity. *Philosophy Today, 44,* 150-159.

Nyberg, S. (n.d.). Untitled poem. http://www.reocities.com/Athens/Acropolis/7952/dikt8.html.

Polkinghorne, Donald (1983). *Methodology for the human sciences: Systems of inquiry.* Albany: SUNY Press.

Ricoeur, P. (1991). *From text to action: Essays in hermeneutics II.* Evanston, IL: Northwestern UP.

Rorty, R. (1979). *Philosophy and the mirror of nature.* Princeton, NJ: Princeton University Press.

Roth, W.-M. (2011). *Passibility: At the limits of the constructivist metaphor.* Dordrecht: Springer.

Smith, J., Flowers, P., & Larkin, M. (2009). *Interpretative phenomenological analysis: Theory, method and research.* London: Sage.

Todres (2007). *Embodied enquiry: Phenomenological touchstones for research, psychotherapy and spirituality.* Hampshire & New York: Palgrave Macmillan.

Van den Berg, J.H. (1955). *The phenomenological approach to psychiatry: An introduction to recent phenomenological psychopathology.* Springfield, IL: Thomas.

Van Kaam, Adrian (1966). *Existential foundations of psychology.* Pittsburgh: Duquesne University Press.

Van Manen, M. (1990). *Researching lived experience: Human science for an action sensitive pedagogy.* London, ON: The Althouse Press.

Van Manen, M (2002a). Phenomenology online: Inquiry. http://www.phenomenologyonline.com/inquiry/.

Van Manen, M. (2002b). *Writing in the dark.* London, Ontario: The Althouse Press.

Van Manen, M. (2007). Phenomenology of practice. *Phenomenology & Practice, 1,* 11-30.

Waldenfels, B. (2006). *Grundmotive einer Phänomenologie des Fremden.* Frankfurt/Main: Suhrkamp.

PART I

Introducing Hermeneutic Phenomenology

2. DEBATING PHENOMENOLOGICAL METHODS

INTRODUCTION

Phenomenological philosophers have been "extraordinarily diverse in their interests, in their interpretation of the central issues of phenomenology, in their application of what they understood to be the phenomenological method, and in their development of what they took to be the phenomenological programme for the future of philosophy" (Moran, 2000, p. 3). This diversity finds reflection in phenomenological research, where the application of philosophical ideas to the empirical project provokes both uncertainty and controversy.

Phenomenological researchers generally agree that our central concern is to return to embodied, experiential meanings. We aim for fresh, complex, rich descriptions of a phenomenon as it is concretely lived. Phenomenological description "must stick close to experience, and yet not limit itself to the empirical but restore to each experience the ontological cipher which marks it internally" (Merleau-Ponty, 1964, p. 157). As Wertz (2005) puts it:

> Phenomenology is a low hovering, in-dwelling, meditative philosophy that glories in the concreteness of person-world relations and accords lived experience, with all its indeterminacy and ambiguity, primacy over the known. (p. 175)

There is a general consensus that we need phenomenological research methods that are responsive to both the phenomenon and the subjective interconnection between the researcher and the researched.

That said, we continue to engage in a spirited debate about how to do phenomenological research in practice. While this debate is healthy, tensions are occasionally created in our community by unduly critical debate where confusion about what constitutes appropriate or "sound" phenomenological research makes our field difficult for novices to access. When commitment to shared scholarly exploration is displaced by dogmatic assertion, both the quality and the potential of phenomenological inquiry are threatened.

Six particular questions are contested: (1) How tightly or loosely should we define what counts as phenomenology? (2) Should we always aim to produce a general (normative) description of the phenomenon or is idiographic analysis a legitimate aim? (3) To what extent should interpretation be involved in our descriptions? (4) Should we set aside or bring to the foreground researcher subjectivity? (5) Should phenomenology be more science than art? (6) Is phenomenology a modernist or postmodernist project, or neither?

In this chapter, I examine each of these areas of contention in the spirit of fostering dialogue and promoting openness and clarity in phenomenological inquiry. In addition to mapping the phenomenological field as a whole, I indicate the routes favoured by hermeneutic phenomenologists, including myself. The

N. Friesen et al. (eds.), Hermeneutic Phenomenology in Education, 17–37.

specific choices we make regarding our methodology arise out of a broader field and it's important we acknowledge that context.

> To prosper and advance, it becomes important for any discipline to evaluate its theoretical and methodological propositions from within its own evolving framework rather than insulate itself from criticism due to threat or cherished group loyalties. (Mills, 2003, p. 150)

WHAT COUNTS AS "PHENOMENOLOGY?"

Many different research methods and techniques are practiced under the banner of phenomenological research. What are the boundaries, the defining characteristics, of phenomenology? What distinguishes our work from other variants of qualitative research that investigate subjective meanings?

Focusing specifically on psychological phenomenological approaches,[1] Giorgi (1989) has stated that four core characteristics hold across all variations: The research is rigorously *descriptive*, uses the phenomenological *reductions*, explores the *intentional* relationship between persons and situations, and discloses the *essences*, or structures, of meaning immanent in human experiences through the use of imaginative variation. Elsewhere Giorgi (1997), more straightforwardly, argues that the phenomenological method encompasses three interlocking steps: (1) phenomenological reduction, (2) description, and (3) search for essences.

Yet, variations in phenomenological methodology flourish. Some adhere reasonably closely to Giorgi's framework based on the reduction and imaginative variation while, at the same time, offering their own emphases (e.g., the open lifeworld approach of Dahlberg et al., 2008; van Manen's, lived experience human science inquiry, 1990; the dialogal approach, Halling et al., 2006; the Dallas approach, Garza 2007; Todres' embodied lifeworld approach, 2005, 2007; and Ashworth's, lifeworld approach, 2003, 2006).

There also exist a number of phenomenological writers who focus on rich descriptions of lived experience and meanings, but which do not explicitly use Husserlian techniques such as eidetic variation. The literary, contemplative, existential-dialectical approach of Jager (2010), Todres (2007) and others offer variants of hermeneutic phenomenology anchored in the poetic tradition of late Heidegger. Smith's Interpretative Phenomenological Analysis (IPA), which has gained considerable purchase in the qualitative psychology field in the United Kingdom, is example of a different hermeneutic approach. Smith argues that his idiographic and inductive method, which seeks to explore participants' personal lived experiences, is phenomenological in its concern for individuals' perceptions. He also, however, identifies more strongly with hermeneutic traditions which recognize the central role played by the researcher, and does not advocate the use of bracketing (Smith, 2004).

The debate about whether or not a method is in fact "phenomenological" pivots on the issue of criteria. Specifically, is it sufficient to strive for rich description of lived experience, or are additional aspects required such as having a special phenomenological stance or attitude? Is Giorgi's Husserl-inspired method the template against which other versions should be measured? When Giorgi (2008a, p. 34) states that he does not consider the ways some colleagues have adapted his own basic method with wider variations to be sound – from either a research or phenomenological perspective – is he more tightly ring-fencing the psychological phenomenological project? In fact, in an earlier paper, Giorgi is clear that his method is neither exclusive nor exhaustive and that it should not be considered paradigmatic (Giorgi, 1975). His complaint would appear to be directed against researchers who either claim their work derives from Husserl when primary sources have not been read or understood, or against researchers who evoke Giorgi's own name and method falsely, thereby misrepresenting his work. More recently, Giorgi (2008b) has critiqued students' illogical tendency to lay claim to ideas stemming from philosophers or methodologists who have irreconcilable differences.

My own position on this question is that phenomenological research is phenomenological when it involves both rich description of either the lifeworld or lived experience, and where the researcher has adopted a special, open phenomenological attitude which, at least initially, refrains from importing external frameworks and sets aside judgements about the realness of the phenomenon. Put another way, I support Husserl's idea that varying modes of "givenness" can only be unfurled through the reduction and, as Marion (2002) puts it, with more reduction we get more givenness. I also think that researchers should be clear about which philosophical and/or research traditions they are following. I have concerns about research which purports to be Husserlian when, for example, there is no evidence of any reductions being attempted. Similarly, researchers who claim to have bracketed and, therefore, transcended their assumptions while using a hermeneutic approach would seem to be both naïve and confused.

In my view, a phenomenological method is sound if it links appropriately to some phenomenological philosophy or theory, and if its claims about method are justified and consistent. For example, in one paper, six researchers (including myself) apply different approaches to – versions of – phenomenology (King et al., 2008). We regard ourselves as practicing phenomenologically-based empirical work as distinct from engaging a philosophical reflection on "things in their appearing" in the philosophical sense. While there are commonalities in our methods of analyses and findings, we also diverge; but in this divergence, we link explicitly and reflexively back to different theoretical and philosophical commitments.

It is perhaps helpful to recognize that a number of qualitative approaches to research have borrowed and built upon phenomenological philosophy and techniques. As Wertz (2005) says, any genuinely psychological qualitative method implicitly uses the descriptive psychological reflection that is characteristic of the phenomenological approach. It he suggests that is perhaps best to accept research which does not fully embrace the phenomenological project's commitment to description along with the researcher having an open *phenomenological attitude* (if not actually applying specific reductions), as phenomenologically-inspired or phenomenologically-orientated. Any research which does not have at its core the description of "the things in their appearing" which focuses experience as lived, cannot be considered phenomenological.

GENERAL DESCRIPTION OR IDIOGRAPHIC ANALYSIS?

Phenomenologists contest what should be the focus of their research. Many, like Giorgi (following Husserl), seek to throw light on the essential and general structures of a phenomenon. One version of this approach is to explicitly focus on the lifeworld, which is seen to be a human universal consisting of essential features (e.g., Dahlberg et al., 2008; Todres, Galvin, & Dahlberg, 2006; Ashworth, 2003, 2006).[2] A variant of lifeworld research is a reflective and practical focus on *lived experience* adopted by many in the pedagogic (see van Manen, 1990) and health care fields (e.g., see Crotty's 1996 review of nursing research). Other phenomenologists concentrate on the *narratives* emerging from data; Langdridge (2008) and his Critical Narrative Approach following Ricoeur is one example.

With these different approaches, the phenomenon in question varies subtly. For instance, in researching the topic of anxiety, one could explore the lifeworld of a person who is anxious; another could aim to explore the general structure (or essence) of the lived experience of "being anxious"; yet another could explore the stories people tell of their experience of feeling anxious. Underlying these different approaches, with their varying points of focus, are questions that ask to what extent the phenomenology practiced aims to describe the experience in general (i.e., as one shared by many), or is it instead focused on explicating individual experience?

Giorgi (2008a) is clear that the purpose of the method he has developed is to clarify the nature of the phenomenon being studied in a more traditional, normative, and scientific sense. He recommends recruiting at least three participants, arguing that the differences between them make it easier to discern the individual experience from the more general experience of the phenomenon. As he puts it: "At least three participants are included because a sufficient number of variations are needed in order to come up with a typical essence" (Giorgi, 2008a, p. 37). In Giorgi's method, idiographic analysis may form part of the process of analysis but the eventual aim is to explicate – eidetically – the phenomenon as a whole regardless of the individuals concerned. Idiographic details are thus discarded or typified and generalized.

In contrast, other phenomenologists explicitly seek out idiographic meanings in an attempt to understand the individual which may or may not offer general insights. In the United Kingdom, the work of Ashworth (e.g., Ashworth, 2006; King et al., 2008) is notable here, as are the contributions of those using Interpretative Phenomenological Analysis (for instance, Smith & Osborn, 2003; Eatough & Smith, 2006). For my part, I have also favored an approach with a strong idiographic, narrative element when exploring how particular health conditions may be experienced by individuals. For example, I was interested in explicating how one woman experienced her particular variant of multiple sclerosis

(Finlay, 2003), and how another coped with her particular journey related to receiving a cochlear implant (Finlay & Molano-Fisher, 2008).

There is also a middle position. Halling (2008) accepts both the particular and general by arguing that idiographic research can also be general in that it may well identify general structures of experience. He suggests that phenomenologists engage three levels of analysis: firstly, they look at particular experience, such as one person's story of being disillusioned; secondly, they concern themselves with themes common to the phenomenon (for instance, the nature of disillusionment in general); thirdly, they probe philosophical and universal aspects of being human, by asking what is it about our nature and relationships that creates disillusionment. Halling counsels researchers to move back and forth between experience and abstraction – between experience and reflection – at these different levels.

Building on Halling's formulation, we could say that single cases may offer insight into individual essences (as opposed to typical or universal essences). Husserl (1913/1983) lends support to this position when he says, "Eidetic singularities are essences which necessarily have over them 'more universal' essences as their genre, but do not have under them any particularization in relation to which they would themselves be species" (p. 25). Thus, the choice of a single case may provide sufficient access to a phenomenon depending on the epistemological goals of the project, and the rigor of the eidetic approach adopted. If the research aims for generality across the field, then a wider sample representing different aspects is required.

Todres and Galvin (2005, 2006) provide an example of research which examines the phenomenon of the "caring narrative" both generically (thematically) and idiographically. Significantly, they also bridge both descriptive and interpretive elements as the italicized example below shows.

DESCRIPTION OR INTERPRETATION?

Phenomenological research characteristically starts with concrete descriptions of lived situations, often first-person accounts, set down in everyday language and avoiding abstract intellectual generalizations. The researcher proceeds by reflectively analyzing these descriptions, perhaps idiographically first, then by offering a synthesized account, for example, identifying general themes about the essence of the phenomenon. Importantly, the phenomenological researcher aims to go beyond surface expressions or explicit meanings to read between the lines so as to access implicit dimensions and intuitions.[3] It is this process of reading between the lines which has generated uncertainty. To what extent does this approach involve going beyond what the person has expressed and enter a more speculative realm of interpretation?

While all phenomenology is descriptive in the sense of aiming to describe rather than explain, a number of scholars and researchers distinguish between descriptive phenomenology versus interpretive, or hermeneutic, phenomenology. With descriptive (i.e., Husserl-inspired) phenomenology,[4] researchers aim to reveal essential general meaning structures of a phenomenon. They stay close to what is given to them in all its richness and complexity, and restrict themselves to "making assertions which are supported by appropriate intuitive validations" (Mohanty, 1983, cited in Giorgi, 1986, p. 9).

Interpretive phenomenology, in contrast, has emerged from the work of hermeneutic philosophers, including Heidegger, Gadamer, and Ricoeur, who argue for our embeddedness in the world of language and social relationships, and the inescapable historicity of all understanding. "The meaning of phenomenological description as a method lies in interpretation," says Heidegger (1962, p. 37). Interpretation is not an additional procedure: It constitutes an inevitable and basic structure of our "being-in-the-world." We experience a thing as something that has already been interpreted.

Thus, a phenomenological method which purports to be "hermeneutic" needs to be able to account explicitly for the researcher's approach and how interpretations are managed. It needs to address how the relationship between researcher and researched – the interface between subject and object – is negotiated.

Interpretation is required, say hermeneutic phenomenologists, to bring out the ways in which meanings occur in a *context*. Firstly, any description of lived experience by participants needs to be seen in the context of that individual's life situation. When a participant with chronic fatigue points to being frustrated with their "lack of energy," the statement takes on more color and significance when we understand the participant is a professional athlete (Finlay, 2011). Secondly, interpretation is implicated as researchers make sense of data by drawing on their own subjective understandings and life experiences. Thirdly, interpretations are filtered through a specific historical lens and arise in a particular social-cultural field including that which relates to the specific co-creating researcher-researched relationship involved.

The division between these descriptive and interpretive or hermeneutic variants of phenomenology finds reflection in research. Giorgi (1985), a proponent of a thorough, descriptive Husserlian method, and prolific writer provided the impetus for what became known as the Duquesne approach or tradition (e.g., Wertz, 1985; Fischer, 1974). Others have embraced more explicitly hermeneutic versions, including the existential, hermeneutic approaches of the Dallas School (Churchill, 2003; Garza, 2007); the open lifeworld approach of Dahlberg et al. (2008); the dialogal approach of Halling and his colleagues (2006); the embodied enquiry approach of Todres (2007); the Interpretative Phenomenological Analysis in use by Smith and his colleagues (Smith, 2007; Smith et al., 2009) and the person-place-architecture phenomenology of Seamon (Seamon, 2010; Seamon & Mugerauer, 1985).

Some scholars, including myself, prefer to see description and interpretation as a continuum where specific work may be more or less interpretive.[5] Van Manen (1990) suggests that when description is mediated by expression, including nonverbal aspects, action, artwork, or text, a stronger element of interpretation is involved. However, drawing on Gadamer's ideas, he distinguishes between interpretation as pointing to something (interpretation suited to phenomenological description) and interpretation as pointing out the meaning of something by imposing an external framework (such as when offering a psychoanalytic interpretation). Ricoeur has made a similar distinction between the "hermeneutics of meaning-recollection" which, he says, aims for greater understanding of the thing to be analyzed in its own terms, where meanings are brought out and the "hermeneutics of suspicion," which involves deeper interpretations needed to challenge surface accounts (Ricoeur, 1970).[6] Wertz (2005) picks up the former sense of interpretation when he argues that "'interpretation' may be used, and may be called for, in order to contextually grasp parts within larger wholes, as long as it remains descriptively grounded" (p. 175).

I agree with other hermeneutic phenomenologists who argue that interpretation is inevitable and necessary because phenomenology is concerned with meanings which tend to be implicit and/or hidden. Interpretation is thus centrally involved in unveiling hidden meanings (rather than being a process whereby external frames of reference are brought in and imposed). That we make a transition from actual experience to a second-hand explication indicates a level of translation and interpretation is involved.

> Phenomenology is seeking after meaning which is perhaps hidden by the entity's mode of appearing ... The things themselves always present themselves in a manner which is at the same time self-concealing. (Moran, 2000, p. 229)

I also agree with Langdridge when he notes that in practice there are no hard and fast boundaries between description and interpretation, as "such boundaries would be antithetical to the spirit of the phenomenological tradition that prizes individuality and creativity" (Langdridge, 2008, p. 1131). An example is offered in the italicized text below which illustrates how description and interpretation might be usefully and creatively blended. Here, Todres and Galvin offer a description and an embodied textural interpretation of the experience of caring for a loved one with Alzheimer's.

> Through numerous experiences of L's memory loss, M first learned that he could not control or stop its exacerbation. Initially he found this extremely irritating and used the term 'nauseous' to express his visceral, angry, emotional reaction to what was, to him, the repetitiveness of her saying or doing something over and over again. His initial angry response to her forgetfulness manifested itself in an attempt to control her into being less forgetful ...

> Embodied interpretation

> To see a loved one change in this way. No ... How deep is the urge to want to stop the exacerbation of memory loss ...? It deserves at least an angry 'No,' a great refusal. It is also a sinking feeling, the 'nausea' of an awareness that relentlessly breaks through .... (Todres & Galvin, 2006, p. 53)

RESEARCHER SUBJECTIVITY

Phenomenologists all accept that researcher subjectivity is inevitably implicated in research – indeed, some would say it is precisely the realization of the intersubjective interconnectedness between researcher and researched that characterizes phenomenology. The question at stake is to what extent, and how, researcher subjectivity should be marshalled in phenomenological research. As Giorgi has firmly stated,

> nothing can be accomplished without subjectivity, so its elimination is not the solution. Rather how the subject is present is what matters, and objectivity itself is an achievement of subjectivity. (1994, p. 205)

Phenomenologists also concur about the need for researchers to engage a "phenomenological attitude." Using this attitude, the researcher strives to be open to the "other" and to attempt to see the world freshly, in a different way. The process has been described variously as disciplined naïveté, bridled dwelling, disinterested attentiveness, and/or the process of retaining an empathic wonderment in the face of the world (Finlay, 2008).

While phenomenologists agree about the need for an open attitude, there remains debate as to whether or not it is necessary to engage the reduction and, if so, what it involves.[7] In other words, there is a consensus that a change of attitude is required but how that change of attitude is to be affected has generated long debate. One particularly divisive issue for researchers is how much attention they should pay to bringing their own experience to the foreground and reflexively (i.e. with self-awareness) exploring their own embodied subjectivity. To what extent should the researcher's attention be on the noetic (manner of being aware) dimension along with the noematic (object of awareness) dimension?

Some phenomenologists emphasize the reduction as a process of rendering oneself as noninfluential and neutral as possible. Here researchers aim to "bracket" their previous understandings, past knowledge, and assumptions about the phenomenon so as to focus on the phenomenon in its appearing. Novice researchers often misunderstand this process of bracketing as an initial first step where subjective bias is acknowledged as part of the project to establish the rigor and validity of the research. In fact, bracketing involves a process whereby "one simply refrains from positing altogether; one looks at the data with the attitude of relative openness" (Giorgi, 1994, p. 212). More specifically, Ashworth (1996) suggests that at least three particular areas of presupposition need to be set aside: (1) scientific theories, knowledge and explanation; (2) truth or falsity of claims being made by the participant; and (3) personal views and experiences of the researcher which would cloud descriptions of the phenomenon itself. Importantly, this "setting aside" is required throughout the research process; it is not just a first step.

Other researchers – particularly those of hermeneutic sensibility – would deny it is possible, or even desirable, to set aside or bracket researchers' experience and understandings. They argue instead that researchers need to come to an awareness of their preexisting beliefs, which then makes it possible to examine and question them in light of new evidence (Halling et al., 2006). Researchers need to bring a "critical self-awareness of their own subjectivity, vested interests, predilections and assumptions and to be conscious of how these might impact on the research process and findings" (Finlay, 2008, p. 17). Researchers' subjectivity should, therefore, be placed in the foreground so as to begin the process of separating out what belongs to the researcher rather than the researched. Colaizzi (1973), for example, argues that researcher self-reflection constitutes an important step of the research process, and that preconceived biases and presuppositions need to be brought into awareness to separate them out from participants' descriptions. Van Manen (2002) proposes a version of the reduction he calls "hermeneutic reduction":

> One needs to reflect on one's own pre-understandings, frameworks, and biases regarding the (psychological, political, and ideological) motivation and the nature of the question, in search for genuine openness in one's conversational relation with the phenomenon. In the reduction one needs to overcome one's subjective or private feelings, preferences, inclinations, or expectations that may seduce or tempt one to come to premature, wishful, or one-sided understandings of an experience that would prevent one from coming to terms with a phenomenon as it is lived through.

Gadamer (1975) describes this process in terms of being open to the other while recognizing biases. According to him, knowledge in the human sciences always involves self-knowledge.

> This openness always includes our situating the other meaning in relation to the whole of our own meanings or ourselves in relation to it ... This kind of sensitivity involves neither "neutrality" with respect to content nor the extinction of one's self, but the foregrounding and appropriation of one's own fore-meanings and prejudices. The important thing is to be aware of one's own bias, so that the text can present itself in all its otherness and thus assert its own truth against one's own fore-meanings. (Gadamer, 1975, pp. 268-269)

Thus, in terms of research, the researcher should shift back and forth, focusing on personal assumptions and then returning to looking at participants' experiences in a fresh way. Wertz (2005) picks up this point when accepting the value of researchers' subjective experience when engaging the epoché of the natural attitude and during the analyses that follow from the phenomenological reduction. He suggests this process allows researchers to:

> recollect our own experiences and to empathically enter and reflect on the lived world of other persons ... as they are given to the first-person point of view. The psychologist can investigate his or her own original sphere of experience and also has an intersubjective horizon of experience that allows access to the experiences of others. (Wertz, 2005, p. 168)

Following Wertz, in a previous paper I discussed the "phenomenological psychological attitude" as a process of retaining a reductive openness to the world while both restraining and using preunderstandings (Finlay, 2008). Here, the researcher engages a dialectic movement between bracketing preunderstandings and exploiting them reflexively as a source of insight. I suggest the challenge for

25

phenomenological researchers is "to simultaneously embody contradictory attitudes of being 'scientifically removed from,' 'open to' and 'aware of' while also interacting with research participants in the midst of their own experiencing" (Finlay, 2008, p. 3). In this context, researcher reflexivity in hermeneutic phenomenology becomes a "process of continually reflecting upon our interpretations of both our experience and the phenomena being studied so as to move beyond the partiality of our previous understandings" (Finlay, 2003b, p. 108). To use Gadamer's metaphor (1975), it involves an active evaluation of the researcher's own experience in order to understand something of the fusion of horizons between subject and object.

> Our understanding of 'other-ness' arises through a process of making ourselves more transparent ... New understandings emerge from a complex dialogue between knower and known, between the researcher's pre-understandings and the current research process. (Finlay, 2011, p. 114)

One critical danger of engaging researcher reflexivity is that of falling prey to navel gazing. The researcher needs to avoid preoccupation with their own emotions and experience if the research is not to be pulled in unfortunate directions which privilege the researcher over the participant. The focus needs to stay on the research participant and the phenomenon in its appearing.[8]

One possible way of avoiding this trap is to embrace the intersubjective relationship between researcher and researched. "There is a reciprocal insertion and intertwining of one in the other," says Merleau-Ponty (1968, p. 138). As researcher and participant intermingle in "pre-analytic participation" (1968, p. 203), each touches and impacts on the other.

> Where more explicitly relational approaches to phenomenological research are adopted, data is seen to emerge out of the researcher-participant relationship, and is understood to be co-created in the embodied dialogical encounter.[9] Researchers who support working in this way argue that what we can know about another arises from that intersubjective space between. Examples of this way of working include the research by Halling and colleagues (2006) using their dialogal method; Churchill's (2003) research on empathy and communication with a bonobo; and my own reflexive-relational phenomenology. (Finlay, 2009; Finlay & Payman, forthcoming)

The passage reproduced in italicized text below is taken from reflexive-relational research on one woman's (Mia's) traumatic abortion-cum-miscarriage experience shows a layered process of how the researcher's (Barbara's) reflexive interpretations formed part of the eventual analysis.

> "Mia integrates layers of monstrous damage, betrayal and abandonment which have replayed themselves through at least two generations. She 'betrayed' her baby and she 'abandoned' herself (psychically in her dissociation), just as her mother 'betrayed' and 'abandoned' her."

Barbara writes reflexively of Mia's miscarriage experience:

"And I curled up and went to sleep with my little glass with the blood in it in the bathroom." I feel myself reacting to Mia's words – it is almost as if I have to remind myself to breathe – somehow her words 'take my breath away'...

I think perhaps it is as if I am being transported into the scene. My empathy for Mia is evoked in such a way that it is almost as if I am somehow 'identifying' with her. I have the sense that so much of her (life) story could be found within those few words ...

The girl (Mia) had to be 'so big' – had to 'look after herself,' no matter how difficult things were emotionally. Somehow 'my little glass' seems to symbolize so much; to carry so much of 'the story' – no matter how bad things got (like 'giving birth' to 'her baby' in the toilet). She still had to get it together herself to look after herself (fish 'the baby' out of the toilet into a glass). And somehow maybe Mia metaphorically captures the 'distance' of mother from child (i.e. the absence of an 'empathic other') in the picture of 'her baby' being 'in a glass,' 'in the bathroom' as she sleeps in the bedroom whilst similarly her own mother has returned to her room to sleep leaving Mia alone." (Finlay & Payman, forthcoming)

SCIENCE OR ART?

All phenomenologists agree on the need to study human beings in human terms. They therefore reject positivist, natural science methods in favor of a qualitative human science approach. As a human *science*, phenomenology aims to be systematic, methodical, general, and critical (Giorgi, 1997). At the same time, phenomenology also pursues the intertwining of science with art, the imparting of a "poetic sensibility" (Ashworth, personal communication) to the scientific enterprise. In this sense, science blends with the stylistic realms of the *humanities*. Where phenomenologists disagree, is about how much weight should be accorded to scientific versus artistic elements.

While Giorgi supports the need to have a "certain openness and flexibility" (2008a, p. 42) when it comes to applying his method, he insists that criteria associated with scientific rigor need to be completely respected. Any discerned meanings that come out of the research need to be seen as based on data and achieved through a systematic process of free imaginative variation which allows a kind of internal validity check.[10] A rigorous application of this eidetic variation involves freely changing aspects of the phenomenon in order to distinguish essential features from particular or incidental ones.

Other phenomenologists, particularly of hermeneutic persuasion, recommend engaging modes beyond the scientific: Art, literary prose, and poetry can be utilized at all stages of research as part of data collection, analysis and writing up. Jager (2010) argues that researchers interested in the human condition need to think in terms that apply to our lived world:

An education [or phenomenology] remains only partial and incomplete as long as it concentrates exclusively on science and technology...and neglects the religious, literary, musical, thoughtful, and artful practices that build a liveable human world ...

> We should remain mindful of the fact that we come face to face and heart to heart with our friends and neighbour or with a work of art only by entering into a covenant and obeying the grammar of an inhabited cosmos. (2010, pp. 80-81)

Hermeneutic phenomenologists like Jager seek methods that retain their concrete, mooded, sensed, imaginative, and embodied nature (Finlay, 2011). Todres, for example, recommends balancing textural and structural forms as part of communicating the aesthetic dimensions of human experience (Todres, 2000, 2007). Hermeneutic phenomenologists in particular will often utilize metaphor in the service of finding words that carry textural, visceral dimensions of lived experience forward. A net may be cast wide across space and time, the cosmos and history, drawing on myths and parables, fable and fiction. "The words must be made to vibrate to the touch of Eros" (Blouin, 2009).

Todres opens such a space in the following passage:

> In living a human life we come with the seasons, with dryness and wetness, with the rhythms of darkness and delight, of going away and coming back, of continuities and great discontinuities, with its Janus-face of both potential anguish and renewal. Framing and permeating all this is finitude; there, in the possibility of not being, and there, in the fragility of flowers, in the beauty of a sunset, and in the passing of a smile. (Todres, 2007, p. 116)

"Phenomenology, not unlike poetry," says van Manen (1990, p. 13), is a "poetizing project; it tries an incantative, evocative speaking, a primal telling, wherein we aim to involve the voice in an original singing of the world." More recently, he suggests that,

> not unlike the poet, the phenomenologist directs the gaze toward the regions where meaning originates, wells up, percolates through the porous membranes of past sedimentations – and then infuses us, permeates us, infects us, touches us, stirs us, exercises a formative affect. (van Manen, 2007, p. 12)

Embracing the Utrecht School tradition, van Manen (1990, 2007) advocates the writing up of phenomenological research as including, ideally, an artistic dimension to "stir our pedagogical, psychological or professional sensibilities" (van Manen, 2007, p. 25). His point highlights how the balance of science-art considerations may shift according to the stage of research.

My belief is that researchers need to attend to the audience they are attempting to communicate with. I value research which has *both* rigor and resonance. I favor reporting research in whatever mode is going to have the most relevance and impact. Broader political, instrumental, or strategic interests cannot be ignored and it behoves phenomenologists to be reflexively aware of the issues at stake when they are presenting their research (Finlay, 2006a). Sometimes, researcher arguments are best presented by emphasizing the systematic nature of research methods applied and the scientific credentials of the research. At other times, the research may be more memorable when creatively presented. As Behar (1996 as cited in Bochner 2001) once said in reference to anthropology, research which "doesn't break your heart just isn't worth doing anymore" (p. 143). A phenomenological text is most successful when readers feel addressed by it (van Manen, 2007):

> Textual emotion, textual understanding can bring an otherwise sober-minded person (the reader but also the author) to tears and to a more deeply understood worldly engagement ... To write phenomenologically is the untiring effort to author a sensitive grasp of being itself. (van Manen, 1990, pp. 129, 132)

Similarly, I value the communicative power of research that challenges, unsettles, and reverberates with our everyday experience of life. I want to be touched by the allusive power of research which resonates and evokes the ambivalence and ambiguity of lived experience. In my view, phenomenology achieves this best when it can turn to aesthetic, literary forms turning the reading of research into an experience in itself.

An example of a hermeneutic entwining of research and literature is offered in in the italicized text below. In his research, Madison (2005, 2010) explores the phenomenon of 'existential migration' both empirically (by interviewing twenty voluntary migrants about their experience) and conceptually (by weaving into his thesis philosophical and literary references). He suggests a number of themes including notions of escape, freedom, belongingness, homelessness and return while drawing on the Heideggerian concept of *Unheimlichkeit* (not-at-homeness). Madison's analysis is further enriched by literary allusions including the epilogue of J.R.R. Tolkein's *Lord of the Rings*.

> "As the main characters return to the Shire homelands, Frodo, in conversation with the wise wizard Gandalf, complains about his shoulder wound. Gandalf sighs: "Alas! There are some wounds that cannot be wholly cured." Frodo continues:
>
> I fear it may be so with mine ... There is no real going back ... I shall not be the same ... To me [returning home] feels more like falling asleep again ...
>
> ... The fact that our co-researchers seem to continue to look for 'home' in some form indicates that they, at least at times, seek the tranquilized 'at-homeness' that they are nonetheless unconvinced by .... (Madison, 2010, pp. 181, 201)

MODERN OR POSTMODERN PARADIGMS?

Denzin and Lincoln (1994) assert that the qualitative research field is "defined by a series of tensions, contradictions, and hesitations" which move back and forth between "the broad, doubting postmodern sensibility and the more certain, more traditional positivist, postpositivist, and naturalistic conceptions of this project" (p. 15). Phenomenology is not exempt and the different variants of phenomenology, with their different supporters are caught in, and articulate, this debate (Finlay, 2011).

Phenomenology is sometimes linked to a modernist agenda (Moran, 2000). Some would argue that it offers an inductive methodology to explore human subjectivity systematically in terms of what individuals are *really* feeling and experiencing. "The main function of a phenomenological description is to serve as a reliable guide to the listener's own actual or potential experience of the phenomena" (Spiegelberg, 1982, p. 694). Here, phenomena are seen to be made up of essences and essential structures which can be identified and described if studied carefully and rigorously enough. In such characterizations, phenomenology can be seen as tending towards being a realist, modernist project where there is a belief in a knowable world with universal properties (at least in some senses), and the aim is to examine the "real world out there."

Others would deny such a simplistic and static view of the phenomenological project. For one thing, attributing fixed immutable properties to human phenomenon is antithetical to the phenomenological project. Philosophers such as Hegel have stressed essence as being a dynamic, dialectical process (Mills, 2005). Also, phenomenological philosophy originally arose, at least in part, in critique of the effects of modern natural human scientific outlook on human beings.[11] If modernism is aligned to a worldview of an ordered universe ruled by mathematical laws which can eventually be uncovered by science (Polkinghorne, 1992), then phenomenology might be better described as postmodern. In this context, many phenomenologists favor an approach which forgoes any search of true fixed meanings, recognizing that truth is a matter of perspective. Instead, they embrace ambiguity, paradox, descriptive nuance, and a more relational unfolding of meanings (Merleau-Ponty, 1968). They recognize the relative, intersubjective, fluid nature of knowledge. They argue that researcher and participant co-create the research; that subject-object/self-other are intertwined in intergivenness (Marion, 2002).[12] In such a paradigm, also, the phenomenological researcher's epistemological authority is disrupted.

Giorgi (1994) engages elements of this debate by highlighting the epistemological rift between "naturalist" and "phenomenological" paradigms. Following Lincoln and Guba (1985), he describes the naturalist paradigm as claiming multiple, constructed, holistic realities where the knower and known are seen as inseparable and interactive. By then contrasting this paradigm with the phenomenological one, he seems to aim to distance phenomenology from any whiff of relativist postmodern sensibility, while favoring a more modernist and grounded critical realist position[13] which admits to a reality independent of consciousness (while accepting knowledge of this can only come through study of consciousness). For him, the phenomenological paradigm involves the researcher describing "the nature of reality as taken up and posited by the research participants. This frees the researcher to discover possible reality claims that may be outside his or her a priori specifications" (1994, p. 203). At the same time, Giorgi supports the Husserlian argument which both insists the groundedness of essential structures and accepts the multiplicity and relativity of appearances,[14] including how these arise in the intersubjective encounter of knower and known – sentiments which seem to come close to the naturalist ideas described by Lincoln and Guba.

The argument about whether phenomenology is a modernist or postmodernist project largely rests on how one defines these concepts (Kvale, 1992). If postmodernism is seen as a perspective which: (i) avoids privileging any one authority or method, (ii) embraces ambiguity, paradox and multiple meanings and (iii) denies that any one approach has a clear window on subjectivity/human experience, then many phenomenologists would feel comfortable with this position. In fact, it could said that even Husserl's early work laid the foundations of the postmodern movement by highlighting varying modes of givenness and relativity of appearances (Rodemeyer, 2008). Here, relativity of understanding is stressed instead of relativism as such (Churchill, 2002).

For some, however, postmodernism involves the dissolution of the autonomous, rational subject: the "self is anesthetized" (Mills, 2005, p. 166). Postmodernism is also associated largely with the poststructural, relativist, deconstructive turn where language is seen as an unstable system of referents, thus making it impossible to adequately capture meanings of social actions or texts leading to messy, critical, reflexive, intertextual representations. Supporters of the turn to discourse argue that we cannot simply see participants' talk about their subjective feelings and experiences as a transparent medium through which to glimpse their (internal) worlds. Instead, they say, we need to focus on the performative and constitutive aspect of language which deconstructs any truths concerning a *subject's* lived experience. While fewer (if any) phenomenologists support this more extreme position, some are working to bridge both modernist and poststructural paradigms. Langdridge (2008), notably, seeks to bring together phenomenology and discursive psychology through Ricoeurian hermeneutics and the application of critical social theory.

The question at stake is: where does phenomenology fit in a postmodern world of ironically shifting boundaries and plurality of perspectives, a world in which construction and deconstruction (of both language and lived embodiment) seem twin imperatives? In the world of qualitative research, where cultural and historical contingency are highlighted, and discursive, poststructuralist, feminist/alternative approaches dominate, is there a plausible space for assertions of authentic selves and universal truths? Or is Langdridge (2008) correct in his critique that phenomenology has continued its mission with "scant regard for the issues raised by contemporary philosophers of language and ... discursive psychology" (p. 1134)? Can phenomenology embrace the 21st century future without casting regretful backward glances to earlier times?

I believe phenomenology needs to move forward and take its place beyond the modernist-postmodernist divide – the era some call post-postmodernism. The goal-posts and language of psychology (and other disciplines) and the qualitative research field have changed over the last few decades. I think it is necessary for phenomenologists to deal with this "new age where messy, uncertain, multivoiced texts, cultural criticism, and new experimental works will become more common, as will more reflexive forms of fieldwork, analysis and intertextual representation" (Denzin & Lincoln, 1994, p. 15). I appreciate the move towards less authoritative, self-critical texts which acknowledge their partial, partisan and socially contingent character. I can enjoy forms of phenomenology where poetic, hyper-reflexive forms offer an ironic counter-point representing our ambivalent, fragmented, multi-colored lived worlds. Ihde's (1993) notion of postphenomenology works well here:

> Postphenomenology is precisely the style of phenomenology which explicitly and dare I say 'consciously' takes multidimensionality, multistability, and the multiple 'voices' of things into account – to that degree it bears a family resemblance to the postmodern. (Ihde, 2003, p. 26)

In the current climate, phenomenologists (along with other types of human science researchers) are challenged to recognize that any knowledge produced is contingent, proportional, emergent, and subject to alternative interpretations. At the very least research which is anchored in a more critical realist, modernist position deserves some healthy questioning and can expect critical challenge. The practice of returning to participants to validate researchers' analyses, for example, could be disputed as a problematic throwback to empirical, realist ideals.[15] At the same time, while phenomenologists may embrace more ironically playful, creative presentations and relativist understandings, they must also ensure they do not lose the speaking, embodied, experiencing subject.

I like the message offered by Gendlin (1997): "Let us enter and speak from the realm that opens where all distinctions break down" (p. 269). We need to go beyond the lines drawn by both modernism and postmodernism embracing both and neither.

CONCLUSION

In this chapter, I have mapped out some of the key areas of confusion and controversy surrounding the application of phenomenology in research. Researchers entering the phenomenological field have to decide for themselves where they stand on questions concerning what paradigm phenomenologists embrace, what their research means, and to what extent interpretation can be involved in the basic descriptive project. They need to work out whether they are seeking normative or idiographic understandings, how to manage researcher subjectivity, and whether phenomenology should be treated as a science, an art, or both.

> The competing visions of how to practice phenomenology stem from different philosophical values, theoretical preferences, and methodological procedures. Different forms are demanded according to the type of phenomenon under investigation and the kind of knowledge the researcher seeks. Given a multiplicity of appearances and meanings, surely a multiplicity of methods is also appropriate. Rather than being fixed in stone, the different phenomenological approaches need to remain dynamic and undergo constant development as the field of qualitative research as a whole evolves: "The flexibility of phenomenological research and the adaptability of its methods to ever widening arcs of inquiry is one of its greatest strengths." (Garza, 2007, p. 338).

Whatever method is embraced, the value of phenomenology remains its ability to bring to life the richness and ambiguity of existence (Finlay, 2011). The magic comes when we see ordinary, taken-for-granted living as something more layered, more nuanced, more unexpected and as potentially transformative; when something is revealed of the *extra*-ordinary.

ACKNOWLEDGMENTS

I am indebted to Steen Halling for being open to dialoguing with me, and so generously offering his time to read and comment on an earlier draft of this chapter.

ENDNOTES

[1] Psychological phenomenological approaches can be contrasted with social phenomenological approaches as advanced by Schütz (1967) and others. In this chapter, I restrict my discussion to psychological phenomenology and I privilege empirical forms of research where participants are involved.

[2] Ashworth (2003, 2006) offers the following list as "fractions" to be employed heuristically in phenomenological lifeworld analysis including: selfhood (meanings of identity, agency, presence, voice); relationships with other people and what others mean to the person (sociality); embodiment (meanings related to one's own sense of one's body); temporality (meanings about past, present and future); spatiality (sense of place, space and bodily scope and possibilities); project (the central concern for the person which reveals itself in the situation); discourse (socially available ways of talking or acting that the person is drawing upon); mood-as-atmosphere (i.e., the feeling tone of the situation).

[3] Technically, the term "intuition" is used in Husserlian philosophy to refer to the experienced presence of any object to consciousness, be it perceived or imagined. Intuition, in this sense, can be understood as general understanding of "fleshy actuality" (Marion, 2002) rather than the more common usage definition as a hunch which is tacit and elusive.

[4] Other commentators such as von Eckartsberg (1998) call the descriptive version "empirical existential-phenomenological" and contrast it with the "hermeneutical phenomenological" approach. He suggests a number of researchers follow this tradition including Amedeo Giorgi, Adrian van Kaam, Paul Colaizzi and William Fischer.

[5] Scholars contest the extent of confluence between Husserlian and Heideggerian philosophy. Some argue that the ontological dimension was present in Husserl's work on life-world and developed with his generative phenomenology; others suggest that Heidegger nudged Husserlian ideas in a different direction. Then there are some who say that positing a "continuum" of description and interpretation may be insufficiently attentive to the radical nature of Heidegger's ontological concerns which moved away from philosophy as a scientific discipline.

[6] Ricoeur's hermeneutics of suspicion go beyond what is given, for example, where Freudian-type analysis brings understanding to bear which is not in the analysand's awareness. Most phenomenologists would argue that the phenomenological spirit is to stay anchored to what is given.

[7] For Husserl, the reduction delivers the philosopher to the "groping entrance into this unknown realm of subjective phenomena" (1936/1970, p. 161). A number of steps or procedures are involved including: 1) the *epoché* of the natural sciences; 2) the *epoché* of the natural attitude; 3) the transcendental reduction; and 4) eidetic reduction. Each of these results in something being put in "brackets" and in a "reduction" of the field which commands one's special focus of attention. The problem remains: how to convert this philosophical method into a practical and empirical one?

[8] Giorgi (1994) offers a more specific argument against the dangers of researchers' overemphasising their own self-awareness and attention to the research relationship – at least in the context of

practising a phenomenological method true to Husserl's project. Giorgi would argue the need to keep clear the intentional objects to which the researcher's acts are directed. He asserts that work like Moustakas' (1990) use of "self-dialogue" in his heuristic research approach is not consistent with the phenomenological project as the goal appears to be a researcher's own growth and self-development rather than the explication of a phenomenon. (For this reason, while some phenomenologists might include "heuristic research" as part of the broader field of phenomenological inquiry, others would not.)

[9] This kind of approach might be criticized for mixing up the focus of the inquiry (i.e., the phenomenon being investigated moves onto the relationship) and for collapsing therapeutic and research interests (Giorgi, 2008b).

[10] Halling (2008) suggests a slightly different version of this free imaginative variation which he calls "empirical variation." Here, emphasis is placed on working collaboratively with others where the group members dialogue about their various perspectives allowing the phenomenon to show itself in new ways. In adopting such an approach, Halling is engaged in a distinctly scientific project. However, he also acknowledges something of the art within the process: "The process is an intermingling of receptivity and creativity, of discovering truth and creating truth" (Halling, 2008, p. 168).

[11] For example, Husserl has argued against rationalism promoting naïve objectivism and naturalizing the spirit; Heidegger's work is conceived as antimodernism; and Gadamer argues that not all truth is encapsulated in the scientific method.

[12] In the relational-centred approach developed by Ken Evans and myself (Finlay & Evans, 2009), for example, data is seen to emerge out of the researcher-coresearcher relationship, co-created in the embodied dialogical encounter. There is an ambiguity and unpredictability that arises in that intersubjective opening between, where anything can appear. Central to this approach is the need to develop awareness of intersubjective research dynamics and parallel processes (where unconscious processes are being re-enacted) through reflexivity.

[13] In between the two poles of realism and relativism is a position variously called "critical realist," "subtle realist" or "new realist." Here researchers tend to be pragmatic. They consider meanings to be fluid while accepting that participants' stories of having an illness reflect something of their subjective perceptions of their experience (if not their actual experience) (Finlay, 2006b).

[14] There are, as Husserl notes in *Ideas 1*, varying modes of givenness. How the givenness is unfurled depends on the extent of the reduction performed – the more reduction, the more givenness (Marion, 2002). Put in other words, the givenness of lived experience can only be captured (in parts and in different appearances) through the reduction.

[15] Colaizzi (1978) recommends participant verification as a final stage of his seven-step analysis. New data emerging from participants' feedback "must be worked into the final product" (1978, p. 62). Giorgi (2008b), on the other hand, argues that such member checking is both misplaced and not trustworthy, as participants in their natural attitude, cannot confirm the meaning of their experiences; nor do they have the relevant phenomenological skills or disciplinary attitude necessary to adequately judge the analysis.

REFERENCES

Ashworth, P.D. (1996). Presuppose nothing! The suspension of assumptions in phenomenological psychological methodology. *Journal of Phenomenological Psychology, 27*(1), 1-25.

Ashworth, P.D. (2003). An approach to phenomenological psychology: The contingencies of the lifeworld. *Journal of Phenomenological Psychology, 34*(2), 145-156.

Ashworth, P.D. (2006). Seeing oneself as a career in the activity of caring. Attending to the lifeworld of the person with Alzheimer's disease. *International Journal of Qualitative Studies in Health and Well-being, 1*(4), 212-225.

Ashworth, A., & Ashworth, P.D. (2003). The lifeworld as phenomenon and as research heuristic, exemplified by a study of the lifeworld of a person suffering Alzheimer's disease. *Journal of Phenomenological Psychology, 34*(2), 179-207.

Blouin, P. (2009). Pornography and eroticism. Paper given at the International Human Science Research Conference, June 2009, Molde, Norway.

Bochner, P.P. (2001). Narrative's virtues. *Qualitative Inquiry, 7*(20), 131-56.

Churchill, S.D. (2002). Stories of experience and the experience of stories: Narrative psychology, phenomenology, and the Postmodern Challenge. *Constructivism in the Human Sciences, 7*, 81-93.

Churchill, S.D. (2003). Gestural communication with a bonobo: Empathy, alterity, and carnal intersubjectivity. *Constructivism in the Human Sciences, 8*(1), 19-36.

Colaizzi, P.F. (1973). *Reflection and research in psychology: A phenomenological study of learning.* Dubuque, IA: Kendall Hunt Publishing. *Phenomenology & Practice,* 21.

Colaizzi, P. (1978). Psychological research as the phenomenologist views it. In R. Valle & King (Eds.), *Existential-phenomenological alternatives for psychology* (pp. 48-71). New York: Oxford UP.

Crotty, M. (1996). *Phenomenology and nursing research.* Melbourne, Australia: Churchill Livingstone.

Dalhberg, K., Dalhberg, H., & Nyström, M. (2008). *Reflective lifeworld research* (2nd edition). Lund, Sweden: Studentlitteratur.

Denzin, N.K., & Lincoln, Y.S. (Eds.). (1994). *Handbook of qualitative research.* Thousand Oaks, CA: Sage.

Eatough, V., & Smith, J. (2006). "I was like a wild wild person": Understanding feelings of anger using interpretative phenomenological analysis. *British Journal of Psychology, 97*, 483-498.

Finlay, L. (2003a). The intertwining of body, self and world: A phenomenological study of living with recently diagnosed multiple sclerosis. *Journal of Phenomenological Psychology, 34*(6), 157-178.

Finlay, L. (2003b). Through the looking glass: Intersubjectivity and hermeneutic reflection. In L. Finlay & B. Gough (Eds.), *Reflexivity: A practical guide for researchers in health and social sciences.* Oxford: Blackwell Publishing.

Finlay, L. (2006a). 'Rigour,' 'ethical integrity' or 'artistry': Reflexively reviewing criteria for evaluating qualitative research. *British Journal of Occupational Therapy, 69*(7), 319-326.

Finlay, L. (2006b). Mapping methodology. In L. Finlay & C. Ballinger (Eds.), *Qualitative research for allied health professionals: Challenging choices.* Chichester, Sussex: John Wiley.

Finlay, L. (2008). A dance between the reduction and reflexivity: Explicating the "phenomenological psychological attitude." *Journal of Phenomenological Psychology, 39*, 1-32.

Finlay, L. (2009). Ambiguous encounters: A relational approach to phenomenological research. *Indo-Pacific Journal of Phenomenology, 3*, 6-25.

Finlay, L., & Molano-Fisher, P. (2008). 'Transforming' self and world: A phenomenological study of a changing lifeworld following a cochlear implant. *Medicine, Health Care and Philosophy, 11*(2). (Online version available from 2007). *Linda Finlay* 22.

Finlay, L., & Payman, B. (forthcoming). "I'm already torn": A relational-centred phenomenology of a 'traumatic abortion experience.' *Janus Head.*

Finlay, L., & Evans, K. (2009). *Relational centred research for psychotherapists: Exploring meanings and experience.* Chichester, West Sussex: Wiley-Blackwell Publishers.

Fischer, W.F. (1974). On the phenomenological mode of researching 'being anxious.' *Journal of Phenomenological Psychology, 4*(2), 405-423.

Gadamer, H.-G. (1975/1996). *Truth and method* (Second revised edition). London: Sheed and Ward.

Garza, G. (2007). Varieties of phenomenological research at the University of Dallas: An emerging typology. *Qualitative Research in Psychology, 4*, 313-342.

Gendlin, E.T. (1997). Reply to Liberman: Liberman, K. Meaning reflexivity: Gendlin's contribution to ethnomethodology. In D.M. Levin (Ed.), *Language beyond postmodernism: Saying and thinking in Gendlin's philosophy.* Evanston, IL: Northwestern University Press.

Giorgi, A. (1975). An application of phenomenological method in psychology. In A. Giorgi, C. Fischer & E. Murray (Eds.), *Duquesne studies in phenomenological psychology: Volume II* (pp. 72-79). Pittsburgh, PA: Duquesne University Press.

Giorgi, A. (ed.). (1985). *Phenomenological and psychological research*. Pittsburgh, PA: Duquesne University Press.

Giorgi, A. (1986). Theoretical justification for the use of descriptions in psychological research. In P. Ashworth, A. Giorgi & A.J.J. de Koning (Eds.), *Qualitative research in psychology: Proceedings of the International Association for Qualitative Research*. Pittsburgh, PA: Duquesne University Press.

Giorgi, A. (1989). One type of analysis of descriptive data: Procedures involved in following a phenomenological method. *Methods, 1*, 39-61.

Giorgi, A. (1994). A phenomenological perspective on certain qualitative research methods. *Journal of Phenomenological Psychology, 25*, 190-220.

Giorgi, A. (1997). The theory, practice, and evaluation of the phenomenological method as a qualitative research procedure. *Journal of Phenomenological Psychology, 28*(2), 235-260.

Giorgi, A. (2008a). Concerning a serious misunderstanding of the essence of the phenomenological method in psychology. *Journal of Phenomenological Psychology, 39*, 33-58. *Phenomenology & Practice* 23.

Giorgi, A. (2008b). Difficulties encountered in the application of the phenomenological method in the social sciences. *The Indo-Pacific Journal of Phenomenology, 8*(1), 1-9.

Halling, S. (2008). *Intimacy, transcendence, and psychology: Closeness and openness in everyday life*. New York: Palgrave Macmillan.

Halling, S., Leifer, M., & Rowe, J.O. (2006). Emergence of the dialogal approach: Forgiving another. In C. T. Fischer (Ed.), *Qualitative research methods for psychology: Introduction through empirical studies* (pp. 247-278). New York: Academic Press.

Heidegger, M. (1927/1962). *Being and time*. Oxford: Blackwell. (1962 text J. Macquarrie & E. Robinson, Trans.)

Husserl, E. (1970). *The crisis of European sciences and transcendental phenomenology*. Evanston, IL: Northwestern University Press. (Original work published in 1936.)

Husserl, E. (1983). *Ideas pertaining to a pure phenomenology and to a phenomenological philosophy. First book* (F. Kersten, Trans.). The Hague: Martinus Nijhoff. (Original work published 1913.)

Ihde, D. (1993). *Postphenomenology: Essays in the postmodern context*. Evanston, IL: Northwestern University Press.

Ihde, D. (2003). Postphenomenology – Again? Retrieved from http://sts.imv.au/dk/arbejdspapierer/wp3.pdf.

King, N., Finlay, L., Ashworth, P., Smith, J.A., Langdridge, D., & Butt, T. (2008). "Can't really trust that, so what can I trust?": A polyvocal, qualitative analysis of the psychology of mistrust. *Qualitative Research in Psychology, 5*(2), 80-102.

Kvale, S. (Ed.). (1992). *Psychology and postmodernism*. London: Sage.

Langdridge, D. (2008). Phenomenology and critical social psychology: Directions and debates in theory and research. *Social and Personality Psychology Compass, 2*, 1126-1142.

Lincoln, Y.S., & Guba, E.G. (1985). *Naturalistic inquiry*. Beverley Hills, CA: Sage.

Madison, G. (2005). *'Existential migration': Voluntary migrant's experiences of not being-at-home in the world*. PhD Thesis, London: School of Psychotherapy and Counselling Psychology at Regent's College.

Madison, G. (2010). *The end of belonging: Untold stories of leaving home and the psychology of global relocation*. Createspace Publications.

Marion, J.-L. (2002). *Being given: Toward a phenomenology of givenness*. Stanford, CA: Stanford University Press.

Merleau-Ponty, M. (1968). *The visible and the invisible* (A. Lingis, Trans.). Evanston, IL: Northwestern University Press. (Original work published in 1964.) *Linda Finlay* 24.

Mills, J. (2005). A critique of relational psychoanalysis. *Psychoanalytic Psychology, 22*(2), 155-188.

Moran, D. (2000). *Introduction to phenomenology*. London: Routledge.

Moustakas, C. (1990). *Heuristic research: Design, methodology, and applications*. Newbury Park, CA: Sage Publications.

Polkinghorne, D.E. (1992). A postmodern epistemology of practice. In S. Kvale (Ed.), *Psychology and postmodernism* (pp. 146-165). London: Sage.

Rodemeyer, L. (2008). The future of phenomenology: Applications. Retrieved from www.newschool.edu/nssr/husserl/Future/Part%20One/Rodemeyer.html.

Ricoeur, P. (1970). *Freud and philosophy: An essay on interpretation* (D. Savage, Trans.). New Haven, CT: Yale University Press.

Schütz, A. (1967). *The phenomenology of the social world* (G.Welsh & F. Lehnert, Trans.). Evanston, IL: Northwestern University Press. (Original work published 1932.)

Smith, J.A. (2004). Reflecting on the development of interpretative phenomenological analysis and its contribution to qualitative research in psychology. *Qualitative Research in Psychology, 1*(1), 39-54.

Smith, J.A. (2007). Hermeneutics, human sciences and health: Linking theory and practice. *International Journal of Qualitative Studies on Health and Well-being, 2*(1), 3-11.

Smith, J.A., & Osborn, M. (2003). Interpretative phenomenological analysis. In J.A. Smith (Ed.), *Qualitative psychology*. London: Sage.

Spiegelberg, H. (1982). *The phenomenological movement*. Boston: Martinus Nijhoff.

Todres, L. (2000). Writing phenomenological-psychological description: An illustration attempting to balance texture and structure. *Auto/Biography, 3* (1&2), 41-48.

Todres, L. (2005). Clarifying the life-world: Descriptive phenomenology. In I. Holloway (Ed.), *Qualitative research in health care*. Buckinghamshire: Open University Press.

Todres, L. (2007). *Embodied enquiry: Phenomenological touchstones for research, psychotherapy and spirituality*. Basingstoke, Hampshire: Palgrave Macmillan. *Phenomenology & Practice 25.*

Todres, L., & Galvin, K. (2005). Pursuing both breadth and depth in qualitative research: Illustrated by a study of the experience of intimate caring for a loved one with Alzheimer's disease. *International Journal of Qualitative Methods, 4*(2), 1-11.

Todres, L., & Galvin, K. (2006). Caring for a partner with Alzheimer's disease: Intimacy, loss and the life that is possible. *International Journal of Qualitative Studies in Health and Well-being, 1,* 50-61.

Todres, L., Galvin, K., & Dahlberg, K. (2007). Lifeworld-led healthcare: Revisiting a humanising philosophy that integrates emerging trends. *Medicine, Health Care and Philosophy, 10,* 53-63.

Wertz, F. (1985). Method and findings in a phenomenological study of a complex lifeevent: Being criminally victimised. In A. Giorgi (Ed.), *Phenomenology and psychological research*. Pittsburgh, PA: Duquesne University Press.

Wertz, F. (2005). Phenomenological research methods for counseling psychology. *Journal of Counseling Psychology, 52*(2), 167-177.

von Eckartsberg, R. (1998). Introducing existential-phenomenological psychology. In R. Valle (Ed.), *Phenomenological inquiry in psychology: Existential and transpersonal dimensions* (pp. 3-20). New York: Plenum Press.

van Manen, M. (1990). *Researching lived experience: Human science for an action sensitive pedagogy*. New York: State University of New York Press.

van Manen, M. (2002). *The heuristic reduction: Wonder*. Accessed November 2007 from: www.phenomenologyonline.com/inquiry/11.html.

van Manen, M. (2007). Phenomenology of practice. *Phenomenology & Practice, 1*(1), 11.

NORM FRIESEN

3. EXPERIENTIAL EVIDENCE: I, WE, YOU

INTRODUCTION

If hermeneutic phenomenology is the study of the meanings of lived experiences, how exactly do we come to *know about* experience and its meanings? In this chapter, I address this question by considering four positions or perspectives evident in common language, and also often implicit in the language of phenomenological research. These are:

- The first-person perspective of the "I," which corresponds to *subjective* knowledge;
- The second-person perspective of "you," which corresponds to *ethical* concerns;
- The third-person perspective of "it" or "one," corresponding to *objective* knowledge;
- The first-person plural perspective of "we," corresponding to *inter*subjective knowledge.[1]

I explore each of these perspectives and corresponding forms of knowledge in turn, focusing first on the subjective and objective (I and it), and then looking at the phenomenologically-significant intersubjective (we) and finally, the ethical (you). In doing so, I sketch out a way in which experience can be studied, and its meanings can be interpreted, employing as my examples experiences and language associated with the use of technology.

To begin, consider this description of student experience in an online context:

> Imagine my surprise when I checked my blog the next day, and saw a comment from someone named Ari in Germany: "Nice story, Janet! I really like the fact that you got some help from others to get your project page done. I think this is very important in wikis." In the days that followed, Ari's comments boosted my confidence and motivated me to complete my first contribution to Wikipedia. (Adapted from Friesen & Hopkins 2008, n.p.)

This passage has many characteristics that make it potentially interesting and effective as an experiential description. One of the most important of these is the *perspective* from which it is told: Grammatically speaking, this is the perspective of the first person singular, of the "I": "Imagine *my* surprise when *I* checked *my* blog ...." First person pronouns appear no less than seven times in this short passage. This description, then, is told from the position of the subject or "active participant," from what has been called the "inner-perspective" (Irrgang, 2007, pp. 23, 27). This is the perspective of subjective knowledge and personal impression. This is a position, for example, from which a person can say that he or she "really

N. Friesen et al. (eds.), Hermeneutic Phenomenology in Education, 39–54.

liked" something, or in which he or she can talk about having (or lacking) confidence and motivation to complete a difficult task. The position of the "I" has traditionally been taken as *the* starting point for certainty and knowledge overall. Descartes's famous phrase "I think; therefore I am" suggests that the thoughts I experience serve directly as the basis for the very existence of that "I." From this understanding, according to Descartes, should follow other certainties about myself and the world around me. However, this way of arriving at knowledge and certainty presents significant problems and challenges. Above all, this first-person knowledge is plagued by its potential to be "just" personal, idiosyncratic or arbitrary. That which is known in such a personal way may be private, or be kept as a kind of secret that is inaccessible to others. The relative "inaccessibility" of this subjective knowledge has led it to be derided as "merely" subjective, as capricious, biased, or idiosyncratic. Of course, this internal, subjective knowledge of the first person is in many ways the direct opposite of *objective* knowledge. Objective knowledge is thought to be independent from the subject or the "I," and is exemplified in the third-person perspective corresponding to the words "he/she/they," "it" or "one"). It is a position of the "onlooker" rather than of the active participant. It is the position, as Irrgang explains, of the "instrumentally-oriented...measuring observer," and is taken for granted as the objective or "natural" stance in the context of quantitative and scientific research (2007, p. 18). In its idealised form, this third-person knowledge is cleansed of any taint of the personal or subjective bias. Objective, independent knowledge of this kind is the operative mode in experimental research that attempts to establish generalizable or universal causal laws and interrelationships. It is gained not through subjective caprice, but by following rules and procedures that are unambiguous and unchanging. These rules and procedures are exemplified in scientific methods and measures that are meant to prove open, repeatable, and verifiable. They serve as a kind of ideal or paradigm for the type of research mentioned earlier that would measure the "statistically significant" difference caused by the introduction of technology in educational contexts. Unlike subjective, first-person knowledge, which is internal and even hidden, third-person objective knowledge is there for all to see. "Objective" realities and conditions persist or change independently, in apparent indifference to one's inner thoughts and feelings.

The perspectives of the subjective "I" and the objective "it" initially appear as mutually exclusive. Each is relatively independent of the other, and one cannot be reduced to the terms of the other. Feelings, impressions, or intimate secrets that may be constitutive of the "I" or self cannot simultaneously be explained away in objective terms. Feelings of pain (or pleasure) do not simply disappear by being accounted for in terms of nerve simulation and the brain's sensory receptors. Merleau-Ponty gives eloquent expression to the irreconcilability of these two ways of knowing in the preface to his *Phenomenology of Perception* (2002):

> I cannot conceive myself as nothing but a bit of the world, a mere object of biological, psychological or sociological investigation. I cannot shut myself up within the realm of science. All my knowledge of the world, even my scientific knowledge, is gained from my own particular point of view, or from some experience of the world without

which the symbols of science would be meaningless. The whole universe of science is built upon the world as directly experienced ... we must [therefore] begin by reawakening the basic experience of the world of which science is the second-order expression. (2002, p. ix)

The "I" appears intrinsically and irreconcilably opposed to the "it": The world of objectivity and science cannot shut subjectivity up within itself. The only way to understand "the precise meaning and scope" of science, Merleau-Ponty says, is "by reawakening the basic experience of the world" (p. viii). However, then the question is: Exactly how can this "reawakening" be achieved? Moreover, how can "the basic experience of the world" be brought to life without a retreat into the privacy of the "I"?

MOVING FROM I TO WE

One way to achieve this reawakening of experience is to recall that in addition to the "I" or "it" of the first- and third-person singular, it is also possible to say "we." Whereas "I" corresponds to the world of the subject and "it" (or he/she) to the world of the object, saying "we" opens up a way of knowing that is *inter*subjective. "We," as the first person plural, represents a kind of expansion of the subjectivity of the "I" across a plurality of first-person perspectives. Instead of designating a world of private, personal impressions and subjective knowledge, it refers to impressions and thoughts that can be shared and held in common by multiple subjectivities. This is the world of culture, both in the elevated sense of the arts, and in the everyday sense of social and cultural norms for speech and behavior.

The intersubjective "we" suggests that instead of being caught in an irreconcilable opposition between the objective and the subjective realm, there is a shared reality that is neither predominantly objective *nor* subjective. One way that the intersubjective realm is brought to life and to light is not through introspection exemplified in the "I" or through the objectivity of scientific investigation, but through *phenomenology* as both a methodology and a practice.[2] Writing again in the preface quoted above, Merleau-Ponty describes, in effect, how "I" becomes "we" in what he calls the intersubjective "phenomenological world":

> The phenomenological world is ... the sense which is revealed where the paths of my various experiences intersect, and also where my own and other people's intersect and engage each other like gears ... It is thus inseparable from subjectivity and intersubjectivity, which find their unity when I either take up my past experiences in those of the present, or other people's in my own. ...We witness every minute the miracle of related experiences, and yet nobody knows better than we do how this miracle is worked, for we are ourselves this network of relationships. (2002, p. xxii)

Intersubjectivity, as Merleau-Ponty indicates, designates the intersection, "blending," or mutual conformity of plural subjectivities (2002, p. xii): "perspectives blend, perceptions confirm each other, a meaning emerges" (2002, p. xxii). The world that is experienced in this mutually engaged or convergent subjectivity is neither the private or inaccessible world of "inner-perspective," nor the immutable, indifferent world of the third-person objectivity. To express its unique experiential status, the phenomenological world of the "we" is called the "life-world": a place where "extreme subjectivism and extreme objectivism" are overcome or "united" (2002, p. xxii). This phenomenological world is one that is available through a shared language, through collaborative action, and in common concerns.

This understanding is again illustrated in the brief descriptive passage quoted above. This passage makes use of the "I" perspective of personal feelings and impressions (rather than explicitly saying "we"), it also illustrates how such personal perspectives intersect or, as Merleau-Ponty (2002) says, constitute a "closely woven fabric" (p. xi). Janet and Ari's interactions show how different "people's [experiences] intersect and engage each other like gears" (Merleau-Ponty, 2002, p. xxii): Ari from Germany tells Janet how much he likes the fact that she got help from others. In fact, these comments boost Janet's confidence, motivating her to complete her first article on *Wikipedia*. In this way, this description shows how the shared life-world is one where it is certainly possible to say "I," and to have feelings and impressions of one's own. Further, it also reflects a context in which the first-person pronoun is constituted through its relation with others. Using the "we" or the intersubjective first-person plural perspective himself, Merleau-Ponty puts it this way:

> *We* witness every minute the miracle of related experiences, and yet nobody knows better than *we* do how this miracle is worked, for *we* are ourselves this network of relationships. The world and reason are not problematical. We may say, if we wish, that they are mysterious, but their mystery defines them: there can be no question of dispelling it by some "solution" (2002, p. xxiii, emphases added)

The *we* represents more than one *I*; *we* connects multiple subjectivities through common concerns and feelings, impressions and meanings that are shared in common.

At the same time, though, the word "we" presents challenges: it has been described by some as a "dangerous pronoun" that is sometimes associated with the suppression of difference and even with acts of hate (e.g., Moss, 2003). Peppers (2006) explains that *we* "is a dangerous pronoun when it hides histories of internal conflict under false or superficial commonality." Leaving little or no opportunity for confirmation or qualification, saying "we" in a text often simply assumes that the reader is a part of the superficial agreement. It tacitly but unmistakably asks the reader to align himself or herself with the "I" of the author. In doing so tacitly or implicitly – rather than forthrightly or explicitly – it does not readily allow for conflict and disagreement. By using "we" in this chapter, I am aware of this dilemma. However, I also believe that it can be addressed, not always fully or completely, but in the ethical terms that are proper to it, through the use of the second-person pronoun, "you." I, therefore, return to this issue in the last section of this chapter, where I consider the ethical implications of saying "you."

DIMENSIONS OF LIFE-WORLD EXPERIENCE

Any study of lived experience or research motivated by a phenomenological question is, in effect, an exploration of a small part of the shared life-world. Exploring this intersubjective realm involves particular techniques that combine elements of inner and outer subjectivity and objectivity. One of these techniques is to understand life-world experience as extending or unfolding along four axes, dimensions or "existentials." These life-world dimensions have wide applicability (without being simply "objective") and are also closely connected to the expression of feelings and impressions (without being reduced to "mere" subjectivity). Working in complex intermixture, these dimensions are a part of the way that life-world experience is organized, or inherent in the way we "live in" or inhabit the life-world. Consequently, they are designated as "lived space," "lived time," "lived body" and "lived relation."

Lived space, of course, is *not* the objective area measured by the square feet in a room or kilometers of distance to be travelled; it is instead the way that a room or a distance is lived in or experienced: as warm and inviting, as conveniently nearby or unreachably distant. Max van Manen (2002) characterizes this life-world dimension as follows:

> this space is ... difficult to put into words since the experience of lived space (like that of lived time or body) is largely pre-verbal; we do not ordinarily reflect on it. And yet we know that the space in which we find ourselves affects the way we feel. The huge spaces of a modern bank building may make us feel small, the wide-open space of a landscape may make us feel exposed but also possibly free. And we may feel just the opposite when we get in a crowded elevator. (n.p.)

"In general," van Manen concludes, "we may say that we *become* the space we are in" (2002; emphasis added).

Lived time is similar to the existential dimension of lived space: it is not "objective" time measured through the indifferent units presented on a clock or calendar, but it is the experience of time as something colored by our own lives. It can "speed up when we enjoy ourselves," or slow down "when we feel bored ... or when we... sit anxiously in the dentist's chair" (van Manen, 2002). Significantly, it becomes inextricably intertwined with the experience of space in a monotonously long journey or in a pleasant stroll.

Lived body correspondingly refers to the experience of our own bodies and those of others. Of course, this experience can be sexual or erotic in character, but more often than not, it is banal or at least ambiguous. The body can be the object of another's scrutinizing gaze, in which case it also often becomes an object of awkward self-awareness. It can be comfortable or uncomfortable, but it often disappears from awareness altogether when engaged in an absorbing task. It communicates and connects with others in powerful but elusive ways. We may be particularly aware of this power when we are trying to create a favorable impression on someone: folding one's hands behind one's back (instead of crossing them on one's chest) to communicate openness, or inching backwards as an expression of discomfort or unease. As van Manen notes, "in our physical or bodily

43

presence we both reveal something about ourselves and we conceal something at the same time-not necessarily consciously or deliberately, but rather in spite of ourselves" (1997, p. 103).

Lived relation refers to the everyday experience of other people, or more abstractly, of the "other." Just as we experience time, space and the body in forms that are colored by emotion and impression, so too do we "live" our relations with others in terms that are charged with feeling, texture, and even flavor. This scenario is illustrated in the language we use to describe our relationships and encounters: "She's a prickly person," "he gives me the creeps," "she's always very sweet," or "that certainly leaves a bitter taste in my mouth!" These kinds of expressions show that we experience relation deeply and even sensuously (in terms of taste and tactility), rather than in more objective, intellectual terms.

EXPERIENCE AS INFORMATION OR EVENT

Speaking specifically of *experience* in terms of the dimensions of lived time, space, relation, and embodiment implies a perhaps uncommon way of understanding the term. Experience is often seen as being grounded in sense data, in "information" that is first received through the five senses, and then given "sense" by being "processed," organized, and analyzed in the mind. This particular understanding of experience is sometimes associated with *empiricism*. Empiricism refers to the belief that knowledge arises primarily or exclusively through the senses and, ultimately, that

> experience is only a matter of data, sense data to be sure but data nonetheless. Considered this way experience is nothing more than a basic component of knowledge that completes itself only through an act of reason, that is, in the establishing of patterns, of generalizations ... it is something [that] stands within the framework of calculation and repeatability. (Risser, 2010, n. p.)

In the context of phenomenology, however, experience is seen very differently: It is not about the accumulation and synthesis of sensory data, but it is understood in terms of an event. It is not a picture we design, gather, or piece together, but it is a phenomenon that occurs, takes place, or happens to us. "The crucial question" for phenomenology, in other words, is "not 'what do I experience?' but 'what *is my* experience?'" (Jay, 2006, p. 94). Experience, accordingly, is not an occurrence that happens outside of us, as something separate from us that is made to impinge upon us as so much sensory information. As Heidegger says, "Experience doesn't pass before me as thing that I set there as an object" (as quoted in Jay, 2006, p. 98). Experience instead is a part of the inseparable connections between the self and the world. It arises through engagement with the world of concerns, actions, and meanings that constitute the life-world. Experience, conceived in this way, is a part of the life-world that we inhabit "naturally" and it partakes in all of the characteristics of this life-world. As Gadamer (2004) explains,

> the world in which we are immersed in the natural attitude ... never becomes an object as such for us, but that represents the pregiven basis of all experience. ... It is

clear that the life-world is always at the same time a communal world that involves being with other people as well. It is a world of persons, and in the natural attitude the validity of this personal world is always assumed. (p. 239)

To put it another way, experience is embedded in the life-world, and because this world, as Gadamer points out, is a "communal world of persons," experience is always much more than a question of unidirectional manipulation and calculation.

Taking this idea even further, one could say that we do not possess our experience, our experience possesses us. Heidegger expresses this concept by saying that

To undergo an experience with something ... means that this something befalls us, strikes us, comes over us, overwhelms us, and transforms us. When we talk of "undergoing" an experience we mean specifically that the experience is not of our making. To undergo here means that we endure it, suffer it, receive it as it strikes us, and submit to it. (1971, p. 57)

Heidegger's conclusion that "experience is not of our making" – taken together with the notion that we submit to it, rather than it submitting to us – is precisely how experience is understood here. Far from being subject to design and measurement, experience is seen as an event that is always embedded in a life-world of other persons.

WRITING AND READING THE LIFE-WORLD

The four life-world dimensions, time, body, space (and/or place,) and relation are bound together by and reflected in everyday language. Indeed, whether it is used in careful description or casual conversation, language is the most common means through which, as Merleau-Ponty says, "perspectives blend, perceptions confirm each other, a meaning emerges" (p. xix). Language provides the most powerful evidence for the existence of a shared life-world; correspondingly, it also forms the most effective tool for exploring it. The simple fact that we can understand one another when speaking of different aspects of experience, feeling, and meaning, is a clear illustration of a shared, intersubjective world.

This dynamic gives language a particular power or potential in hermeneutic phenomenological research. This aspect is the potential of the "evocation" or even the "simulation" of experience. Writing, for example, "Ari's comments boosted my confidence" show the potential of descriptive and everyday writing to present an experiential moment to the reader. Longer and more detailed passages have the potential to extend this power and to draw the reader into an experience, to evoke an experience for the reader, or even to enable the reader to "experience" it vicariously. Realizing this potential involves the use of linguistic or descriptive techniques that are closer to fictional writing than they are to the objective "third-person" forms of description. It involves writing, in other words, that draws from the shared subjective and personal experiential characteristics that constitute the common world of the "we" rather than the objective world of factual or academic texts. These techniques, in turn, are intended to give the reader the opportunity to "participate" in the experience described, to become part of the plurality that is implied in the word "we."

There are other similarities linking this type of description to fictional writing: A novel and its characters and events, for example, can lie dormant on the shelf, to be given semblance of life when the novel is picked up and read. Descriptions used in hermeneutic phenomenological research are similarly dependent on the reader. The reader is asked to help "breathe life" into these descriptions, to encounter these passages with the expectation and sensibility of someone reading fiction, from an orientation of involved receptivity rather than analytic detachment. Of course, this request is by no means an appeal for the reader to abandon all possibility of independent disagreement or critique. What these kinds of descriptions instead ask for is a similar kind of reading to that of engaging in a work of fiction or viewing a motion picture.

The word "I" is accordingly used in this description in a manner similar to the way it would be used in fictional passages written in the first person. It is not meant to emphasize the inward-looking or introspective possibilities of selfhood, but rather, is an attempt to make the descriptions as direct, recognizable, and compelling as possible, and to encourage the overlapping of different first-person perspectives. Like Merleau-Ponty (above) and Husserl (just below), phenomenological texts also uses the word "we" in a similar manner, to invoke the intersubjective position of the third-person plural. Any hermeneutic phenomenological study, then, is an exploration of the shared life-world that is invoked or simulated through descriptive, evocative language. However, while this "sharing" of a common life-world is an important goal, the ultimate aim of this type of research is even more ambitious: To bring these shared experiences and meanings to explicit and reflective attention. In doing so, this study aims to more than just describe, it also aims to reflect upon and interpret these descriptions. Phenomenological writing, such as is provided in the chapters of this book, frequently alternates between descriptive passages (which are indented and italicized in this text) and text that is reflective and interpretive in character.

Despite its unconventional ambiguity and informality, this type of inquiry can be both valuable and accessible: As I have already indicated, it can address familiar issues and questions in ways that are quite different from conventional research. This method can be particularly valuable in cases where conventional research has asked the same question again and again, only to repeatedly receive the same answers.

PHENOMENOLOGICAL DESCRIPTION OF THE UTRECHT SCHOOL

The quasi-fictional descriptive method explained above was initially conceived in the context of the Dutch Utrecht School and has been developed further and given explicit articulation by Max van Manen, a Canadian educational researcher. This section provides an overview of the way that evidence is collected and then presented and analyzed through writing, using the method of hermeneutic phenomenological description, as developed by van Manen. The Utrecht school, which flourished only for a decade or so (from 1946 to 1957), represented a loose grouping of scholars who applied aspects of hermeneutic phenomenology as a research method to a wide range of disciplines. Writing together with Utrecht scholar Bas Levering, van Manen explains:

> The Utrecht School consisted of an assortment of phenomenologically oriented psychologists, educators, pedagogues, pediatricians, sociologists, criminologists, jurists, psychiatrists, and other medical doctors, who formed a more or less close association of like-minded academics. (Levering & van Manen, 2003, p. 278)

In recent years, as van Manen observes, the work of this group "… has inspired … variations of a practice-based phenomenology especially in psychology (e.g., Giorgi [2009] and Moustakas [1994]), in nursing (e.g., Benner [1994]) and in education (e.g., van Manen)" (2002).

One of the notable characteristics of the work of the Utrecht School is the way its members would "write up" their research in an informal, even conversational way. The research publications that are most characteristic of this school skillfully interweave informal descriptive writing with more formal reflection and analysis. This task was accomplished so successfully in some cases that the careful and painstaking research, writing and re-writing efforts of the authors are difficult for the reader to detect. In addition, these researchers did not produce any writings that explicated their methodology. Thus, despite the existence of some exemplary pieces associated with the Utrecht School (e.g., Langeveld, 1983; Buytendijk, 1988; Bleeker & Mulderij, 1992), the very accessibility of the writing of these texts effectively "closed the possibility for others to exercise these same practices" (Levering & van Manen, 2003, p. 278). The apparent simplicity of accomplished writing, in other words, all too easily hid the complexity of the research processes beneath it.

In this context, van Manen's work can be characterized as an attempt to "reopen" the possibility of exercising these same practices of research and writing for others. In *Researching Lived Experience: Human Science for an Action Sensitive Pedagogy* (1997), van Manen explains in some detail how researchers can work toward the close and apparently effortless interweaving of analysis, reflection, and informal description that typifies the texts of the Utrecht School. In this same book, van Manen also explains how to collect, combine, and refine interview and other descriptive material to serve as experiential data in this kind of research. As the title of van Manen's book indicates, pedagogy is a subject particularly germane to this type of research.

"Phenomenology," as van Manen says, "is the active and reflective participation in meaning" (2002). The phenomenological researcher in this sense does not typically have a data gathering phase with an explicit beginning and ending set in advance but instead "dwells" with his or her question as it is being formulated, while he or she may be away from her desk and studies, during formal interviewing and analysis activities, and throughout the writing process. A film, a novel, or a radio program may suddenly speak to the researcher and the question with which she is dwelling, shedding light on one aspect or another of the phenomenon in question. As a result, it is often not possible to give an exhaustive account of data sources or even a clear-cut enumeration of a single sample set or collection of interviews. It would be in some ways more in the spirit of the research method to describe the relevant contexts and experiences engaged in while dwelling with the problem.

The sources of potential meaning or relevant data are numerous. The researcher can develop and cultivate experiential meaning as it arises in a range of sources, including "historical, cultural, literary" and aesthetic materials (e.g., historical accounts, novels, and films), as well as a range of linguistic sources, including metaphors, sayings, and etymological and definitional distinctions both from everyday speech and formal writing (2002). For example, a popular movie such as *You've Got Mail* (1998) has been used in one hermeneutic phenomenological investigation of "keeping in touch by electronic mail" (Dobson, 2002).

These sources are used to create the types of first-person, written descriptions discussed above. When these descriptions are carefully developed and refined to constitute short, self-contained, quasi-fictional accounts, they are referred to by van Manen as "anecdotes." The anecdote as van Manen defines it is a brief, simple story, a vividly particular presentation of a single incident that is intended to stand out precisely through its incidental nature, in its compressed but concrete particularity. Again, the very short description provided above is a good, if somewhat brief, example of an anecdote: it are very particular and concrete, and it focuses, however briefly, on a specific incident. It presents an everyday kind of event and experience, highlighting one aspect that stands out for the person involved in it. The term *anecdote* has been deliberately chosen by van Manen for its colloquial overtones and its obvious distance from any validated and authoritative sense of "truth" or "evidence":

> Anecdotes have enjoyed low status in scholarly writings ... Evidence that is "only anecdotal" is not permitted to furnish a proper argument. But empirical generalization is not the aim of phenomenological research. [In fact, anecdotes] ... express a certain distain for the alienated and alienating discourse of scholars who have difficulty showing how life and theoretical propositions are connected. (p. 119)

It is useful also to characterize an anecdote can by what it is *not*: it does not present general principles, statistical patterns, or theoretical constructs. It is not used as evidence in the sense of an historical incident that "really happened" at a given point in time. Thus, an anecdote can be "adapted" from another text or description, as is the case with the second short anecdote provided at the outset of chapter one. Speaking specifically of technology use, the anecdote should also be differentiated from the vivid ethnographic accounts of computer use of the kind provided by Sherry Turkle in *The Second Self* (1984, 2005) or *The Life on the Screen* (1995), which Turkle (2005) characterizes as "portraits of what can [and does] happen when people enter into very close relationships" with the computer (p. 25). When employed as a means of studying engagement with computer technology, anecdotal accounts generally do not serve as evidence of what can happen with this technology. Instead, they attempt to provide the reader with recognizable experiences of this kind of engagement. Anecdotes are not presented to the reader with the tacit claim, "This really happened"; they instead bring with them the tacit appeal: "Is this experientially recognizable or resonant?" More specifically then, the anecdote is told with the intention of raising the further question: "What is the experiential meaning of what happened?"

Despite the reach and variety of potential sources in writing anecdotes and in carrying out hermeneutic phenomenological research, the principle supply of meaning or of experiential data is often presented by open-ended, "qualitative" interviews. As a data-gathering technique generally, this type of interview is marked by its unstructured and unscripted nature. One of the most important challenges in such an interview is not for the interviewer to stick to a particular script, but for him or her to remain responsive, "flexible and attentive to the ... meanings that may emerge as the interview progresses" (Warren, 2001 p. 87). Such an interview also tends to take the form of a kind of an "interpretive" or "guided conversation" that unfolds with very few pre-determined questions. It relies on the unscripted use of "probes to clarify answers or [to] request further examples, and follow-up questions that pursue implications of answers to main questions" (van Manen, 2002; Warren, 2001, pp. 85, 86–87).

Using the term *hermeneutic interview* (1997, pp. 98–99; 2002) van Manen describes the point of such an interview as follows:

> A hermeneutic interview is an interpretive conversation wherein both partners reflectively orient themselves to the interpersonal or collective ground that brings the significance of the phenomenological question into view. The art of the researcher in the hermeneutic interview is to keep the question (of the meaning of the phenomenon [under investigation]) open: to keep himself or herself and the interviewee oriented to the substance of the thing being questioned. (2002, n.p.)

In the course of such an interview, it is important for the researcher to be on the lookout for descriptive material having potentially anecdotal or "quasi-fictional" qualities. These brief descriptions take the form of a short account or a notable or unusual incident that captures or says something about the experience or phenomenon in question.

Interviewing in hermeneutic phenomenological research often presents a number of significant challenges. The first of these is that participants or interviewees generally do not see experiential categories as being relevant in research contexts; they do not describe their experience in terms of "incidents" or according to an experientially attuned vocabulary. To help both interviewee and interviewer to maintain a focus on the experiential, it can be useful to employ certain ways of asking questions or setting up "probes" that guide the conversation away from theory and explanation and keep it firmly anchored in the concrete. One of these ways is to explore the experience with the interviewee in terms of the four fundamental life-world themes or dimensions: lived space, lived time, lived relation, and lived body. A second way of addressing this difference is to ask questions that lead the interviewer to switch from a conventional vocabulary of intellection and thought to one of feeling and impression. Thus, asking a question like "what did you *think* when that happened" would be replaced with the question: "how did you *feel* when that happened?" Allowing participants to speak in terms of thinking and of the intellect can provide responses that may, in effect, theorize colloquially the phenomenon in question. On the other hand, focusing the participant on his or her feelings and responses can help to orient and open the interview to questions of situated attunement and "dwelling."

In keeping with the implications of "dwelling" with a question and data, the data gathered from the participant or interviewee in hermeneutic phenomenological research is typically not seen as coming to an end with the conclusion of the initial interview session. Van Manen encourages researchers to include participants in the ongoing, cyclical, hermeneutic development of experiential meanings as these unfold in subsequent stages in the research. This dynamic includes discussing interview notes or interview transcripts with the interviewee and exploring together themes or important, common meanings that might emerge from these provisional documents. Involvement of the interviewee also extends to the review and discussion of more developed and refined descriptive material and drafts of the research text itself. According to van Manen, the question "Is this what the experience is really like?" should ground all such discussions (2002).

WONDER VERSUS THE "NATURAL ATTITUDE"

Gathering, compiling, writing and re-writing descriptions in order to make aspects of the life-world clearly available for reflection is not easy; for what is often most noteworthy about the world of shared human meanings is precisely the fact that it is *not usually regarded as worthy of note*. In this section, I introduce a few concepts that are indispensable to hermeneutic phenomenological research: the natural attitude, intentionality and wonder (the last of these is also known as "the reduction"). Our sharing of everyday meanings and the overlapping of common experiences is something that is readily forgotten, overlooked, or ignored. One could say that we are to the life-world as a fish is to water: The life-world is the environment that surrounds and sustains us, but because it is everywhere, it tends to be the last thing to receive our notice. Consequently, we are not often in a good position to explore it or even to acknowledge its reality. It disappears all too easily between the opposed domains of the objective and the subjective. Edmund Husserl explains:

> the lifeworld, for us who wakingly live in it, is always there, existing in advance for us, the 'ground' of all praxis, whether theoretical or extratheoretical. The world is pregiven to us, the waking, always somehow practically interested subjects, not occasionally but always and necessarily as the universal field of all actual and possible praxis, as horizon. To live is always to live-in-certainty-of-the-world. (1970, p. 142)

"Living-in-certainty-of-the-world" generally comes to explicit attention only when an extraordinary event occurs – when the figurative "gears" mentioned by Merleau-Ponty become disengaged. Such an event may occur when travelling in a foreign country or entering for the first time into a situation that is very different or "other" from what is familiar: we are confronted by practices or conventions that may violate our "living-in-certainty-of-the-world" or our unarticulated "common sense."

An important constituent of this commonsensical "living in certainty" is called "intentionality." Intentionality refers to the meanings, plans, and purposes that constitute our connection with the world around us and give the world its familiarity. Extending from unconscious habits and actions (like turning a page or clicking a link) through to the most complex tasks of focused (self-) awareness, intentionality designates to a kind of "directionality" that links self to the world: "Intentionality" derives from the Latin verb "intendere," which means "to point to" or "to aim at," and ... the intentionality of mental states and experiences ... [are] accordingly characterized ... [as] being "directed toward something" ... i.e., a mental state of "aiming" toward a certain state of affairs. (McIntyre & Woodruff Smith, 1989, p. 147)

While phenomenological research begins with the recognition that self and world are connected through intentionality, it focuses particular attention on those moments when intentionality is disrupted. When the purposive powers of the mind are disrupted, miss their target, or are exposed to strangeness or otherness, the completion of intended actions comes to a halt. Merleau-Ponty speaks of phenomenology as working to encourage these moments. He describes it as an attempt to "slacke[n] the intentional threads which attach us to the world and thus [bring] them to our notice..." (2002, p. xv). Slackening is deliberately cultivated as part of a particular methodology or technique, or more accurately, as an attitude or *disposition*. This technique or attitude is known as "the reduction." The reduction refers to the suspension of both commonsense and scientific understandings or explanations. Husserl describes it as "the bracketing" of the "natural attitude." Cultivating this disposition or sensitivity to that which is "out of the ordinary" is central to the research, writing, and re-writing that have occurred in putting together many of the studies collected in this book. However, it is crucial in reading such a study as well.

The highest goal of the writing and reflection undertaken here is to remove the reader as far as possible from what Husserl has called the "natural attitude." The ultimate aim of this type of writing in this sense is to bring the reader to a place where the phenomena being investigated are no longer simply taken for granted and accepted as ordinary. The goal is to take the reader to a place where the natural attitude is suspended; ultimately to a place of wonder. As van Manen (2002) explains, the goal of the type of hermeneutic phenomenological writing practiced here is to

> shatter the taken-for-grantedness of our everyday reality. Wonder [in this sense] is the unwilled willingness to meet what is utterly strange in what is most familiar. It is the willingness to step back and let things speak to us, a passive receptivity to let the things of the world present themselves in their own terms. When we are struck with wonder, our minds are suddenly cleared of the clutter of everyday concerns that

51

otherwise constantly occupy us. We are confronted by the thing, the phenomenon in all of its strangeness and uniqueness. The wonder of that thing takes us in … (n.p.)

To respond to a text with wonder, to meet the "utterly strange" in a phenomenon that may be otherwise thoroughly "known" and familiar, however, is to ask a great deal of both the researcher/writer and the reader. Reacting in this fashion is not automatic, and, of course, it cannot be forced. As a result the intention or hope of the phenomenological researcher and writer therefore to invite, rather than in any way to compel, the reader into a suspension of the mundane. To extend this invitation to the reader is to ask him or her to enter into a different personal perspective, that of the "you," of the relational and the ethical. Only in this way is it ultimately possible to share the world of the "we."

SAYING "YOU" AND THE ETHICS OF ADDRESS

The relational, ethical aspects of the first-person plural perspective become important, even unavoidable, when we address someone as "you." In saying "you," the person speaking offers, establishes, or elaborates a relation to the person addressed. "You" implies relation; it is a word spoken by an "I" to another. When Ari says to Janet, "I really like the fact that you got some help from others to get your project page done. I think this is very important in wikis," he is engaged in relational action that has clearly ethical implications: his figurative path intersects (to use Merleau-Ponty's terms) with Janet's in a way that affects her noticeably and meaningfully. As a result, Ari's address or relational action can also be interpreted in terms of what is good or bad, right or wrong: The effect of Ari's words on Janet might lead readers to conclude that it was the *right* thing to say or do. A different response or a different end result – for example, appearing to be too enthusiastic, leading Janet to question Ari's seriousness – might result in a different ethical judgement.

The "you" perspective is relevant to hermeneutic phenomenology because the descriptive and interpretive passages in the various chapters of this book have been written with the intention of addressing the reader individually, as an "I" would address a "you." In writing hermeneutic phenomenological text, I am consequently aiming, ideally, to bring the reader to the text in a "you" relation with me. Together the two, the you and the I, *may* form an intersubjective "we." This dynamic implies that "I" as author has an ethical responsibility in relation to "you" as the reader.

This responsibility can be best understood in linguistic terms because language not only has substantial power to suggest, evoke, and simulate; it also presents significant peril in that it can mislead and, above all, reinforce the "natural attitude" that does not see beyond received common sense. As indicated above, my aim in writing is not to use language and description to compel readers to arrive at certain experiential meanings and understandings; my aim instead is to invite readers to share a range of experiential possibilities. Such an invitation is intended when I use the sometimes dangerous first-person pronoun "we": I do not do so without acknowledging the suppositions that this word brings with it, and the power it has to cover over conflict and disagreement with a superficial sense of commonality.

Thus, I simultaneously invite the reader to disagree with what is suggested when I use the term *we* and to approach the text and the author behind it in a manner that is active and engaged.

NOTES

¹ I owe this particular account of personal perspectives and knowledge forms to Bernhard Irrgang; it is articulated briefly in the first chapter of *Gehirn und leiblicher Geist*, and was also discussed in the context of a series of seminars held at the Technical University Dresden in November of 2008. Related discussions of personal perspectives can be found, most notably, in Martin Buber's *I and Thou* (1958).

² Phenomenology here designates what would be more accurately but more awkwardly termed "hermeneutic phenomenology." Referring to the art and science of interpretation, hermeneutics has been combined with phenomenology to constitute an interpretation or investigation of the *meaning* of lived experience. Exemplary treatments of hermeneutic phenomenology can be found in the writings of Martin Heidegger and Hans-Georg Gadamer.

REFERENCES

Benner, P. E. (1994). *Interpretive phenomenology: Embodiment, caring, and ethics in health and illness.* Thousand Oaks, CA: Sage.

Bleeker, H., & Mulderij, K. (1992). The experience of motor disability. *Phenomenology + Pedagogy, 10*, 1–18.

Buber, M. (1958). *I and thou.* New York, NY: Scribner's.

Burgess, T.F. (2001). A general introduction to the design of questionnaires for survey research. Retrieved from http://www.leeds.ac.uk/iss/documentation/top/top2.pdf.

Buytendijk, F. J. J. (1988). The first smile of the child. *Phenomenology + Pedagogy, 6*(1), 15–24.

Chiu, K.-Y., Stewart, B., & Ehlert, M. (2003). Relationships among student demo-graphic characteristics, student academic achievement, student satisfaction, and online business – Course quality factors. NAWeb. Retrieved from http://www.unb.ca/naweb/proceedings/2003/PaperChiu.html.

Dobson, T. M. (2002). Keeping in touch by electronic mail. In Max van Manen (Ed.), *Writing in the dark: Phenomenological studies in interpretive inquiry* (pp. 98–115). London, ON: Althouse Press.

Friesen, N., & Hopkins, J. (2008). Wikiversity; or education meets the free culture movement: An ethnographic investigation. *First Monday, 13*(10). Retrieved from http://www.uic.edu/htbin/cgiwrap/bin/ojs/index.php/fm/.

Gadamer, H. G. (2004). *Truth and method* (2nd rev. ed.). New York, NY: Continuum

Ginsburg, S. (2011). *Designing the iPhone user experience: A user-centered approach to sketching and prototyping iPhone apps.* Boston, MA: Pearson Education.

Giorgi, A. (2009). *The descriptive phenomenological method in psychology: A modified Husserlian approach.* Pittsburgh, PA: Duquesne University Press.

Heckman, R., & Annabi, H. (2003). A content analytic comparison of FtF and ALN case-study discussion. Proceedings of 36th Hawaii International Conference on Systems Science. CD-Rom. Washington, DC: IEEE Computer Society Press.

Heidegger, M. (1971). The nature of language. In *On the way to language* (pp. 57–108). New York, NY: Harper & Row.

Hiltz, S. R., & Shea, P. (2005). The student in the online classroom. In S.R. Hiltz & R. Goldman (Eds.), *Learning together online: Research on asynchronous learning networks* (pp. 145–168). Mahwah, NJ: Lawrence Erlbaum Publishers.

Husserl, E. (1970). *Crisis of European sciences and transcendental phenomenology.* Evanston, IL: Northwestern University Press.

Irrgang, B. (2007). *Gehirn und leiblicher geist. Phänomenologisch-hermeneutische Philosophie des Geistes.* Stuttgart: Franz Steiner Verlag.

Jay, M. (2006). The lifeworld and lived experience. In H.L. Dreyfus & M.A. Wrathall (Eds.), *A companion to phenomenology and existentialism.* Malden, MA: Blackwell.

Jurczyk, J., Kushner-Benson, S. N., & Savery, J. (2004). Measuring student percep-tions in web-based courses: A standards-based approach. *Online Journal of Distance Learning Administration, 7*(4). Retrieved from http://www.westga.edu/~distance/ojdla/winter74/jurczyk74.htm.

Levering, B., & van Manen, M. (2002). Phenomenological anthropology in the Netherlands and Flanders. In A.-T. Tymieniecka (Ed.), *Phenomenology world wide: Foundations – Expanding dynamics – Life-engagements: A guide for research and study* (pp. 278–286). Dordrecht: Kluwer Academic Publishers.

McIntyre, R., & Woodruff Smith, D. (1989). Theory of intentionality. In J.N. Mohanty & W.R. McKenna (Eds.), *Husserl's phenomenology: A textbook* (pp. 147–179). Washington, DC: Center for Advanced Research in Phenomenology and University Press of America.

Merleau-Ponty, M. (2002). *Phenomenology of perception.* London, UK: Routledge.

Moss, D. (2003). *Hating in the first person plural: psychoanalytic essays on racism, homophobia, misogyny, and terror.* New York, NY: Other Press.

Moustakas, C. (1994). *Phenomenological research methods.* Thousand Oaks, CA: Sage Publications.

Peppers, C. (2006). The dangerous pronoun: An ecopoetics of "We." *International Journal of the Arts in Society, 1*(2), 93–100.

Picciano, A. G. (2002). Beyond student perceptions: Issues of interaction, presence, and performance in an online course. *Journal of Asynchronous Learning Networks, 6*(1), 21–40. Retrieved from: http://www.sloan-c.org/publications/jaln/v6n1/pdf/v6n1_picciano.pdf.

Risser, J. (2010, August). Where do we find words for what we cannot say? On language and experience in the understanding of life. Paper presented at the meeting of the International Human Sciences Research Conference, Seattle, WA.

Tullis, T. & Albert, W. (2008). *Measuring the user experience: Collecting, analyzing, and presenting usability metrics.* Amsterdam: Elsevier.

Turkle, S. (1984). *The second self: Computers and the human spirit.* New York, NY: Simon and Schuster.

Turkle, S. (1995). *Life on the screen: Identity in the age of the Internet.* New York, NY: Simon and Schuster.

Turkle, S. (2005). *The second self: Computers and the human spirit* (20th anniversary ed.). Cambridge, MA: MIT Press.

van Manen, M. (1997). *Researching lived experience: Human science for an action sensitive pedagogy,* 2nd ed. London, ON: Althouse Press.

van Manen, M. (2002). *Phenomenology online.* Retrieved from http://www.phenomenologyonline.com.

Warren, C.A.B. (2001). Qualitative interviewing. In J.F. Gubrium & J.A. Holstein (Eds.), *Handbook of interview research: Context & method* (pp. 83–101). Thousand Oaks, CA: Sage.

4. "AN EVENT IN SOUND"[1]

Considerations on the Ethical-Aesthetic Traits of the Hermeneutic Phenomenological Text

INTRODUCTION

In this chapter, we endeavor to describe some of the linguistic textures of hermeneutic-phenomenological writing and, in so doing, point to the close connection between lived experience and the ethical-aesthetic traits in interpreting and writing the experience.

Our starting point for considering phenomenological writing to be an ethical-aesthetic responsibility of the researcher is Heidegger's (2001) understanding of existence as a poetic[2] dwelling and Wivel's (1953) postulate that the ethical outlook comes from within, from the poetic outlook. Awareness of the ethical-aesthetic dimension is, of course, of importance to all phenomenological research. However, it becomes even more imperative for researchers who follow the scholars of the Utrecht School and van Manen's orientation to hermeneutic phenomenology, which use an expressive/aesthetic language to turn informants' lived experiences into anecdotes. The dilemma here is how and why we can trust aesthetic language to be ethical.

Our primary interest in phenomenology is methodological, methodical and pragmatic, not philosophical. In this sense, we follow Ricoeur's (1998) declaration that he does not "adhere to the letter of Heidegger's philosophy but shall develop it for my own purposes" (p. 109). Our purpose here is not to tarry in philosophical discourse but to focus on the methodological significance of *writing the experience* rather than writing about the experience. In so doing, we focus on language and its potential to give expression to the meaning of recollected lived experiences.

This chapter begins by focusing specifically on the phenomenology of the Utrecht School, particularly as it has been developed as a "research orientation" by Max van Manen (1997b). The scholars who share this orientation (e.g. Buytendijk, Langeveld, and Linschoten) are typically known for at least three things: their choice of everyday, common and situational subjects; their use of experiential material in their texts; and their unconventional writing style. One key notion in the methodology developed by van Manen (van Manen 1989, 1997b) is the *anecdote*: an experiential description that is carefully crafted by the researcher and that is based on informants' accounts of lived experience. We employ the notion of the anecdote when we explore the linguistic features of writing the experience. When we move from writing the experience to the raw material provided by informants, we employ the term *lived-experience description* (van Manen, 1997b) interchangeably with *experiential accounts.*[3]

N. Friesen et al. (eds.), Hermeneutic Phenomenology in Education, 55–78.

I am not alone in this desire to understand those moments of life that are invisible even and precisely in practice,. In their text *Becoming Aware* (Depraz et al., 2002) the authors (a phenomenological philosopher, a neuroscientist–Buddhist practitioner–phenomenologist, and a psychologist) confront in/visibility head on.

A "FINE" HUMAN SCIENCE

The scholars of the Utrecht School gained reputations for their evocative and insightful texts on a variety of common human experiences, such as "On Falling Asleep" (Linschoten), "The Meaning of Being Ill" (van den Berg), and "The Psychology of Driving a Car" (van Lennep).[4] What united the original group of like-minded academics was an inclination to integrate the diverse social disciplines and their experiential practices; they were all "sailing under the flag of the personal responsibility and social engagement of the individual human being" (Levering & van Manen, 2001, p. 278, emphasis in original). However, the methodological underpinnings of their work were kept hidden or in petto.[5] Thus, the profound existential orientation of the Utrecht School has since been misunderstood as an arcane, impressionistic, and exclusive form of phenomenology. As phenomenological writers, they appear to have simply practiced phenomenology with earnestness and sensitivity, rather than overtly teaching or explicating its substance. The lack of methodological self-awareness of the Utrecht School phenomenology might belong to what Merleau-Ponty (2002) interprets as a characteristic of European phenomenology in general. According to him, phenomenology is a practiced and acknowledged movement that involves a style of thinking and writing before reaching philosophical and methodological self-awareness. Despite the criticism of the Utrecht School, by becoming familiar with their reflective and often beautiful texts, the power of their methodology is almost self-evident. But how did they write like this? Can the skill of beautiful and perceptive writing be acquired through a persevering and sympathetically insightful practice? Our endeavor to understand begins in the world of aesthetics.

Things speak of the beautiful

The concept of "the beautiful" was once a universal metaphysical concept that had a function in the universal doctrine of being. Even today, the concept of "the beautiful" has significance for contemporary methodology of the human sciences. The original Greek word kalon translates to fine, as in "the fine arts." The adjective fine distinguishes these arts from natural sciences and human sciences. "In fine art the art itself is not beautiful, but is called so because it produces the beautiful," Heidegger claims (2001, p. 35). How does fine art produce what is beautiful? Heidegger demonstrates to us that a piece of art can bring into nearness the nature of a thing – a pair of shoes, for example (van Gogh, 1885). By unveiling the shoe-ness of the shoes, the painting, in its beauty, sets to work the truth about shoes. Under Heidegger's and van Gogh's guidance, we perceive a pair of worn-out shoes, shabby and dirty from daily toil and the worker's contact with water, soil and dust. Before our eyes, these shoes are transformed and we realize that they are not just a pair of shoes but also appear meaningfully as shoes to us. The artist is "a passageway" (Heidegger, 2001, p. 39) to the work, and the work itself guides us to an open space where the authentic being of the shoes is at work. The shoe-ness of the shoes, the "is-ness" of the thing, is not a representation of a corresponding object that we can verify by matching the depiction correctly to the object depicted.

The is-ness of the thing is not fully accessible to us, but is constantly alternating in its revealing and concealing of itself beyond human control and prediction. As Heidegger notes, "There is much in being that man cannot master. There is but little that comes to be known. What is known remains inexact, what is mastered insecure" (p. 51). In the midst of things, situations and events, there are spaces, openings, and rifts. It is in these gaps of interpretation and understanding that "truth happens" (p. 56), and meaning is disclosed as beauty. Van Gogh's painting is not the expression of an isolated pair of shoes, but an appearance, as Shelley might say, of that which lies beyond perception, as it has been blunted or annihilated through routine. Because we tend to recognize things from their most practical and prominent characteristics, we rarely look closer to see what they really are.

To the Greeks, to know something was to uncover its being. They called this uncovering aletheia, which can be translated as truth, or literally as unconcealedness (Heidegger, 1998, p. 11). In the fine arts, beauty is exactly this unconcealedness and disclosure. Its appearance is related to the idea of "shining." The verb to shine requires something to shine upon. Thus, to shine means to make that on which the light falls appear. Since this light falls in the realms of both the visible and the intelligible, shining also brings into appearance the meaning of phenomena upon which this light has fallen (Gadamer, 1985). Heidegger (2001) points to the space where beauty occurs as a "lighting" or "clearing." He says, "That which is can only be, as a being, if it stands within and stands out within what is lighted in this clearing" (p. 51). Things appear to us in a bright glade, but simultaneously they withdraw themselves. We pass along the things of the world and we dwell with them as they alternate between self-disclosure and self-concealment by the light of what they are. "Light of this kind joins its shining to and into the work. This shining, joined in the work is the beautiful. Beauty is one way in which truth occurs as unconcealedness," says Heidegger (2001, p. 54, italics in original). He continues:

> Truth is the unconcealedness of that which is as something that is. Truth is the truth of Being. Beauty does not occur alongside and apart from this truth. When truth sets itself into the work, it appears. Appearance – as this being of truth in the work and as work – is beauty. Thus the beautiful belongs to the advent of truth, truth's taking of its place. (p. 79)

As Heidegger sees it, beauty can be the passage to truth. He objects to any understanding of aesthetics that would reduce it to merely an affective term. A piece of art is not beautiful because it is enjoyable, admirable or precious, but because of its essential ability to let truth happen, which means to reveal "the isness of what is" (2001, p. 79).

Language speaks in the anecdote

An anecdote speaks to us much in the same way as a good novel or a beautiful poem does. It evokes feelings of recognition, points to experiential possibilities that we have never encountered before, or leads to thoughts whose possibility we were not earlier aware of. When a well-written phenomenological text establishes a relationship with the reader "language is no longer an instrument, no longer a means. It is a manifestation, a revelation of intimate being and of the psychic link which unites us to the world and our fellow men," (Merleau-Ponty, 2002, p. 196). In the hands of a talented phenomenologist, the meaning of words is given a new twist. Or rather, as Heidegger notes, a phenomenologist has learned "to live in the speaking of language" (2001, p. 207). Much like Heidegger's own evocative response to Georg Trakl's poem A Winter Evening, the intention of a phenomenologist is to have the reader receive and respond to the otherwise concealed meaning of the lived experience which can be evoked in the honed anecdote. Van Manen, like Heidegger, makes substantial use of experiential material – such as literature and other artistic work – in order "to refer beyond the realm of what can be said clearly and distinctly [...] and to make present a meaning which we are unable to express clearly in any other way" (Kockelmans, 1987, p. ix). To listen and respond to the things of the world through language, to let language itself speak is, according to Heidegger (2001), the only way that human beings can truly say something. By listening to the speaking of the things of the world, the vocatio of a text, we feel addressed by the experience. The vocation, or call, of a text is sensed as an implicit, felt understanding that is non-cognitive as well as cognitive, sensed as well as reflected.

Language, seen not primarily as expression, utterance or action (Heidegger, 2001) but, rather, as a disruption or a peal of the stillness of things, can be both evocatively inventive as well as commonly accessible. In reflecting on the phenomenological text, van Manen (1997a) identifies five vocative qualities, which strikingly resemble the fictional devices of the novelist. His methodological shift of focus, from content to form and beyond, shows that content and form are indivisible for phenomenological writing: "When we turn from thematic meaning to expressive meaning then the question we ask turns from 'what does the text speak about?' to 'how does the text speak?'" (van Manen, 1997a, p. 345). How the text speaks is a matter of letting the mantic dimensions of the language come to expression, a perspective also noticed by Heidegger, Merleau-Ponty and Wittgenstein. The mantic-expressive language first and foremost speaks in the concreteness, the addressiveness, the embeddedness of meaning, and by the transformative qualities of the text. The evocative dimensions belong to our common day-to-day language and might be so close to us in speech and reading that we miss what they say. Heidegger notes, "Everyday language is a forgotten and therefore used-up poem, from which there hardly resounds a call any longer"

(2001, p. 205). The experiential account brings a possible human experience into nearness by mediating the tension between the particular and the universal of this experience. As they occur in phenomenological writing, anecdotes are, thus, not mere illustrations to embellish an otherwise boring text. The anecdote can be understood as "a methodological device in human science to make comprehensible some notion that easily eludes us" (van Manen, 1997b, p. 116). When the anecdote tells us something about a particular experience, a unique person, or an individual life, it also reveals something universal. "And vice versa, at the hand of an anecdote fundamental insights or truths are tested for their value in the contingent world of everyday experience" (p. 120).

An open, accessible style of writing and way of relating experiences harmonizes with phenomenological philosophy and phenomenological writing. Accordingly, this style of scientific writing is based on conversations and dialogues with others, with oneself as an author, and with language itself because "its speaking speaks for us in what has been spoken" (Heidegger, 2001, p. 207). The ideal of phenomenological writing is the literary prose style, the vague and the equivocal, the quote and the collage, the question and the provocation, the void and the vision (Cooley, 1981, our translation). No matter how much effort we put into describing the experience and interpreting its possible meaning, phenomenological texts can never be heard as completed symphonies; well-conducted they may be, but they are eternally bound to be etudes. There will always be another, alternative interpretation. In that sense, phenomenological texts are, simultaneously, conversations that open into the future, and ongoing dialogues about the ethical-aesthetic dimensions of the texts.

How it speaks

Roland Barthes (1981) once said that a text needs to have *punctum*; it needs to have a point. Phenomenological texts can make something new; they can invent perspectives, connections, compositions, thoughts that have not been presented in that way before. The phenomenological text aims to present a difference (Heidegger, 2001) to bring forth something by discerning it from the rest, to present something unique or previously unthought-of. It seeks to bring something forth, to bring something into light, to let something shine, or as Barthes (1981) notices, to point out the particular meaning of something and establish a punctum. A snapshot, he says, becomes a photograph when it has punctum. An unfocused, random "snap" cannot make sense on its own since *it* does not speak to us. Instead, the photographer speaks to us through his or her engagement in the act of creating the photograph. A snapshot cannot make sense on its own since *it* does not speak to us – the *photographer* does. It needs the photographer to explain what it portrays.

No image presents the original. Although it is always a representation, it has analogous qualities. In the case of a photograph or a snapshot, it might be a perfect *analogon*. There is however, a profound difference between a snapshot and a photograph with regards to what they tell and the language with which it is said. While the familiarity and immediate identification of an event in a snapshot creates a recognizable atmosphere that we may approve by experience, a photo has a stranger, more intriguing, perhaps even hostile influence. A snapshot is fixed in place and time, and depicts a particular moment. We may wonder about the particular content of the moment of a snapshot, but nothing emerges from the picture that brings forth a counter-image or a sense of a deeper questioning. A snapshot points to itself. Its lack of uniqueness might lead to confusion with other snapshots, and its reality is analogous in a corresponding way to the truth of the image.

A photograph has punctum insofar as it pricks us, touches us, disturbs us, moves us, and addresses us. A photograph speaks for itself while the photographer is silent. Barthes (1981) notes that a photograph is "a message without a code ... the photographic message is a continuous message" (p. 196). The photograph with punctum is not a correct and complete analog for reality, but rather a transformative image that speaks beyond the reality captured in it. More than a mere representation of the world "as it is" like a random snapshot, a photograph causes the viewer to question its existential meaning. A photo with punctum prompts us to wonder and, at the same time, involves us in self-reflection. According to Heidegger (2001), artwork, like photos, can "place us in that lighted realm in which every being stands for us and from which it withdraws" (p. 51). The meaning of the photograph is continuous, open, inexhaustible, and not immediately accessible as a totality to sensation and thought. The photograph, unlike the random snapshot, is a not transparent or translucent representation, but has a transformative effect on the viewer.

Quotations from a qualitative interview may fall somewhere in between the random snapshot and the photograph with punctum: It can require some interpretation by the reader, but generally does not simply work on its own to prompt the reader to self-reflection or wonder. An anecdote in phenomenological writing, on the other hand, is meant to touch us, to address us. It makes contact with something inside us and, if well written, imbues us with wonder. A compelling anecdote has the duality of pre-reflexivity and interpretation; "it simultaneously pulls us in but then prompts us to reflect" (van Manen, 1997b, p. 121). The compelling anecdote renders possibilities for the researcher to unveil themes in an experience since the anecdote is not *about* the experience. For the involved reader, it *is* the prereflective experience, the experience as lived through.

The scholars of the Utrecht School did not hesitate to turn to the world of aesthetics in their attempt to describe human experiences. They were inspired by poetry, literature, music and art in their scientific texts. It is striking how their texts, by combining the rigor of science and the beauty of poetry, evoke a pathic sense of grasping the described phenomena. Decades before Roland Barthes (1989) talked about *integral writing* as a sort of holistic writing – the merging of more traditional academic language and the language of literature – the scholars of the Utrecht School were already practising it. They already knew and adhered to the idea that:

> [Human] science will become literature, insofar as literature – subject, moreover, to a growing collapse of traditional genres (poem, narrative, criticism, essay) – is already,

has always been, science; for what the human sciences are discovering today, in whatever realm: sociological, psychological, psychiatric, linguistic, etc., literature has always known; the difference is that literature has not said what it knows, it has written it. (Barthes, 1989, p. 10)

For that reason, we do not hesitate to call the phenomenology of the Utrecht School, and the development of the orientation, a *fine human science*. By "linking the poetic word with everyday speech as an intensification of the latter" (Gadamer, 1985, p. 470), hermeneutic phenomenology lets us see the phenomenon as it shines forth. By interpreting insights, phenomenology serves as a deeper understanding of meanings. Although phenomenological inquiry, as experience itself, lacks fulfilment (Kuhns, 1970, p. 68), a systematic and intersubjective methodological phenomenology concerns itself with the same questions, and also structures experience in the same way as art.

The light of subjectivity

An evocative text shines in itself and, simultaneously, it shines upon the phenomenon it evokes; it brings the phenomenon out of concealment. Luijpen notes, "Unconcealedness requires a certain 'light' ... This 'light' is the 'light' of man's subjectivity" (1960, pp. 137-138). Phenomenologists have, from time to time, been upbraided for treating truth as being merely subjective and relative. However, to the phenomenologist, the truth is not primarily to be found in the normative elements of justice and systems, but is intertwined in the relational existence of human beings. By living one's life and by reflecting on existence, the human being brings it out of concealedness, merely by living its intentional meaning. In accordance with Heidegger, Luijpen (1960) names our conscious existence the *lumen naturale*, or the natural light. It constitutes the very nature of persons, the human being as "a being unveiled" (p. 143). This lumen naturale, called *logos* by the Greek, translated by Gadamer as both reflection and language, is the *aletheia* that takes being out of the concealedness of human existence (Heidegger, 1962). In the natural sciences, person and object are kept at a distance from each other, and the world is a world upon which human beings act. In phenomenology the two melt into each other (Merleau-Ponty, 1997). In a profound way, the meaning of the world is inseparable from the things of the world, and also from the meaning of being a human. Language is not a device that we create to name the world according to our own sweet will, but rather something we take part in, something that is ahead of each subject – the world in which the subject unfolds. Derrida (1992) notes that words are more than simply information, communication, or disclosure. Language is testifying, witnessing. What is said, orally or written has a meaning beyond itself, because it speaks of "what I will tell." Language is a testimony of my point of view, my understanding, my interpretation and, ultimately, of whom I am. My language may, to some extent, be experienced as subjective, and yet it is still part of the human community constituted by a linguistic meaning community, and as such, it interprets both subjective and intersubjective meaning.

Dreyfus (1991) maintains that the human reflective attitude is always secondary and derivative, while the immediate subjective is primary. Merleau-Ponty (2002) notes that we cannot separate ourselves from the world, but are a part of the world which we understand and are related to. He says, "For we have the experience of ourselves, of that consciousness which we are, and it is on the basis of this experience that all linguistic connotations are assessed, and precisely through it that language comes to have any meaning at all for us" (pp. xvi-xvii). The experience has meaning for us and we express that meaning in language. Merleau-Ponty urges us to trust our experience of the world, and the impossibility of a catatonic, in order to avoid skepticism. In fact, we might too easily come to trust intellectual and scientific knowledge, and begin to distrust the world as reveals itself to us in language and by its very existence. "We must not, therefore, wonder whether we really perceive a world, we must instead say: the world is what we perceive" (p. xviii). We share a lifeworld that is intersubjective and relate to this mutual lifeworld in our constant experiential interpretation of meaning.

The texts written by the Utrecht School could be described as distilled, refined accounts of lived experiences, and as such, they shine forth by the light of subjectivity. The mere use of words such as *beauty*, *light*, and *shine* points us to the intrinsic and enigmatic relation between the experience and the expression of the same, and between description and interpretation, all of which are embedded in the elusiveness of language. Gadamer (2002) sees a connection between the concept of *intuition* and that of *vividness*, since intuition (as an aesthetic problem) cannot be understood merely from an epistemological standpoint. Rather it is related to the "free" play of imagination and cognition. Gadamer (2002) asserts:

> It is here, in the use of language, in rhetoric and literature, that the concept "vivid" is truly at home: namely, as a special quality of description and narration such that we see "before us," so to speak, what is not as such seen, but only told. That is clearly an aesthetic quality. (p. 158)

What is being told and is not seen is an *event in sound*. Moreover, such an event has the ethic-aesthetic virtues of both beauty and truth; the telling that is this event unveils qualities that display the scene freely before us, vividly addressing our intellect as well as our senses and sensations. As phenomenologists, who wish to show, describe, and understand human experiences, we dwell in the borderland between vivid descriptions, free imagination, and intellectual intuition. Phenomenology and art seem to share experiential structures, (Kuhns, 1970) and might be seen to reinforce one another, rather than being "separate in scholarship" (Kuhns, 1970, p. 53). Phenomenology and art share the desire to present and represent the aesthetic and truth of the events of the world. Kuhns notes that "taking philosophical accounts together with literary art allows us to entertain different approaches to the same kind of experience. Philosophy argues its possibility; literary art offers it whole" (p. 81). If this is indeed the case, phenomenological writing might lead beyond the solely aesthetic stand of performance indicated by modernity, toward an ethic-aesthetic textual practice that, at its best, is beautiful as well as morally bound.

MEMORIES AND RECOLLECTIONS

Speaking of the human sciences, Barthes (1989) writes, "Science speaks itself; literature writes itself; science is led by the voice, literature follows the hand; it is not the same body, and hence the same desire, which is behind the one and the other" (p. 5). For hermeneutic phenomenology, it *is* the same desire. Through the hand, we wish to give voice to that which experience speaks of: memories of moments lived through. One of Sartre's projects is relevant in this area: When one is inside an event, one is not thinking of it. To *live* a story and to tell a story are different experiences. "One can live or tell; not both at once" (Murdoch, 1953, p. 11). Thus, a telling of lived events is a recalling of the *lived* in the shape of a memory. As a result, phenomenological telling is retrospective, looking beyond or behind what is currently at hand, distinguishing between appearance and essence, facticities and facts.

Facts, van den Berg (1961) holds, are the "skeleton of the past" and to recollect facts of the past is not to retrieve memories: "We know that the war began on the 10th of May, 1940.[6] But this knowing is still not a memory; we are only remembering a fact, nothing else" (p. 33). The invasion of the Netherlands is a fact duly proved and archived by media, history books and other historical documents. History (*Die Historie*), Heidegger claims (1962), is what actually happened. The story (*Die Geschichte*), on the other hand, is what happened to the singular subject, the meaningful and lived-through experience of the subject. Recollection of the invasion of the Netherlands as a historical fact is different from the experiential accounts of the day of the invasion. Thus, actual memories of the day, May 10th, 1940, are another matter altogether. We could not do without the day itself, van den Berg (1961) says,

> The day as it began, the warm day in spring with clear blue sky and whirring metal planes in it; the early hour and all the pyjama-clad people looking at the sky. We need all the attributes of the event, we can hardly omit even one of them if we are to tempt the day to show itself. And then, suddenly, there it is, the day, just as it all happened; thousands of impressions are there at the same time, unabridged and full of meaning, still nameless. And before they get a name, they have sunk back in that immense grave called the past. (pp. 33-34)

So what do van den Berg's thoughts on recalling memories mean for the gathering of experiential accounts? First, the problem with lived experiences is that they often hide deep down in our memory where they sometimes stubbornly resist our struggle to bring them to light so we can reflect on and articulate them (Henriksson, 2009). A memory can be as elusive as the Cheshire cat; all we see is its teasing smile. However, van den Berg holds that "the past is not unavailable to us and we come to realize that when, in precious moments, the past 'jumps or flies at us in a smell or a sound'" (van den Berg, 1961, p. 34). He goes on to say that the past is always ready for us, "only a word is needed, a chord, a small constellation of things, something incidental, whatever it is. It seems as though the past can only come to us through a back entrance; the front door is closed" (p. 34). How do we find the back entrance to memories of the past? Is there a key somewhere? Can we *make* memories jump or fly at us?

The roundness of the memory

The past is already ready for us; a back entrance is half open, only a particular chord needs to vibrate for a memory to flash back on us. In her novel *Sartre Romantic Rationalist*, Murdoch (1953) attends to the semblance of the novelist and the phenomenologist to speak in ways that may echo the tone of evocative and vivid memories:

> The novelist proper is, in his way, a sort of phenomenologist. He has always implicitly understood, what the philosopher has grasped less clearly, that human reason is not a single unitary gadget the nature of which could be discovered once for all. The novelist has had his eye fixed in what we do, and not on what we ought to do or must be presumed to do. He has as a natural gift that blessed freedom from rationalism which the academic thinker achieves, if at all, by a precarious discipline. He has always been, what the very latest philosophers claim to be, a describer rather than an explainer; and in consequence he has often anticipated the philosopher's discoveries. (p. 8)

Being a phenomenological describer and a hermeneutic interpreter – both aspects being the leading desire of the Utrecht School phenomenologist – clearly influences the phenomenological language and the textual expression of which we are depending to somehow approach the experience as it was lived through in the past. Human experience, not being a unitary process to be experientially accomplished and fulfilled, nevertheless is experientially concentrated and focused as an instant entity. The human experience is not the observant observation of things or events, but the immediate lived thoroughness of a moment before it is reflected. The experience is from the inside, and as Bachelard (1994) notes, "devoid of all exterior features, being cannot be otherwise than round" (p. 234). Being isolated in a particular momentous description the memorable moment of young Proust is an entity that is concentrated upon itself, and thus, in Bachelardian terms becomes spherical, centralized, rounded, a unity of meaning.

> One day in winter, on my return home, my mother, seeing that I was cold, offered me some tea, a thing I did not ordinarily take. I declined at first, and then, for no particular reason, changed my mind. She sent for one of those squat, plump little cakes called "petites madeleines," which look as though they had been moulded in the fluted valve of a scallop shell. And soon, mechanically, dispirited after a dreary day with the prospect of a depressing morrow, I raised to my lips a spoonful of the tea in which I had soaked a morsel of the cake. No sooner had the warm liquid mixed with the crumbs touched my palate than a shudder ran through me and I stopped, intent upon the something isolated, detached, with no suggestion of its origin. ... this new sensation having had on me the effect which love has of filling me with a precious essence; or rather this essence was not in me it was me. I had ceased now to feel mediocre, contingent, mortal. Whence could it have come to me, this all-powerful joy? I sensed that it was connected with the taste of the tea and the cake, but that it infinitely transcended those savours, could, no, indeed, be of the same nature. Whence

did it come? What did it mean? How could I seize and apprehend it? (Proust, 1970, p. 48)

The now-famous paragraph from Proust's *In Search of Lost Time*, illustrates how memories *are* able to jump or fly at us, even beyond our "wanting and doing" (Gadamer, 1985, p. xxviii). The taste of the Madeleine cake did not just stir a memory, "this essence was not in me it *was* me," Proust writes. The memory, which came through what van den Berg calls "a back entrance," did not come as a temporal single fact or recollection of a time past, it came as a corporeal, spatial, relational and concentrated lived experience which pervaded his whole being. The essence of the memory *was me*, Proust says. It is exactly this essence (as meaning) of a memory that is the target for hermeneutic phenomenological inquiry, this is what we, as researchers, try to "seize and apprehend" and this is also, ironically, what we are doomed to fail at. We are always too late to catch the pre-reflective meaning of an experience as lived in the past. Yet, we continue to try.

Not just our senses including smell, taste, and sound, but also objects could open the back entrance to memories and, thus, function as mediators between the past and present. Previously, Socrates argued that both objects and people are mediators of recollections. Like Proust's madeleine cake, objects can cause us stumble on memories accidentally.

> And what is the feeling of lovers when they recognize a lyre, or a garment, or anything else which the beloved has been in the habit of using? Do not they, from knowing the lyre, form in the mind's eye an image of the youth to whom the lyre belongs? And this is recollection: and in the same way anyone who sees Simmias may remember Cebes; and there are endless other things of the same nature. (Plato, 1973, p. 506)

The word *recollection* is etymologically related to the word *remember*, meaning recall to mind, be mindful of. The word also has the meaning "to evoke memories." Recollection, Plato says, is "a process of recovering that which has been forgotten through time and inattention" (p. 506). So, if we are mindful of our recollections, we might find that memories jump or fly at us as van den Berg (1961) holds. To memorize has the original meaning of "commit to writing" and that is precisely the task of phenomenology; we ask our informants to "memorize," to recall a specific moment, a moment that we then try to capture in writing.

Narrating the past in the present

Our memory is, however, more than a mental force that enables us to recall personal experiences. The memory is, in fact, what "makes shared experience possible" which allows us to "participate with other minds in an enlarged awareness" (Kuhns, 1970, p. 107). Recollections, as Socrates describes them, might turn into memories by the sight of something that we associate with something else – for example, people, objects, places, feelings – and help us open up the intersubjective space of shared experience:

Sometime during the evening one of the children found an old photo album and started to ask questions about people who she did not recognize in the photos. My sister-in-law walked over to help identify people. Suddenly she exclaimed, "Look! The old blue bucket!" Suddenly, the child with the photo album found herself surrounded by adult relatives. "We used to carry the fish from the boat to Aunt Amelia's house in it. Remember how it reeked of fish?"

"Oh yes, we kept it in the garden shed because of the smell!"

"Aunt Amelia really hated when we brought her eels, especially if they were small!"

"Still, her pickled eel was one of the best in the village ...." More and more relatives gathered around the table to join in the conversation. "Didn't we use that bucket when we bricked your garage, Andy?"

"Yes, we did! I had forgotten that. Remember when Marge brought us coffee and you fell of the ladder when you tried to reach the mug! God, how we laughed!"

"Who bought Aunt Amelia's house when she died?

"Wasn't it the son of the next door neighbor?"

"Yes, maybe it was."

"Whatever happened to the bucket? Do you think it is still in the garden shed?"

"Maybe the new owners use it now ...."

The blue bucket was not just a conversation piece; it became a mediator of past events and it evoked memories of people, places, and moods. The Past was no longer the past that had been, but a past alive in the Now. Undoubtedly, several lived experiences were recollected and turned into memories that evening. Perhaps these lived experiences were also told, shared and interpreted.

Although memories can be happy, they might also be sorrowful and wistful, something we need to keep in mind as researchers. What memories and emotions do we awake in the informants when we ask them to recall a specific moment? Neither the informant nor the researcher could know the forces that might be let loose when we ask for a lived-experience description; embodied memories could be dormant or suppressed but the body has its own way of dealing with memories.

Perhaps the body has its own memory system, like the invisible meridian lines those Chinese acupuncturists always talk about ... Maybe the pain of memory is encoded into our marrow and each remembered grievance swims in our bloodstream like a hard, black pebble ... perhaps the body is this hypersensitive, revengeful entity, a ledger book, a warehouse of remembered slights and cruelties. (Umrigar, 2007, pp. 103-104)

As researchers we need to tread lightly both when we borrow other peoples' lived experiences and when we set out to write and interpret these experiences. In addition, as the different steps of the reduction urges us, we need to keep a close eye on our own lived experiences of the phenomenon under investigation. We, too, have bodies with their own knowledge and memories, bodies which may lead us astray when we try to describe and understand possible meanings of the phenomenon. If memory and recollections are etymologically connected to the act of "committing to writing," then the mere act of writing down the memory would result in a "Eureka!" But, to catch that which "shines forth" in a phenomenon with words is, at times, as impossible as trying to catch a sun beam. We may find that we "see the words fly about the room in all directions" (Abrams, 1953, p. 216). Yet, we hold with van Manen (1997b) that writing is the method of coming to understand the meaning in lived experience.

Writing the experience

In hermeneutic phenomenology, there is a compelling connection between reflection on the meaning of experiential accounts and the writing process. A phenomenological text is not so much a traditional research report, but a wilful wandering into a more profound understanding of the taken-for-granted; the text aims to be a questioning experience for the reader (as well as the writer). Gadamer, by reference to Vico, the Italian 18th century philosopher, points to the old truth of common sense, and the classic human ideal of wisdom as a mode of knowledge: "Talking well (eu legein) has always two meanings; it is not merely a rhetorical ideal. It also means saying the right thing, i.e. the truth, and is not just the art of speaking or saying whatsoever well" (Gadamer, 1985, p. 19).

The truth based on common sense and wisdom is a knowledge not based on argumentation, but is a practical knowledge, *phronesis*, that shows itself to us as obvious and trustworthy. Aristotle (384–322 B.C.E) considered phronesis to be an intellectual virtue and a "determination of moral being, which cannot exist without the totality of the 'ethical virtues,' which in turn cannot exist without it" (Gadamer, 1985, p. 22).

The *vita memoriae*, the truth in "convincing examples as only history can offer them" (Gadamer, 1985, p. 23) is, to Aristotle, a moral knowledge that might also be operative in recollected lived-experience descriptions. Gadamer suggests that Aristotle's digging into the epistemological significance of the senses was "intended ultimately to correct the exaggeration of philosophical speculation" (p. 25). The buffer effect of the credible lived example against abstract, conceptual knowledge is relevant in contemporary phenomenology as well. The lived experience is a "living feeling" (p. 57), is "the unit of what is given" (p. 59) and has an "inner relation to life" (p. 61) – qualities that makes the lived experience a meaningful rounded whole. A lived experience is "taken out of the continuity of life and at the same time related to the whole of one's life" (p. 62). The phenomenologically meaningful lived example is distinguished from the rest of life's web by being told, written, honed and increasingly made sense of. And at the same time, the lived example inserts itself in life and adds sense to the self and the life of the person.

In research, however, we do not ask our informants to sit down and try to recall just *any* lived experience. We want them to share with us, in speech or in writing, a memory of a *specific* moment when they experienced something that something being a subject singled out by the researcher. Once the memory of the lived experience has surfaced we face another predicament: How is it best described? What words do we use to name the unabridged and meaningful memory?

"An Event in Sound"

In her book on Sartre, Murdoch (1953) argues that the difference between poem and prose is not found in their aesthetic properties – imagery, language, word-order, thought, movement, or argument. "What makes a poem separate is not just the mode of language-using of which it is an instance, but the quality and integrity of the poetic thought of which it is an incarnation" (p. 72). The distinction is not between poetry and prose, she argues, but between substance and the lack of substance, between "disciplined aesthetic uses" and "formless non-aesthetic uses of language" (p. 72). The poetic reflection tunes us in toward the inner disturbance and interference of existence and "directs attention to the things of the world, [it] alters courses of action, [it] arouses feelings and conveys information" (p. 73). Addressing the description below, one may wonder if the "world changes first and pulls language after it, or [if] a new awareness of language suddenly makes us see the world differently" (p. 28).

> After just a few months in second grade, our son announced at dinner, "I hate writing!" Since I consider him a verbal little person, I was surprised at his outbreak.
> "What's so terrible about writing? Isn't it nice to see your thoughts on paper?"
> "Mom, it takes forever to put words into sentences and sentences into paragraphs! And Mrs. Peterson wants me to write about our winter holidays. It's so tedious!"
> "Well, why don't you try to express your thoughts in a poem, then?"
> "What's a poem, Mom?"
> How much would a seven-year-old understand about the difference between prose and poetry? I tried to explain in as uncomplicated a manner as possible. "You see, when you write a story you need to put all the words you use in a certain position, you cannot just pile them up. You need to get the order of the words right otherwise they don't make sense. Now, in a poem you don't necessarily have to do that. A poem is meant to leave empty spaces, and these spaces are for the reader to fill with imaginations of their own."

My son looked a bit puzzled, but silently finished his meal and
then disappeared into his room. Half an hour later he was still in
his room, door closed. My knock on the door was answered by a
muffled, "Who is it?"
"It's Mom. May I come in?"
"Uhuh..."He is curled up by his desk, his posture indicating
concentration. On the floor around him, heaps of papers are
floating. On his desk, yet another sheet of paper is the target for
his profound attention.
"What's all this?"
"It's poems, Mom."
"May I have a look?"
"Sure."
I pick one paper randomly from the floor. While I read the poem,
my son stops writing, lifts his head, and listens as I pronounce his
words and give voice to his experiences:

> *"Winter night*
> *Wolves howling to the moon*
> *Fireworks!!!! Boom, boom!*
> *Cold stars*
> *Winter Night*
> *Happy new year!"*

I pick up sheet after sheet from the floor. An army of poems are
marching over the pages; steadfast and unwavering they carry
variations on the same theme across the pages: winter nights.
"These are beautiful poems!"
"Yes, I know," he beams. "This is real writing, Mom!" Since
that day he has not – at least to my knowledge – written any more
poems, but neither has he complained about the agonizing act of
writing. The very few times he lets me read anything he has
written in school, I am amazed by his vocabulary, his
thoughtfulness, and the eloquence of his texts.

What did this young boy experience while he was producing all of these poems
which described his feelings on New Year's Eve? Did he relive the winter nights
through the words? Perhaps he met himself as a person for the first time, a human
being standing in the midst of fireworks and wolves' howling, hailing the words
which were suddenly there for him? Perhaps, that evening, he found what Barthes
(1989) calls "the Eros of language" (p. 9). "This is *real* writing, Mom!" he said.
What is *real* writing? Is there *fake* writing too? Judging from the comment,
experientially there is. What, then, is the difference between *real* and *fake* writing
in human science texts? How do we, the writers-researchers-interpreters, do justice
to the meaning of the lived-experience descriptions? What language do we use?

Poetic writing or writing poetry?

The adjective *expressive* has as synonyms *eloquent, empathic, lively, lyrical, meaningful, poignant, revealing, strong, thoughtful, vivid* – all of which signal that the role of the researcher in hermeneutic phenomenology is not that of a mere writer of a scientific report. In addition to analytic, interpretive, and methodological skills, we need a skill involving semantics, the sense of the value of words, and an awareness of how fringes and halos surround words and expressions. But does that mean that phenomenologists are also poets? Before we continue, some semantic distinctions are necessary.

The word *poesie* has its roots in the Greek word *poiēsis* which means *making, fabrication, poetry,* and *poem*. But poesie also has a narrower meaning than the original *poiēsis* that applies especially to writing in verse as opposed to prose. Heidegger's notion of *Dichtung* has its etymological roots in the Latin word *dictare,* meaning *to invent, to write,* or *to compose verses*. This notion has a wider meaning than *poesie* and applies to all creative writing. Heidegger uses *Dichtung* in a narrow and in a broad sense: in the narrow sense it refers to poetry; in the broad sense it refers to the original meaning of inventing, writing, and composing (Inwood, 2006). For scholars within the tradition of the Utrecht School, it is this latter meaning of the Heideggerian *Dichtung* that establishes language as poetic and expressive. For Heidegger (2001), there is also a close unsurpassable relationship between poetic language and thinking:

> When thought's courage stems from
> the bidding of Being, then
> destiny's language thrives.
>
> As soon as we have the thing before
> our eyes, and in our hearts an ear
> for the word, thinking prospers.
>
> Few are experienced enough in the
> difference between an object of
> scholarship and a matter of thought.
>
> If in thinking there were already
> adversaries and not mere
> opponents, then thinking's case
> would be more auspicious. (p. 5)

The phenomenological effort of writing ingeniously, the endeavor to initiate or originate a resonant language rich with experiential meaning, comes from the way we dwell with the things of the world. When a phenomenological text speaks to us, like a poem or a novel does, it is because it evokes in us recognition or thoughts which are new and at the same time conversant. Heidegger's (2001) persistent experience that "language speaks" (p. 188) somehow puts the human being in a position where he or she becomes a witness to the act of writing. Language calls things into nearness and each thing presents and represents a whole world of meaning. The phenomenologist is the dative of life and the world of things, the *who* to whom something is given.[7] The phenomenologist as well admits with Heidegger (2001) that "the world grants to things their presence. Things bear world. World grants things" (p. 199). The intimate relation among things, world, human being and expression, is an incisive experiential proximity, a genuine but neglected inseparability. Experiential accounts collected from fictional literature, novels, poetry, or from the world of aesthetics, art, films, or music may assist in presenting and describing the richness and subtleties of phenomena in human life. A phenomenological text combines "the power of philosophic or systematic discourse with the power of literary or poetic language ... a tension between the pre-reflective and reflective pulls of language (van Manen, 1997b, p. 121).

Literature and poetry are frequently evocative mediators for a deeper understanding of human experiences. Just think of how Shakespeare, in *Macbeth,* brilliantly underscores power corruption, how Euripides, in *Medea*, illustrates the fury of a woman scorned, and how Strindberg, in *The Pelican*, shows the lifelong deception and the collapse of a family. It is, though, important to bear in mind that "poems and novels do not 'prove' anything. But both can be enormously helpful in bringing certain phenomena closer to us and thus in making us 'understand' them, helping us to understand ourselves and the world in which we live" (Kockelmans, 1987, pp. viii-ix).

SCIENCE AND LITERATURE

For a long time, humans have made a clear distinction between science (natural as well as human) and literature. Science has been ascribed its own characteristics distinctly apart from those of literature. The differences – but also the similarities – become decidedly noticeable when we look at the role of language. In science and in literature language does not constitute itself in the same way.

For the scientist who wishes to write up his report, content tends to precede form. Only when the content is clearly stated does language enter the report. Language becomes a tool, an instrument, which the scientist wishes to make as neutral as possible. But language as a neutral device is nothing but a mere illusion, a self-deception on behalf of the scientist. Writing is not merely a cognitive, pragmatic act. "Language itself, however, has something speculative about it ... as the realization of meaning, as the event of speech, of mediation, of coming to an understanding" (Gadamer, 1985, p. 469). Writing could be liberating, inspirational; in writing the words construct, confirm – and challenge – your world. For the writer, though, language never pre-exists social, emotional, or scientific reality. "No, language is the *being* of literature, its very world: all literature is contained in the act of writing, and no longer in that of 'thinking'" (Gadamer, 1976, pp. 4-5). It would seem that Gadamer crosses swords with Heidegger (2001), who sees a close link between poetry and thinking. However, Gadamer (2002) also argues, when he

71

addresses the difference between what he calls "intentional words" and the words of poetic language, that "there are transitional cases that stand between poetically articulated language on the one hand and the purely intentional word on the other" (p. 67).

What is the difference between Johan's voice in Strindberg's *The Maid's Son*, when he describes his lived experiences of school, and the voice of a student who does not feel recognized by his or her teacher in a qualitative, scientific study (e.g., Henriksson, 2008; Saevi, 2003)? What is the difference between the voice of a sick, bed-ridden woman in Axelsson's novel *The April Witch* and the experience of bed-ridden patients, who are being fed in a scientific study (e.g., Martinsen, Harder, & Biering-Sorensen, 2008)?

One could argue that a difference is that literature speaks to our senses while science speaks to our intellect. Or one could argue that the difference is a question of validation. Although a novel or a poem can touch us, or even transform us, it could be shrugged off by thinking "it's just make-believe," something not true, not valid. In contrast, a scientific report is subject to serious scrutiny by academic peers, referees, or supervisors. Thus, literature and science deal with different realities; a novel is ultimately the subjective fantasy of one person, while science presents us with the ultimate objective matter-of-fact truth. Yet another difference, we hold, is the usability of the different kinds of texts: what pragmatic use do they have? Scientific reports explicitly or implicitly suggest a solution to a problem; the text has, or points out, The Answer. A novel or a poem, on the other hand, is likely to evoke reflection, to point *to* questions and not to point *out* answers. Furthermore, when we read scientific reports and literature, we do it with different attitudes towards the text. When I sit down to read a novel, there are some taken-for-granted features at work: It is not real, but fantasy. Although the author may vividly describe persons, actions, and milieu, it is in *my* mind that the images are born, there is no external verification of what the text says. Gadamer (2002) shows this concept using Dostoevsky's novel *The Brothers Karamazov* as an example.

> The staircase that Smerdjakov falls down plays a major role in the story. Everyone who has read the book will remember this scene and will "know" exactly what the staircase looks like. Not one of us has exactly the same image of it and yet we all believe that we see it quite vividly. It would be absurd to ask what the staircase "intended" by Dostoevsky really looked like. (p. 111)

No, we do not want to see the "intended" staircase. We demand that authors of fiction present us with words, which we, the readers, can turn into images that are ours, and ours alone. At the same time, our images can be curiously shared with other readers. What happens if the author of a novel imposes the "intended" upon us?

In her novel *The Shape of Snakes*, Minette Walters (2000) portrays a black woman in a white community, "Mad Annie," who suffers from Tourette's syndrome and alcoholism. Walters uses different literary techniques (handwritten letters, newspaper clippings etc.). Although these techniques are somewhat atypical for fiction, they are not uncommon, and as readers we accept them as the poetic freedom of the writer. What makes Walter's novel stand out, is something else altogether. Eighty pages in, when the readers are well acquainted with the characters, their thoughts, their surroundings, and how they are related to each other, when the readers have formed images of the lives and faces described, Walters defaces these personal images by forcing the "intended" upon us. She presents photos of the main characters. In so doing, Walters manipulates a world, which we, up until the moment we first lay eyes on the photos, thought was ours. As readers, our original attitude or intention toward the text is thwarted by the author's intention. There is a loss of equilibrium as Walters, through the photos, declares our images "wrong" or invalid. Suddenly, there are no clear lines between fiction and what is (allegedly) real, and we lose our foothold and our "mindhold," our attitude. We simply cannot figure out what attitude to adopt toward this text. Is it fiction? Is it real? How do we receive the message of the book? We seem to adopt different attitudes depending on whether something *actually* happened or whether it *could have* happened. Is Walter's book true writing or fake writing? We feel an urge to know. How else can we know how to relate to the content of the book?

In a similar way, we tend to separate science from literature, which shows that we are still burdened by the Cartesian dualistic heritage; some things belong to the brain, some things to the mind. And yet, we are not fully able to understand how perception interacts with thought or our bodily senses. This compartmentalization of spheres disregards the Husserlian belief that science, too, is a part of our lifeworld. Our lifeworld is not compartmentalized, fragmentized; it is a complex whole, as we live, interact, speak – and write. "Today we have often to labor to regain the awareness that the word is still always at root the spoken word. Early man had no such problem: he felt the word, even when written, as primarily an event in sound ..." (Ong, 1967, p. ix). Could it be, Ong asks, that we have become relatively deaf, that we have adjusted to the post-Newtonian silent universe, and that words that existed in a sensorium have grown utterly strange to us?

PHENOMENOLOGICAL WRITING AS A MOVING BEYOND

Within hermeneutic phenomenology, writing is the method; it is how phenomenological research is done (van Manen, 1997b) and it is through language and writing that we can hope to come to understand some aspect of life. Hermeneutic phenomenology is not just a matter of reporting research findings in the conventional way. Here we employ quotes from two scholars to illuminate the difference between a traditional research report and a phenomenological study:

> The element of discovery takes place, in non-fiction, not during the writing but during the research. This makes writing a piece very tedious. You already know what it's about. (Plimpton, 1981, p. 352)

> Once one has started to write a paper, it often looks very different from what the raw data suggested to you. Sometimes ... you suddenly find that you are, in fact, espousing quite a different doctrine to what you did when you started writing the

paper ... As I write ... I see something in an entirely new light ... The act of writing is ... where you do analyse your data. (Rymer, 1988, p. 239)

The quote from Plimpton highlights two distinct features which distinguish hermeneutic phenomenology from traditional research reports. The first is that we do not separate research from writing. The second is that we do not "already know what it's about." Quite the contrary, we, as Rymer says, analyse the informants' lived-experience descriptions through the act of writing. To enter the world of lived experiences through the world of language is to embark on an adventurous endeavor, which sometimes proves to be an amazing discovery as the meaning of an experience unfolds before our eyes, on paper or on the screen. However, there is an ironic paradox in writing for discovery: we discover nothing at all.

Building on the myth of Orpheus and Eurydice and Blanchot's (1982) interpretation of it, van Manen (2002) describes phenomenological writing as "falling forward into the dark" or as "writing in the dark." It is not uncommon for writers of phenomenological texts, van Manen argues, to find that "every word kills and becomes the death of the object it tries to represent ... language kills whatever it touches ... there is nothing to say ... it is impossible to truly 'say' something" (p. 244). There is, says van Manen "no soaring height to reach from which things could be seen in Heideggerian brightness" (p. 246). The quote, which van Manen most likely refers to when he talks about Heideggerian brightness, reads:

> Language is – language, speech. Language speaks. If we let ourselves fall into the abyss denoted by this sentence, we do not go tumbling into emptiness. We fall upward, to a height. Its loftiness opens up a depth. The two span a realm in which we would like to become at home, so as to find a residence, a dwelling place for the life of man. (Heidegger, 2001, pp. 189-190)

"Language speaks." Language always speaks. Not of darkness or of emptiness, but of a realm in which humans dwell. The Heideggerian height symbolizes the space where language is in fact born, employed, and communicated. It lets the things speak and it permits us, as phenomenological writers, to be "bespoken by language" (p. 190).

Even though van Manen's line of thought is well grounded and carefully argued, it does bring to mind a certain linguistic nihilism which implies that language occults the object it strives to represent (e.g., Donato, 1993). To name the project of writing "writing in the dark," which allows neither clear views nor compelling words to be distinguished or verbalized also implicitly, places phenomenological writing in a romantic tradition, in the wake of Plato's world of ideas – where the writer dwells, quite content in his or her subjectivity. To ask of phenomenology that it make anything or everything clear is to remain in the realm of Husserl's transcendental phenomenology, where essence precedes existence. But there is no original meaning, just possible meanings and shadows on the wall of the cave, which we as researchers can try to describe, interpret, and bestow meaning upon. Hermeneutic phenomenology is not a romantic project; it is very much a realistic project. It is an exploration into the lifeworld – the puzzling, the complex, and sometimes the unintelligible world we live in and experiences we live through. The phenomenon is not a meaning but a thing, a substance. Like when we read a poem we attend to what is there, to the very speaking of the substance, for "what the thing *is* is there," Murdoch (1953) notes. She continues:

> The image which suggests itself is that of language as an opaque coagulated substance to be contemplated for itself alone, or else as a transparent glass through which one looks at the world or a tool with which one prods it. (pp. 71-72)

The language that is spoken by the things and events of the world is a language that speaks clearly, but if we attend to the world with a phenomenological rather than with a natural attitude (Sokolowski, 2000), language can leave us with "an opaque coagulated substance." Heidegger, in fact, demonstrates with his awareness of language that phenomenology takes away the transparency of things as well as of language itself. It is of course true, that sometimes the act of writing is a "curling up with language" (Jelinek, 2004), but if we remain curled up with language, the whole phenomenological project, as research on practice, is at jeopardy. To write phenomenology is not a matter of quenching some thirst for poetic writing in the researcher. In that case we would truly be writing in the dark, and the widespread misunderstanding that phenomenology is "anti-scientific, not based upon analysis and description but originating in a kind of uncontrollable intuition or metaphysical revelation" (Schutz, 1979, p. 55) would be a diehard misconception.

Phenomenology does not claim privileged access to truth or accurate insights, nor should we ask of ourselves, as phenomenologists, whether what we unveil is a definite truth. We must, as Sartre (1949) argues, give up "the impossible dream of giving an impartial picture of Society and the human condition" (p. 23). Then, and only then, can writing phenomenologically be a strenuous pleasure that challenges the strength of our attention (Weil, 1990), and thus implicates a shared difference in our common existence (Luijpen, 1960) instead of remaining merely the "poet's" personal pain. Only then, can we get out of the grip of "curling up with language" where we see nothing, or simply see through making the world and our lived experiences transparent, invisible, as Lewis (1986) notes:

> The whole point of seeing through something is to see something through it. It is good that the window should be transparent, because the street or garden beyond is opaque. How if you saw through the garden too? It is no use trying "to see through" first principles. If you see through everything, then everything is transparent. But a wholly transparent world is an invisible world. To see through all things is the same as not to see. (p. 48)

Phenomenological writing is the practice of going beyond what is immediately apparent by directing attention to the is-ness of what is there. As such, writing phenomenology is the approval of perceptive and linguistic non-transparency. Furthermore, writing is the transitional practice of letting human experience pass beyond the abstract, conceptual, cognitive condition of a traditional scientific practice in order to let experience reverberate immediately beyond everything we think we already know. It is to carefully "touch the depths before it [experience] stirs the surface" (Bachelard, 1994, p. xxiii). Writing phenomenology can never simply be to "iterate what is already given and understood in lived experience in the way that it is given and understood" (Burch, 1989, p. 4). Writing, as a hermeneutic phenomenological endeavor, constantly aims at transcending the natural attitude of things by going beyond their transparent obviousness and "re-achieving a direct and primitive contact with the world" (Merleau-Ponty, 2002, p. vii). For Løgstrup (1971), the natural attitude equals *triviality*, which is our unreflected way of seeing things. As a contrast to triviality, Løgstrup offers the concept of *beauty*:

> Because triviality is false, unclear, and imprecise, and because beauty overcomes triviality, which otherwise is the atmosphere in which everything is seen. The world, nature, things are brought close to us in a manner which is revelational in character ...
> It is revelation and nearness; and beauty is so to speak its means in that beauty destroys triviality. (p. 206)

In an expressive (aesthetic) language, Løgstrup also sees a deep ethical commitment when he holds that a beautiful text brings a message from an existence in which we already find ourselves and that expressive writing reveals that "we are blind and deaf to the world in which we live" (p. 218). Thus, phenomenological writing is the interlacing of the ethical and the aesthetic.

When we try to abide by Merleau-Ponty's postulate, we dwell in the space between a *poetic* attitude, in which the writer has "a silent contact with the things, touching them, testing them, palping them" (Sartre, 1949, p. 14), and a *utilitarian* writing style in which words are domesticated and honed to express the lived experience. However, we are never quite capable of expressing what we want to say. We say "too much or not enough; each phrase is a wager, a risk assumed" (p. 37). Sartre's statement could indeed be seen as rather disheartening, but at the same time, it is immensely inspiring; it urges us, forces us, and pushes us to write evocatively of lived experiences – with even more careful circumspection – and deeper devotion.

NOTES

[1] We have borrowed the title from a quote in Ong, W. J. (1967). The presence of the world. New Haven: Yale University Press.

[2] Here we see "poetic" as Heidegger's *Dichtung*, which has a broader meaning than "poetry." See the side heading *Poetic writing or writing poetry?*

[3] Some experiential accounts in this article are, if not otherwise stated, drawn from the authors' own lived experiences.

[4] Translated versions from Dutch to English are available in Kockelmans, 1987.

[5] From the Latin *in pectore*, "in the breast." To do something privately and not announced to the general public.

[6] Van den Berg is writing from a Dutch perspective, thus the date and year.

[7] Dative, from Latin *dativus*, meaning *appropriate to giving*.

REFERENCES

Abrams, M.H. (1953). *The mirror and the lamp: Romantic theory and the critical tradition.* Oxford: Oxford University Press.

Bachelard, G. (1994). *The poetics of space.* (M. Jolas, Trans.) Boston: Beacon Press. (Original work published 1958.)

Barthes, R. (1981). *Camera Lucida: Reflections on photography.* (R. Howard, Trans.) New York: Hill and Wang.

Barthes, R. (1989). *The rustle of language.* (R. Howard, Trans.). Berkeley: University of California Press. (Original work published 1984.)

Burch, R. (1989). Phenomenology and its Practices. *Phenomenology + Pedagogy, 7,* 187-217.

Cooley, C.H. (1902). *Samhället och individen.* Göteborg: Korpen.

Derrida, J. (1992). *On the name.* California: Stanford University Press.

Dreyfus, H. (1991). *Being-in-the-world. A commentary on Heidegger's being and time.* Division Cambridge: Massachusetts University Press.

Donato, E. (1993). *The script of decadence: Essays on the fictions of Flaubert and the poetics of romanticism.* New York: Oxford University Press.

Gadamer, H.-G. (1985). *Truth and method.* (G. Barden and J. Cumming, Trans.). New York: Crossroad. (Original work published 1960.)

Gadamer, H.-G. (1976). *Philosophical hermeneutics.* (D. E. Linge, Trans.). Los Angeles: University of California Press.

Gadamer, H.-G. (2002). *The relevance of the beautiful and other essays.* (N. Walker, Trans.). Cambridge: Cambridge University Press. (Original work published 1977.)

Heidegger, M. (1962). *Being and time.* (J. Macquarrie & E. Robinson, Trans.) Oxford: Basil Blackwell. (Original work published 1926.)

Heidegger, M. (2001). *Poetry, language, thought.* (A. Hofstadter, Trans.) New York: Harper & Row. (Original work published 1971.)

Heidegger, M. (1989). *Parmenides.* Indianapolis: Indiana University Press.

Henriksson, C. (2008). *Living away from blessings. School failure as lived experience.* London, Ontario: The Althouse Press.

Henriksson, C. (2009). Curriculum in abundance – A phenomenological reading. *Journal of the American Association for the Advancement of Curriculum Studies, 5,* www.uwstout.edu.

Inwood, M. (2006). *A Heidegger dictionary.* Oxford: Blackwell.

Jelinek, E. (2004). *Nobel lecture.* Retrieved from www.nobelprize.org.

Kockelmans, J.J. (Ed.). (1987). *Phenomenological psychology: The Dutch school.* Dordrecht: Kluwer.

Kuhns, R. (1970). *Structures of experience. Essays on the affinity between philosophy and literature.* New York: Basic Books.

Levering, B. & van Manen, M. (2001). Phenomenological anthropology in the Netherlands and Flanders. In Teresa Tymieniecka (Ed.), *Phenomenology world-wide* (pp. 274-286). Dordrecht: Kluwer Academic Publishers.

Lewis, C.S. (1943/1986). *The abolition of Man.* London: Collins.

Luijpen, W.A. (1960). *Existential phenomenology.* Pittsburgh: Duquesne University Press.

Løgstrup, K.E. (1971). *The ethical demand.* (Trans. J. M. Gustafson). Philadelphia: Fortress Press.

Martinsen, B., Harder, I., & Biering-Sorensen, F. (June 2008). The meaning of assisted feeding for people living with spinal cord injury: A phenomenological study. *Journal of Advanced Nursing, 62*(5), 533-540.

Merleau-Ponty, M. (2002). *Phenomenology of perception.* (C. Smith, Trans.) New York: Routeledge. (Original work published 1945.)

Merleau-Ponty, M. (1997). *The visible and the invisible.* (A. Lingis, Trans.). Evanston: Northwestern University Press. (Original work published 1964.)

Murdoch, I. (1953). *Sartre Romantic Rationalist.* Cambridge: Bowes & Bowes.

Ong, W.J. (1967). *The presence of the world.* New Haven: Yale University Press.

Online Etymology Dictionary. (2004). Retrieved from www.etymologyonline.com.

Plato (1973). *The republic and other works.* (B. Jowett, Trans.). New York: Anchor Books.

Plimpton, G. (1981). *Writers at work. The Paris review interviews.* Harmondsworth: Penguin.

Proust, M. (1970). *Rememberance of things past. Swann's way.* (C. K. S Moncrieff &T. Kilmartin, Trans.). New York: Vintage Books. (Original work published 1913.)

Ricoeur, P. (1998). *Hermeneutics & the human sciences.* (J.B. Thompson, Trans.). Cambridge: Cambridge University Press. (Original work published 1981).

Rymer, J. (1988): Scientific composing processes: How eminent scientists write journal articles. In D. A. Jolliffe (Ed.), *Advances in writing research, Volume 2: Writing in academic disciplines.* Norwood, NJ: Ablex.

Sartre, J-P. (1949). *Literature and existentialism.* (B. Frechtman, Trans.). New York: Citadel Press. (Original work published 1949).

Sævi, T. (2005). *Seeing disability pedagogically. The lived experience of disability in the pedagogical encounter.* Bergen: University of Bergen, Norway.

Schutz, A. (1970). *On phenomenology and social relations.* Chicago: The University of Chicago Press.

Sokolowski, R. (2000). *Introduction to phenomenology.* Cambridge: Cambridge University Press.

Umrigar, T. (2007). *The space between us.* London: Harper Perennial.

Van den Berg, J. H. (1961). *The changing nature of man. Introduction to a historical psychology.* (H.F. Croes, Trans.). New York: Dell Publishing. (Original work published 1956.)

Van Manen, M. (1989). By the light of anecdote. *Phenomenology+Pedagogy,* 7, pp. 232-253.

Van Manen, M. (1997a). From meaning to method. *Qualitative Health Research: An International, Interdisciplinary Journal,* 7(3), 345-369.

Van Manen, M. (1997b). *Researching lived experience.* London, Ontario: The Althouse Press.

Van Manen, M. (2002). *Writing in the dark.* London, Ontario: The Althouse Press.

Walters, M. (2000). *The shape of snakes.* London: Macmillan.

Weil, S. (1990). *Ordenes makt.* Essays i utvalg. Oslo: Solum.

Wivel, O. (1953). *Poesi og eksistens.* Copenhagen: Gyldendal.

5. HERMENEUTIC PHENOMENOLOGY AND COGNITION

Tracking the Microtonality in/of Learning

INTRODUCTION

How might I investigate phenomena of knowing and learning relevant to everyday school (mathematics and science) contexts? How might I do it knowing that the principle audience of my research consists of individuals steeped in classical (constructivist) epistemology and methodology? How might I conduct phenomenological research on knowing and learning phenomena without risking the charge of introspection and navel gazing *in the context of* my *research community*, where members are suspicious when they hear the word phenomenology? Although there has been a historical reticence to admit phenomenology as a method and topic, over my career I have been able to assist some teacher colleagues with reports that could be considered phenomenological.

Nearly a decade and a half ago, I began to seriously engage with the problematic of cognitive phenomenology. I already had a successful career publishing and conducting research that employed a wide range of quantitative – I am a trained statistician – and qualitative research methods, on ways of knowing and learning in science and mathematics. My interest had been sparked a few years earlier during a three-month-long research stay in Australia where I investigated knowing and learning in a high school physics course. Together with my colleagues, I had set up an experiment generally referred to as *POE* – predict, observe, and explain. The students in the class were confronted with a situation. We asked them to predict what they would be observing when a person sitting on a rotating stool would spin a bicycle wheel. Following their predictions, we performed the demonstration and then asked the students to note what they had seen. Finally, we asked the students to explain what they had seen.

What stood out for me from the results was the fact that five students wrote down that they had seen the person at rest. These five then provided explanations for why the person should have remained at rest while the bicycle wheel was spinning. Eighteen students, however, had seen the experimenter move and they all explained that the stool should have rotated. I was baffled at the time: How could it be that there is such a split between the two groups of students? Each categorically stated that they have seen or not seen the person on the stool move. In this chapter, I not only offer a description of cognitive phenomenology as I have developed it for my purposes but also invite readers to engage in a practice of what could be called tracking precisely that which forever escapes us: The radical foreign/strange [*radikal Fremdes*] is precisely that which no subjective expectations [*Erwartungen*] and no trans-subjective conditions of possibilities can anticipate"

N. Friesen et al. (eds.), Hermeneutic Phenomenology in Education, 79–103.

(Waldenfels, 2006, p. 30).[1] Inquiring into the conditions of seeing and into the phenomenality of the visible, I work towards understanding what remains forever invisible. This, as some phenomenological philosophers have argued, is life itself (e.g., Henry, 2000). The chapter itself, therefore, is a sustained inquiry on the topic of: the praxis of doing phenomenology.

AN EXPERIMENT IN LEARNING

During a stay at the "Neurosciences and Cognitive Sciences" division of the *Hanse Institute for Advanced Studies*, I began to work on the problematic that had arisen from my work in Australia. While analyzing the videotapes collected during a 20-lesson tenth-grade high school physics course on static electricity, I also conducted an inquiry into the experience of learning and into the process of *coming to know*. I had been inspired by a series of publications concerning first- (phenomenological) and third-person methods (e.g., Varela, 1996; Varela & Shear, 1999). I therefore kept daily notes not only about the learning occurring while I was analyzing the video but also about things I noticed while riding my bicycle through the countryside for pleasure or while riding to the university for transportation. I designed an experiment for the purpose of tracking knowing, learning, memory, noticing, and the like. In this experiment, I would take the same 25-kilometer tour for 20 days in a row. Each time preceding the trip, I would write down everything I anticipated seeing. My first day's entry was because I had never been where the trip would take me. Upon returning, I would note what I remembered having seen.

  Among all the things I learned and among all the experiences I had, one incident stands out in particular. It occurred on the seventh day of my experiment. I am riding along Wildeshausener Landstraße when all of a sudden I am struck by what I see. Not even 200 meters to my left, there are two giant silos across the field and at the edge of a wooded area that I had not seen before. It comes as a shock. How could it have been that two such immense structures – they are so big that they can easily be seen on the aerial map of Google – had escaped my attention on the first six trips? My heart starts to pound as I begin to realize that the twin silos, which had not existed for me until this day, already begin to have predated my experience and taken on a permanent existence ("twin silos … that I had not seen *before*"). They have become independent Galilean objects, divorced from my perception that has just enabled them.[2] Another idea almost simultaneously zips through me: if a teacher had tested me about the twin silos, I would have failed after the first six "lessons." In fact, I did fail. There is no record of these structures in my research notes. I remember to this day the intensity of the shock that came with the first appearance of the silos in my consciousness as well as the subsequent shock based on the realization that my previous world has gone lost forever. This world I inhabit now was populated with the two silos. A sudden 'amnesia' has befallen me since the world I appeared to have been so familiar with no longer is accessible; I have forever lost this world of yesterday and of the five days before that. I cannot even imagine this part of my trip, and so the world, without the twin silos. And another shock hits me: because I have forgotten and lost this previous world, I would have had a hard time empathizing with students, for whom the silos do not exist – if I not had had *this* experience. (The silos have since become symbols for all mathematical and scientific learning I in which I did and still have interest.) How could I possibly teach when I do not even experience the world that my students inhabit? And another shock: How did these twin silos come to exist independent of me, outside of me, even though they *appeared* and *disclosed themselves to me and within me*? It is only years later that I realize: Piaget's object permanence is precisely this phenomenon where objects come to exist independent of their appearance, independent of the process of phenomenalization that occurs some time between 8 months and 1 year and is perhaps the most important developmental step in the life of an individual.

All of this, all of these realizations happened in a fraction of a second. At the time I immediately know that I am onto something. The initial shock is followed by a number of aftershocks in the form of a rapid succession of realizations that emerge into my consciousness and that are not the result of a "construction" – just as I have not (intentionally) "constructed" the silos: they are just there, all of a sudden, being given.[3] I have lived these experiences with a certain excitement. There is an emotional response associated with the realization that I have learned something that had escaped my in more than 15 years of researching students in the process of learning science and mathematics. It had escaped me although I had been pouring over videotapes featuring students in science classes almost daily and although I have analyzed hundreds of hours of classroom tapes. It had escaped me although I was sensitive to the person's point of view, and although I have been familiar as a teacher with the common presupposition that students could learn science (and mathematics) just by doing hands-on experimentation. But characteristic of my work, I began to focus on learning rather than on the emotional response. In fact, the feelings and emotional response are secondary to the phenomena that I was and still am primarily interested: the role of emotion, orientation, and movement that brings about the experiences rather than the emotional *responses* (to these primary experiences) that other researchers are interested in. To elaborate on the nature of this primary interest, consider the following excerpt from an evocative anecdote from a book on hermeneutic phenomenological method.

> Later in the day, I check my email again, and am surprised to see that I have received a message from myself! I click on it only to see that it is the message I earlier sent to my friend. I feel an embarrassed blush as I realize what I have done: I've sent my message to everyone in the class, including the instructor! The message that I originally replied to was actually one that my friend sent to our class email list! I feel like an idiot! (Friesen, 2009, p. 143–144)

In this anecdote, the author writes about the experience of an "embarrassed blush" and the sense of feeling "like an idiot" that followed the realization of what the writer had done. While not the aspect of emotions that I am personally pursing in my work (e.g., Roth, 2007), these feelings and emotional responses certainly are interesting topics of research. I am interested in the *pre-noetic* emotional make-up out of which the person sent the email in the first place, their orientation toward action (writing the email) or the way in which reality appeared in and to their consciousness. Below I argue that this could be considered emotion "on the pre-noetic side of the fold." Colleagues steeped in hermeneutics favor explanations that 'everything' is the result of an interpretation. I argue, however, and in line with Heidegger, that interpretation is not the basic mode of being. Practical understanding [*Verstehen*] always already exists at the instant interpretation comes into play: as the process of "development of understanding" "which we shall call *interpretation*" (Heidegger, 1977b, p. 148). In this process, "understanding appropriates in an understanding way what it [already] understands. In interpretation, understanding does not become something else, but itself" (p. 148). That is, interpretation can develop understanding because it is already enabled in and by the design of understanding. The primordial nature of understanding is particularly evident in more recent hermeneutic phenomenology that has articulated the *process* of interpretation. I understand interpretation to be a cyclical, hermeneutic process consisting of two parts:

> Strictly speaking, explanation alone is methodical. Understanding/comprehension is instead the non-methodical that – in the sciences of interpretation – combines with the methodical moment of explication. This moment precedes, accompanies, and concludes and thereby *envelops* explication. In turn, explication *develops* understanding/comprehension analytically. (Ricœur, 1986, p. 200)[4]

That is, all of my explication is *enveloped* by my practical comprehension of the world that comprehends (comprises) me and an understanding of which it *develops*. This practical comprehension "precedes, accompanies, and concludes explication"; it completely *envelops* explication. There is a true dialectical phenomenon, whereby two processes are related. Each is a manifestation of a unitary process. This relation is embodied in the verbs, deriving from the lower Latin *faluppa*, a ball of wheat, which continues to exist in both the verbs enfold and unfold. Because of this all-encompassing nature of practical comprehension, I am interested in researching it and all the pre-noetic orientations and conditions that lead to the feelings, emotions, and moods that realize themselves on the reflective side of a fold (Varela & Depraz, 2005). To understand the phenomena of learning that I am interested in, I have to pursue how actions and understandings emerge from modes of affect that precede what appears as cognized emotion on the reflective side of the fold. In a sense, I have to attempt to access modes of being that the person is not even aware of. (Voice recordings and the analysis of prosody allow the tracking of emotional valences of which the persons themselves are not [yet] conscious [e.g., Roth, 2007].) When I was struck by the sight of the twin silos that suddenly appeared for me, *affected* me, I was in a receptive state but I *could not have intended* these entities to emerge; I *could not have engaged* them as intentional objects. At this state, something yet to be determined happened so that the twin silos could be and were given to me even though I did not attend to them. More importantly, there was a pre-noetic sensibility and affection that allowed me to track down the *phenomenalization* of the twin silos. It is *this* context, in which learning occurs, that is of interest to me rather than the bewilderment and the excitement that I felt after the first few seconds. After a few seconds, a *realization* had set in that I was coming to understand something of importance to learning science research. But before continuing here, I will articulate a broader framework for the phenomenological study of learning as it has arisen for me from more than two centuries of relevant work. Most recently, this framework has lead to my development of an epistemology that is grounded in *incarnation*, that is, a radical approach to the question of embodiment of cognition (Roth, 2010a).

TOWARD A RADICAL PHENOMENOLOGY OF LIFE

For years, I struggled in an attempt to bring together and understand the various directions in which phenomenological philosophers have been taking the study. Perhaps because of my interests in the role of the body *in and for* communication and learning, and perhaps because of my science background, I am interested in epistemologies that are possible on evolutionary grounds (explication and interpretation are latecomers, historically, in the natural world). My interest lies in how we know and learn given that culturally and historically, we did not begin with language and concepts. Before we know to produce language, we know to move; before we can have any (cognitive) intention to move, we already need to know to move. A phenomenology that takes into account such constraints has to be concerned with the body – or, rather, with the flesh (*Leib, chair*) – that makes anything we are interested in possible in the first place. Over two decades, a period that covers the years when I conducted research on "situated cognition" and "embodied cognition," two aspects of my work have allowed me to arrive at a deeper and at an increasingly integrated understanding of the role of the body/flesh in knowing and learning.

On the one hand, I took the time to read many of the original texts that one might relate to phenomenological investigations of cognition: *Vorlesungen zur Phänomenologie des inneren Zeitbewusstseins* (Husserl, 1928/1980), *Phénoménologie de la perception* (Merleau-Ponty, 1945), *Autrement qu'être ou au-delà de l'essence* (Levinas, 1978), *Chair et corps: Sur la phénoménologie de Husserl* (Franck, 1981), *Étant donné: Essaie d'une phénoménologie de la donation* (Marion, 1997), *Incarnation: une philosophie de la chair* (Henry, 2000), and *Grundmotive einer Phänomenologie des Fremden* (Waldenfels, 2006). Much less known but equally, if not more, important to my theoretical understanding, which in turn influenced my approach to the data, were the analyses of the non-intentional body that had been produced in the early parts of the 19th century including *Influence de l'habitude sur al faculté de penser* (Maine de Biran, 2006) and *Essai sur les fondements de la psychologie* (Maine de Biran, 1859). Finally, I was influenced by a number of contemporary phenomenological analyses of time that explicitly recognize the accomplishments of Heidegger, Merleau-Ponty, Levinas, Henry, and Marion as their point of departure (Varela, 1999a; Varela & Depraz, 2005). Much of this literature is grounded in a European tradition, especially coming from France where the engagement with Husserl and Heidegger has probably been the most intense and, from my perspective much truer to the spirit of the German philosopher than the literature that has emerged in Anglo-Saxon countries generally and in North America specifically. One American philosopher deserves mention, though, because her detailed inquiry in the phenomenology of dance movements have led her to the same or similar conclusions that Michel Henry has evolved through his phenomenological analyses and his readings of Pierre Maine de Biran: Maxine Sheets-Johnstone (e.g., 2009). She is the only North American philosopher who has arrived at an understanding of the distinction between *Körper* and *Leib* that is similar to European scholars. This distinction allows her to ground our originary knowledge and understanding in a *pathic Leib* that precedes any transcendent feeling that we might have in this or that part of our bodies.

On the other hand, I engaged closely with hundreds of hours of video recordings of individuals of all ages (the youngest about 1 year, the oldest a scientist in his late 60s) and in analyses of first-person experiences. Bringing together these two strands of inquiry, both being keen observations of individuals involved with others in the pursuit of some goal, I was inspired by work of other natural scientists and mathematicians. After all, Husserl did have his Ph.D. in mathematics – and he was interested in establishing common ground between fields that are often held to be incommensurable: the hermeneutic and the natural sciences. Thus, the merging of third- and first-person perspectives allows me to investigate phenomena of the *Körperleib* (Varela, 1999b), or, phenomena that *integrate* the different ways in which the body appears to us. Thus, three main threads need to be woven together on an equal footing to provide a seamless braid of continuity between the material and the experiential, the natural and the transcendental:

(I) the formal level because eidetic descriptive structures and implementation partake of the same mode of ideality and hence are effectively on common ground;

(II) the natural bodily process at the right level spanning across two levels of global emergence and local mechanisms that assure a direct relevance to both the psychological content if examined phenomenologically and to a detailed scientific examination;

(III) the pragmatic level of the *Leib/Körper* transition because it, and it alone, can have a situated bivalence, that excludes neither and provides the relevant basis for the preceding threads. (Varela, 1999a, p. 151–152)

This aspect of my work, which merges the two approaches, therefore, has a strong *empirical* orientation – which is not unfamiliar to those familiar with *Experimental Phenomenology* (Ihde, 1986). For many, the perhaps most surprising of my influences in this empirical work has been two philosophers that others might not link to empirical work at all: Martin Heidegger and Jacques Derrida. More than other philosophers that I am familiar with, these two engage in sustained, *slow* and meticulous readings of the texts that they have chosen as the objects of their attention. For example, the former produces chapter- and book-length texts while working through textual fragments of ancient Greek philosophers that have been handed down to the present day – including Parmenides (Heidegger, 1942/1982), Anaximander (in Heidegger, 1977a), and Heraclitus (in Heidegger, 2000). Following in his footsteps, the French philosopher employs a similar style, always reminding his readers as much as himself that a/his reading needs to be slowed down to unearth what the text at hand has to offer. Most relevant to my research on mathematical cognition, Derrida (1962) engages in a book-length reading of Husserl's (1939) essay "Die Frage nach dem Ursprung der Geometrie" or he responds in a book-length text to the criticism John Searle had voiced to Derrida's (in 1972) "signature, événement, contexte": *Limited Inc* (Derrida, 1988). Reading is always too fast and too slow at the same time: "To say it provisionally, and again too quickly and conscious of the limits, of misunderstanding or unjustifiable exclusions" (Derrida, 2000, p. 210). It is through slow and meticulous readings of everyday situations recorded on videotape that we can have access to the manner and conditions of human *praxis* in order to unfold them – in time and by making time.

When I now look across that wide and varied literature, through the lens of the concrete investigations that I have conducted on knowing and learning across the life span and across phenomenological experiments (both sketched in concrete examples below), an integrative framework of the body and the relation between cognition and emotion emerges for me (Figure 2.1). At the heart of *life* is movement. This original movement, the original deployment, however, does not occur in time or space: it *is* the origin of time and space. This is what I understand *écriture* [writing] to be a metaphor of: the movement that produces spacing, *khora*, and, with it, time and space.[5] Or rather, life is movement: no movement and repetition, no life (Henry, 2004). This originary moment[6] of life is undifferentiated, the unity of the original being, the subjective body before the spacing that produces the organic body in its transcendence (Figure 3.1):

> In the radical immanence of the absolute subjectivity of life, that is, in its non-differentiation from itself, resides the condition of the possibilities and the essence of all action, which is nothing other than the actualization of a force in its principle immanence to itself and rendered possible by it. (p. 173)

If we experience the world as one – if there is but one world despite the different sense impressions that we have from our senses of seeing, hearing, touching-feeling, smelling, tasting – then this is because of "a *single* and *unique* power … a power that is our body" (p. 192, my emphasis). *It* manifests itself in the different modalities in which this power realizes itself. This power, leading to the movements, constitutes our original being, our subjective body, which is given to us in total passivity. These originary movements auto-affect so that they are remembered but not however by means of some mediation or by means of a transcendent moment that somehow *stands out*. This auto-affection is an auto-*donation*: life gives itself to itself. Auto-affection is the origin of differentiation of the Self [*Selbst*], which cannot be achieved by means of unification of a transcendent body and by its self-identification (Waldenfels, 1999). It is that moment that may have existed before *Seiendes* has been taken as a surrogate for

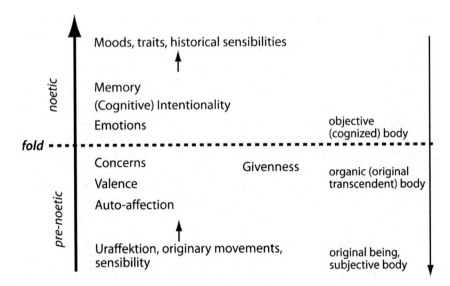

Figure 3.1. Research framework grounded in a phenomenology of the flesh.

(supplement of) *Sein*, before the spacing of *khora*, before the Lacanian bar unfolds into the relation of signifier and signified. This is the instant before signification, "the one-for-the-other that certainly shows itself in the said, but does so only after the event, betrayed, foreign to the said of being, shows itself as a contradiction" (Levinas, 1978, p. 213). It is an instant of affect *before* we cognize something *as* this or that emotion. It is thus that the hand remembers a telephone number that the mind has long forgotten; and it is thus that the ear remembers the dial tone melody that the conscious mind would have never been able to remember (Roth, 2011a). It is *in* the execution that my flesh remembers; it is the performance that is remembrance. This original motion is associated with a form of e-motion, a valuation that will select some movements over others because they meet some basic need already at the emergence of life and with the first one-cellular organisms (Leontyev, 1981).

From the original being emerges the differentiation of the organic body into the powers of its organs. The movements are different when they occur in the eyes or in the neck, arms or legs; a pain is *felt* in a particular location at a pre-noetic level (I am not in pain because I interpret some raw stimulus but rather I can talk about a pain because I am already affected.) This organic body is a transcendent body with a series of differentiations (including the emotions) that are not yet present in the (invisible) subjective body, or, the source of all powers. It gives rise to "the emergence of contours of a world with its fundamental orientations" (Varela & Depraz, 2005, p. 64). At this level,

I am affected by some sense-data, attracted by some affective tendencies that enable me to orient myself passively and receptively in the space and in the world. ... The very first appearance is *already* pervaded by affective tendencies: some form of a pre-egoic source is already affected, a world is already sketched. (p. 64)

The result is that there already is an irreducible relation "between affect and cognition, between values and living itself" (p. 65).

It is on this basis that the noetic moments of the human life form can establish themselves. What I do not see sufficiently appreciated in a lot of scholarly writing from a hermeneutic perspective is an acknowledgment of passivity that underlies what we do. It is not just that we take passivity as our object and write about passivity and affect. Underlying the emotions we write about – the ones we capture in a statement such as "I feel like an idiot" and that we have felt or feel empathetic with – are on the reflective side of the fold. They are enabled by affective processes that are non-intentional or that occur *despite oneself* prior to reflection and interpretation. This "*despite oneself* marks this life in its very living. Life is life despite life: in its patience and its aging" (Levinas, 1978, p. 86). We notice its effect in our own speech, whereby we discover our thoughts in what we have said rather than saying what we have thought (Merleau-Ponty, 1945; Vygotskij, 2005). This passivity is not the counterpart of will. This "passivity proper to patience – more passive thus than any passivity correlative to the voluntary – signifies in the 'passive' synthesis of its temporality" (Levinas, 1978, p. 87). This is a "radical form of 'originary passivity' [*Urpassivität*] that arises from af-fection, which can be ascribed to an experience [*Erfahrung*] that emerges from befalling [*Widerfahrniss*]" (Waldenfels, 2006, p. 48). The associated temporality is the result of af-fect, something done (Lat. *facēre*) to (Lat. *ad-*) us in a manner that we cannot anticipate, something we do not put into play or initiate, and which has a "temporal unfolding of self-affection [that is] from the very start traversed by alterity" (Varela & Depraz, 2005, p. 62). It is the shock when the twin towers suddenly appear to me where there had been no such thing before. This response is one moment of an event [*Ereignis*] provoked in the encounter with the foreign/strange [*Fremde*] - an event diastatically shifted with respect to itself, its complement being *pathos* (Waldenfels, 2006). At its very heart, therefore, affect is "altered" - an effect "rooted in the fact that self-affection is always an affection including an other, even if it is, as it is the case here, a self-alterity" (Varela & Depraz, 2005, p. 62). This shock is a phenomenon that allows us, like the phenomenon of attention, to understand "that there is something happening *between me and the things, between me and the others* that does not have one-sidedly its origin within me, even though I am part of it" (Waldenfels, 2006, p. 100, original emphasis, my underlining). We retain from this quote that things and other human beings do not have their origin within me; this would be a "one-sided" position. That which I do not know or can deduce from what I know, the radically other, the foreign/strange [*Fremde*], af-fects me and I respond in shock. The temporal order of this experience is of the increment of much less than a second.

Emotions and moods (Figure 3.1), on the other hand, appear on this, the conscious side of the fold (Varela & Depraz, 2005). The level of moods especially is tied to a dimension of time that is characterized by its socio-historical dimensions (which is a temporal dimension of our experience that is very different from the micro-temporality underlying *praxis*). From a third-person neuroscientific perspective, microtonality is due to neuron processes that occur at the order of 10 milliseconds to 100 milliseconds (the "1/10" scale), whereas descriptive narrative assessments require neuronal coherences orders of magnitude longer (the "10" scale) (Varela, 1999a). Cognitive acts of everyday behavior and decision-making occur on time scales that are of the order of seconds (the "1" scale). This immediately allows us to understand that our research findings will differ when we analyze what research participants tell us about their emotions *after the fact* versus analyzing what research participants do while doing it at the "1" scale i.e. the level of actions members of a setting engage in by tracking their micro-emotionalities on a scale of 10–300 milliseconds by means of analysis of prosody (e.g., Roth & Tobin, 2010). Thus, I could show how solidarity and conflict, experiences at the "10" scale, emerge from events at the "1/10" scale that I tracked using voice analysis of videotapes.

We therefore see that third-person investigations provide us "objective" access to a micro-tonality that manifests itself in the rates and quality of speaking. But micro-tonality can also be analyzed through first-person study, however, and thereby provide us with a means of *cross-validation* of research results. Analyzing an instant of musical exaltation of one of the authors, Varela and Depraz (2005) differentiate these time scales and the different but related ways in which these express themselves. Thus, at a microlevel, events occur with the playing of the first few notes of a sonata. This is different from what is happening at the scale of the length of a sonata movement: "By the time the first variation of the musical theme starts the feeling tone is fully formed and the first waves of thought-wandering have begun" (p. 68). Evidently, the order of events is exactly the opposite of what others describe in saying that "a certain mood is present to me" that "gives a color or shade to the whole of the immediate context" (Ihde, 1986, p. 43). My own theoretical inclinations are more in line with the non-intentional phenomenology developed by such authors as Levinas, Marion, Henry, and, more recently, Waldenfels or Varela and Depraz rather than with the intentionalist philosophy that Husserl had originated and that influenced a significant amount of phenomenological work (including Merleau-Ponty).

It would be wrong to assume that there is only upward "causation," that there is a flow from microtonality to macrotonality, micro-emotionality to macro-emotionality. Rather, as shown in Figure 3.1, there is also "downward causation," whereby events at the "10" scale, the results of interpretive-hermeneutic analysis, change *praxis* ("1" scale) and microtonal events that arise at the "1/10" scale. The lived experience emerges at that latter scale, which

> is rooted in and arises from *a germ or source* of motion-disposition, *a primordial fluctuation*. That this has to do with a primordial fluctuation motivates our notion here that affect *precedes* temporality: affect implicates as its very nature the tendency, a "pulsation" and a motion that, as such, can *only* display itself in time and thus *as* time. (Varela & Depraz, 2005, p. 69)

There are therefore different levels of affect that tend to be studied by and attributed to different fields: affection, which in evolutionary neurobiology is referred to as "valence," but appears as "emotion" in psychology, and is studied in phenomenology from the perspective of its phenomenalization, that is, at the crease that produces the fold between pre-noetic and noetic experience (Depraz, 2008).

Returning to the opening anecdote, we can now differentiate between those realizations that occur right there, at the instant that the twin silos come to exist, the experiences of shock and the aftershocks that follow, and those that subsequently follow when I subject this experience to hermeneutic analysis. The fundamental realization occurs at a scale where interpretive analysis *cannot* occur because of biological constraints arising from the level of organization at neuronal levels (some of which is local and fast whereas others require very different regions of the brain - making integration much slower). In my own work, I have strived to achieve cross-validations even though my primary discipline is not keenly interested in phenomenological studies of cognition (though some colleagues might accept an occasional study from the related methodological framework of phenomenography).

THIRD-PERSON INVESTIGATIONS OF PERCEPTION

In my analyses of learning conducted during the stay at the Hanse Institute of Advanced Studies, I had many opportunities to note instances where students saw themselves confronted with surprising discoveries – though they did not engage in the kinds of inquiries that the twin silos had spawned in me. For example, the students were asked to generate static electricity using a variety of materials – rods from different plastics, cloth of different material (e.g., wool, cotton, silk), transparency sheet – and to test for its presence using a small glow lamp. In the course of one 45-minute lesson, the four students in one of the recorded groups do a total of 162 trials: bringing into contact (rub, pull past each other, or re-used previously rubbed materials) two materials and subsequently testing them for charges. Although the teacher has shown them what to do – rub the transparency sheet with a piece of cloth or pull it through clasped knees and "test" the sheet with a glow lamp – the four pupils do not get the investigation to work in a consistent manner. Although in some instances the lamp glows, most of the time it does not.

Birgit then makes a significant discovery about the glow lamp. She repeats what the teacher had demonstrated in trials number 116 and 117. As she and her group mates have just jotted down the conclusion that the experiments do not work with old (i.e., used) transparency sheets, Birgit suggests doing the investigation again using a new transparency sheet. She reaches out and pulls closer to herself one of the two glow lamps that they share in the group. Her gaze comes to rest on the device held between the thumbs and index fingers of both hands (Figure 3.2). The gaze does not move for what seems to be an interminable 1.8 seconds.[7] She then puts the lamp back on the table. She takes the other one. Birgit then pulls the transparency through her clasped knees and takes the glow lamp. She stops. Birgit looks at the lamp intently again (1.3 seconds). And then she tests the transparency.

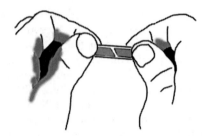

Figure 3.2. Birgit intently looks at the glow lamp in her two hands. It is at that instant that the gap between the two filaments becomes salient to her.

The lamp does not glow. Birgit gazes intently at the lamp (1.0 second). She then turns to the teacher and asks: "Is it not broken? Because this is not connected on the inside?"

Up until this point, the students have used the glow lamp as they have used their pens to write down the results i.e. tools to be used for a certain purpose. The teacher has shown them how to use the tool and has demonstrated the presence of charges using the same lamp that Birgit has been using. But here something significant occurs. Birgit actually perceives, for a first time, the internal structure of the neon glow lamp. Her surprise announces itself – after the fact – in the sequence of gazes and trials. She communicates her discovery of the gap between the two electrodes. This gap then becomes the explanation of the failure to observe the presence of electrical charges in an experiment that appears to be exactly like the one that the teacher has demonstrated. Birgit's articulation is associated with two experiments that have not worked and the close inspection of two lamps. The articulation makes available an articulation of the lamp, a gap between the electrodes that surges into her conscious awareness precisely at this time.[8] She asks the teacher about the tool: Is it not broken? She asks at *this* time because it has just become salient, or, stood out as an articulation [*Gliederung*] that could be articulated [*artikuliert*]. Birgit links the lack of success of getting the lamp to light up to the possibility of it being broken; and she brings together the possibility of the malfunction with some feature on the inside of the lamp. Why does the gap stand out? Does Birgit expect the wire to be continuous, such as in a regular incandescent light bulb? She notices the gap *as gap* and perhaps in its difference to other lamps that she is familiar with.

Readers certainly are familiar with the analyses of everyday being, where the things we use (objects, tools) do not appear to us as they do the person with a theoretical gaze (Heidegger, 1927/1977b). Use is tailored to the tool; it is therefore only in use that hammering reveals the nature (*Sein*) of the hammer (a *Seiendes*) in everyday use. Use does not grasp the hammer (*Seiende*) in a thematic manner i.e., in the manner it would reveal itself to the theoretical gaze of the scientist, who, nevertheless, use tools in the same way when they do not gaze at them.[9] Thus, "use does not know the structure of the useful thing as such" (p. 69). In this episode, we see precisely that. As long as the glow lamp is taken to be working – the teacher has shown it to work, and sometimes it lights up for the students as well – the tool *does not reveal its (inner) structure*. The inner structure of the lamp is not required for successful use. "That which is at hand is neither grasped theoretically at all nor is it in itself initially thematic in a circumspect way for circumspection" (p. 69). It is in the breakdown, it is the possibility of breakdown itself – that calls on circumspection to make the lamp thematic in a circumspect way just as it is when there is a problem with Heidegger's hammer that its properties manifest themselves in a transcendent way: it is too heavy, the handle is broken, or the handle has come loose.

In saying "Is it not broken? Because this is not connected on the inside?" Birgit makes a statement that isolates and brings to the fore a property of the tool. A property however is not the thing itself. It is rather the way in which the thing shows itself from itself, or, transcendentalizes and phenomenalizes itself. *Logos*, Heidegger suggests, has for the ancient Greek the sense of *apophansis*: "Letting *Seiendes* show itself from itself" (p. 154). In Birgit's statement "This is not connected on the inside" we may say with Heidegger that "that which is discovered for sight is not 'sense' but a *Seiendes* in its mode of being at hand" (p. 154). This statement is a derivative – as it should be according to Heidegger – of the experience of a sudden realization of something that had not existed for her before: a gap between the electrodes, which, for a regular incandescent lamp would mean that it no longer works. The recognition of the gap as gap is the response to being affected,. The response cannot be separated because recognition and response are the irreducible parts of a unitary but diastatic event [*Ereignis*].

In looking at the videotapes featuring Birgit and her peers, I see many instances of this same type. The students see something that they *could not have anticipated* or intentionally learned precisely because they have not known about it. They could not have known about the internal structure and arrived at it through process of construction and interpretation for at least for three reasons. One: it is in one of these lessons that they have encountered the device for a first time. They do not know the device and therefore have no reason to look for an internal structure of which they know not. Two: they come to interact with the glow lamps as tools in their everyday (laboratory) use. As long as the lamps do what they have been demonstrated to do – to glow – there is no reason to investigate the inner structure much. We do not investigate the inner structure of the blender we use in the kitchen until we have some reason to do so. Three: because they do not know the device they cannot have an intent to reveal a particular property and interpret it. Birgit is confronted with the gap between the two electrodes much in the same way that I am confronted with the twin silos. The gap and the twin silos *are given in and to perception*. They have become figure against a more diffuse ground. But there is more to it, for figure and ground are dimensions of the visible, whereas the radically new requires us to consider the invisible, the unknown and therefore foreign/strange [*das Fremde*].

TRACKING PERCEPTION AND PERCEPTUAL LEARNING

The three closely related rules ... (a) attend to phenomena as and how they show themselves, (b) describe (don't explain) phenomena and (c) horizontalize all phenomena initially – tell us something about how a phenomenological investigation must begin at the first level. (Ihde, 1986, p. 38)

Now that we have ascertained that the original appearance of the physical world is not a result of an interpretive process, we need to understand how something heretofore invisible can arise from or by means of the ground. From Ihde (1986) I have learned not only how to generally orient with respect to phenomenological analysis but also – because of my interest in learning from experience in science laboratories and from mathematical hands-on tasks – some of the particular experiments. But in contrast to him, I have followed others in accepting the non-intentional as an integral aspect of noesis (e.g., Henry, 2004). It does not yet help me to think that material things arise from the ground when we change our gaze. This would mean that we accept the world in some definite form of being and that all we have to do is engage in a different way of looking or interpreting to make a different figure appear from the same ground. The ground, because of its very phenomenality, is not and cannot be the source of what we come to know however; it is already visible but not attended to consciously while something is a figure. What we need to track is the phenomenalization of something *invisible* to becoming visible. Phenomenological analyses show that the ground *is* the locus of the crossing between invisible and visible (Marion, 1996). Moreover, that which is invisible and unknown is inherently foreign/strange [*fremd*] (Waldenfels, 2006). As a learning scientist, I need to better understand this encounter of what is inherently foreign/strange [*fremd*]: that which students are supposed to learn precisely because they do not already know it. This foreign/strange [das *Fremde*] constitutes a challenge to the hermeneutic process, for if explication is enveloped by practical understanding, then the absolutely foreign/strange [das *Fremde*] cannot be aimed at, resists, and is *inaccessible* to interpretation that always already is grounded in the familiar.

Driven by the interest to understand how we come to see something *as something* – the emotionality underlying such a state of being driven might be an interesting object of study in its own right – I began conducting phenomenological studies of perception generally and perception in problem-solving situation more specifically. I "fell" into one of these investigations while sitting on a plane returning from a conference. At the time, I am hanging onto some thoughts about perception when I am confronted all of a sudden with the image that appears in my mind's eye: the well-known Müller-Lyer "illusion" (Figure 3.3). Not having read any scientific studies concerning the phenomenon, I begin to wonder why we might see the lines as different in length. Again, an unintended idea surges into my consciousness: use the drawing software on my computer to make representations suitable for an inquiry.

a.   b.

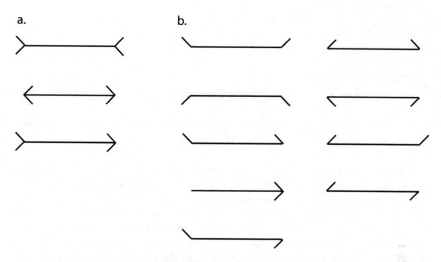

Figure 3.3. The Müller-Lyer phenomenon (a) and some variations on its basic shapes (b) produced during a flight on a laptop computer.

I begin by drawing the original design (Figure 3.3a), a line with arrows on each end that point inward or outward. I immediately see "the illusion," I succumb to the illusion. I know the lines are of equal length, as I have just drawn the first one and then copied it twice. I squint – Sideline: Why do I squint? Because I intend? Where does the intention come from? Is there an intention of an intention? – in the attempt to overcome the illusion. Squinting clearly is a practice that produces variations that allow *structural* features or behavioral *invariants* to stand out as figures against ground. It is *praxis* of the "fourth hermeneutic rule": "*Seek out structural or invariant features of the* phenomena" (Ihde, 1986, p. 39, original emphasis). I close one eye, then the other. I move the three shapes about. But whatever I do, the three lines look different in length. I then have an idea. (Where did it come from? Wasn't it given to me?) I copy the basic shapes and then produce variations by removing parts of the arrowheads (Figure 3.4a). I compare the resulting shapes pair-wise. All of a sudden I notice that there is a substantial difference in the perception whether I pair a partial upper arrow with a lower arrow from which the lower (Figure 3.4b) or upper part of the arrow (Figure 3.4c) is removed. Moving back and forth, I realize that my eyes are following the truncated lines of the arrowheads. That is, rather than staying on the baselines to be compared, the eyes follow and extend the truncated lines. I can gloss the result in this way: In the upper case of each pair in Figures 3.4a, b, the eyes "find the horizontal line in the distance, so that the line appears larger, because if I were close up, I would see it in its real size, that is, larger." In the lower case of each pair in Figures 3.4a, b, "the eyes find the horizontal close up, so that it would be smaller in the distance." "It's like railroad lines, but of different gauge!"

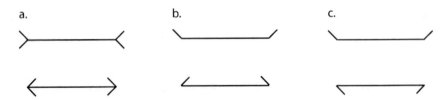

Figure 3.4. The Müler-Lyer configuration (a) and two variations (b, c) that immediately preceded the insight.

I begin to analyze. It is not that I interpreted the two arrows (Figure 3.4a) differently. "I" was not involved at all. The ("my") eyes moved, and as a result of their movement, "I" saw two arrows of different length. "I" had nothing to do with this. These events happen at a scale much below that of the things I tend to be conscious off. I know that they occur however because I can provoke perceptual experiences by actively moving the eyes so that one or the other experience results (e.g., Roth, 2011c). The "illusion" is the result of the movement that my eyes have learned. This is a movement the memory of which lies in its performance (Henry, 2000). These are forms of movements that they remember without requiring re-presentation to be recalled. Their memory is in the movement itself! The eyes move because they have an immanent memory of movement. The Müller-Lyer effect is not an illusion but the result of the eyes doing what they do best! They do what they do because it serves the organism ("me") in navigating a three-dimensional world where trees look smaller when I walk away from them and become bigger the closer I get.

I do one more thing – a very difficult one indeed but one that can be practiced. I anticipate the results from experience. I fixate an image on my retina by staring at it so that the eye no longer moves with respect to the object. I copy one of the arrows. I turn off the grid of the drawing program. I bring the screen closer to my face so that the surroundings no longer distract the eyes and encourage them to move. Within a fraction of a second the arrow disappears and my visual field dissolves until there is nothing but light grey: *If the eyes do not move, there is nothing to be seen.* The movements of my eyes make the world appear in the way it does. The retina is not a mirror in which the world reflects itself. It is not a medium where something appears that my mind "interprets." The movement of the eyes is part of what produces the world we experience – the capacity and memory for which is immanent in their performance. An object is figure against some ground and the eyes move back and forth between the two to *make* the figure stand out. Each arrow comes to stand against the ground because of the eye movements between figure and ground; and the arrows appear to be of different length because of the movement within the figure.

> And yet perspective, in its proper mode, also provokes a paradox. Or rather, it imitates the paradox, by inverting the relation it has established between the visible and invisible. In the two operations, the gaze arrives at seeing what it should not be able to see, but differently: the paradox offers a counter-appearance, while perspective

suggests a breakthrough of the gaze. The paradox poses a visible that belies the visible, perspective a gaze that pierces through the visible. ... The gaze in perspective carves the visible to install there the invisible distance that makes it something that can be aimed at [*visable*], and initially, simply, visible. (Marion, 1996, pp. 12, 16)

Perspective is invisible and yet the eyes arrive at making it possible. But how? "It is the painting that brings the gaze to life, not the other way around. It is the painting that grants the gaze the ability to make this crossing, as well as the climb from the unseen toward the visible" (p. 78). At that instant on the plane, I remember the twin silos. I realize that to see the twin silos, the eyes have to find them or know that they are there. The silos are silos only because of their internal structure that the eyes establish through their movements. They exist as silos only because the eyes stabilize the figure against everything else as the ground. My analysis has not yet established, however, *how* the eyes (can) find and *found* the figure in the first place. The original twin silo experience could be analyzed to reveal an answer. We could also investigate how figures emerge when we look at fields of spots such as the well-known puzzles from which emerge, after some time, a Dalmatian dog or a Holstein cow. We would then come to know that it is the world that brings my gaze to life. It is because the movements of my eyes have been *entrained by* the affordances of the world. Paraphrasing Marion we might say that it is not so much that I have learned to see the twin silos but that the twin silos, in having given themselves, have taught my eyes how to see and re-see (reproduce) them. They have shown and revealed themselves, from themselves, and for themselves without my intention intervening. It is only *after* cognizing them that I could *re*-cognize the figure *as twin silos*. Another phenomenological analysis supports this approach and result:

> The ingenious intuition of abstract painting was to invert the psychological explication, to show that all associations that form themselves around a color rest upon it rather than having the power to explain its particular tonality. It is the pathos proper to each color that produces the variable bundle of images that it normally evokes, it is the permanence of this tonality and its link to a color that explains the totality of the associations that gravitate around it. (Henry, 2004, p. 132)

That is, the access to the associations arising from perceptual experiences is not to be found in the (interpretive) associations we make, the *ekstatic* sense of this or that impression. I attribute this to the effect of a microtonality of experience, which is the source of subsequent associations, the latter being the effect of the microtonality rather than its explanatory cause. That is, it is the tonality proper to the color and the permanence of this tonality around which our associations gravitate. The *pathos* is proper to the color. That is, "the living present is *suffused* with the affective" (Varela & Depraz, 2005, p. 65; original emphasis?).

I have been citing above from a chapter entitled "Ce que cela done," which the English translation renders as "What Gives." The translation does not do justice to the title, which is a formulaic expression that a hobby cook might use when saying, "I will change these ingredients and then see what that will come of it [*voir ce que cela donne*]." Can we ever know what something we do will give rise to, will yield, will show itself in the results? We do not, because otherwise we would not write emails that we are subsequently ashamed of and "feel stupid" about. Already, "The question '*what* shows itself?' is put by that one himself *who* looks, even before he thematically distinguishes the difference between being [*être*] and things [*étants*]" (Levinas, 1978, p. 44).

The perspective we have arrived at here is very different from the "ocularcentric" approach that dominates current learning sciences research and constructivist understandings of learning. The eye is not a mirror of the world, nor the organ of an intentional agent that goes out to construct itself a world. It is in and through the movements that the world comes to be as it is, but these specific movements that produce my figure|ground experiences are the results of an initial entrainment and the immanent memory of their performance resulting from an auto-affection of the flesh. The mind is not producer of the world precisely because it is confronted with the unknown or the foreign/strange [*das Fremde*], which, curling up upon itself, forever withdraws into itself.

DA CAPO AL CODA

> That which he [the painter] does not invent is the pathos that corresponds each time with this graphism, with this configuration – *the pathos of the force that produces this graphism*, which is its interior sonority. (Henry, 1988, p. 96, emphasis added)

What the visitor to a museum observes is the painting, its structures, configurations, and its graphisms. What the visitor does not see is the *pathos* of the force from which the visible has emerged. In *Voir l'invisible* [Seeing the invisible], Henry shows how it is precisely the *non-figural* abstract painting that makes the invisible visible – in part because it focuses on the role of the ground against which the figure emerges but which constitutes only a crossing between invisible and visible (Marion, 1996). In the same way, the reader of a text is confronted with configurations or graphisms of a different type. Again however, the *pathos* of the force that created the work remains invisible – though engaging in the same inquiries with/for the same purpose as the original one may put this pathos in relief. In this chapter, I repeatedly refer to the emotions that have come with and in fact mark an instant where I felt to have discovered something significant. This, of course, is an interesting phenomenon in its own right. But perhaps more interesting is the question about the inquiry itself. Why has it been so sustained, allowing me to pursue questions of learning over decades even though there have been repeated instances of "success"? There is an underlying affective moment that cannot be dissociated from the (learning) movement but that does not express itself in the *ekstatic*, phenomenalizing manner of the "I feel stupid," "I feel happy," or "I feel good." It constitutes the pre-noetic tonality of the movement and is inseparable from it. It is this aspect of affect that I am not aware of while writing that I am really interested in, rather than the feelings I might have when I have completed this chapter. This aspect is the *pathos of the force* that produces this text at the very moment that I am producing it at this instant.

In the course of my inquiries, after early efforts to the contrary, I have attempted to develop theories of learning that were consistent with my own learning about learning. When I looked around in the early 1990s, I saw a lot of learning research that could not have been consistent with the things my colleagues wrote about the learning of students. This became very evident to me, for the first time, when I read the literature about the teacher as a "reflective practitioner" and the distinction between reflecting in practice and reflecting on practice. Perhaps because I was a teacher at the time, the concept of "reflecting in practice" made sense to me only for understanding those instances of my classroom life when there was space for taking time out from teaching itself and making what I *had done before* the object of my attention. I could reflect on something only when it was already available to me in objectified (*ekstatic*, transcendental) form. In the thickets of things, however, neither my colleagues nor I – or any other practitioner for that matter, including dancers, athletes, or scientists – had time at our hands to begin thinking about what we were doing. The theory just did not make sense and did not capture the micro-temporality of teaching. In the same manner, I felt that the available learning theories did not capture what learning is about because they failed to describe how researchers themselves actually came to know the microtonality of *their* learning. The relevant aspects of knowing and learning that I came to understand only more recently are the irreducibility of affect and cognition and the radical passivity with respect to intentions and learning objects. What I learned about learning in the course of reading and conducting first- and third-person investigations cannot be separated from the affectivity that oriented and gave tonality and valence to the movement. It is not that the movement is merely shaded by an emotional tonality: emotion and movement are two faces of the same coin: "emotional affects in the auto-movement of the flow of consciousness" (Depraz, 2010, p. 227). What I learned I could not have constructed intentionally as this would have required my previous knowledge of *what* I wanted to construct – much like the carpenter can anticipate the results of the building work with the materials and tools at hand.

The movement occurs in and is directed to an emotional quality of hope or expectation of learning something and is paired with a moment of surprise (shock) experienced at the instant of a realization of the new. This experience confronts us with a paradox:

> How do we knowingly allow ourselves to be surprised? Ultimately, it is this very paradox which we call auto-antecedence – a surprise that knows itself as such, a knowledge so intimate that it accepts no longer having purchase on (mastery of) itself. (Depraz, 2010, p. 224)

Anticipation is based on continuity, or, that something not yet the case will eventually occur. Current learning theories are premised on the intentional engagement of the learner with the learning object, a subject who can anticipate in some sense what it is that s/he "constructs." I would not have needed all these years of inquiry, dead ends and sudden surprises if there had been, 25 years ago or some time since, anything in my life that would have allowed me to anticipate what I know today, or allowed me to "construct" my life in a different manner.

CODA

I know that merely pursing descriptions of experience will not lead us to what I pursue without fully knowing what it is. In fact, some scholars suggest that "[f]rom several individual lived-experience descriptions it is possible to distinguish essential themes from incidental themes: What do lived-experience descriptions have in common?" (Henriksson, 2008, p. 42–43). Given my extensive work in linguistic studies of learning and interview analysis, my hunch is – because the analysis is one of *descriptions* – that the answer to such a question is shaped by the possibilities of language, its genres, grammatical and semantic forms (Roth, 2010b). Thus, "essential experiences of school failure" always already are enabled by language. There is little further that the analysis of a *description* qua description can take us. Auto/biography therefore constitutes a genre that tells the tellable and intelligible. This is so because "'language is as old as consciousness' … and language is practical consciousness for others and therefore for myself" (Vygotskij, 2005, p. 1017). In a strong sense, we therefore do not have to ask real people as long as we have an appropriate sample of language. As I developed elsewhere to a considerable extent: Rendered in language, *any* and *all* experience is inherently shared and no longer singularly mine (Roth, 2011b). In the saying, a spacing has occurred that presupposes itself as difference between being (*Sein, Être*) and Lao Tse's "ten thousand things" (*Seiendes, étant*). Text "will no longer repeat a *present*, *re*-present a present that is elsewhere and before, the plenitude of which is much older, absent from the scene [text] and rightfully capable of doing without it" (Derrida, 1967, p. 348). I am fully in agreement with others who emphasize the pathic as a constitutive moment of our life generally and of knowing more specifically (van Manen, 2007). I propose a phenomenology of *praxis* (the term I prefer over practice[s]) to understand how people learn and what they learn. I also differ from some others, however, in that these are modes of knowing that are *invisible* and that only *manifest* themselves in particular ways. This is fundamental to the approach Michel Henry takes in his material phenomenology or to the approach of understanding the essence of human *praxis* in terms of habits [*habitudes*] (Maine de Biran, 2006) and *habitus* (Bourdieu, 1997). As I describe above, the movement of my eyes, their self-movement, produces *what* I see, or, the phenomenality of the world even though this movement is not visible to me in my worldly *praxis*. Similarly, the affordances and constraints language offers for describing experiences is invisible to the interviewer and interviewee talking about the latter's experiences, where they might reveal that they "felt [so] stupid" or "a complete failure." This, therefore, distinguishes my work (without inherently making it better) from that of others interested in phenomenological perspectives on learning.

I am not alone in this desire to understand those moments of life that are invisible even and precisely in practice,. In their text *Becoming Aware* (Depraz et al., 2002) the authors (a phenomenological philosopher, a neuroscientist–Buddhist practitioner–phenomenologist, and a psychologist) confront in/visibility head on:

"How do you know that by exploring experience with a method you are not, in fact, deforming or even creating what you claim to 'experience'? Experience being what it is, what is the possible meaning of your so-called 'examination' of it?"

We can call this the "excavation fallacy," or in philosophical terms, the *hermeneutical* objection (inspired as it is by a Heideggerian move). In still another formulation, this is the *deconstructive* objection, based on post-modern philosophical analysis (mostly derived from Derrida). All these objections go to the heart of our project here. They all emphasize the claim that there is no such thing as a "deep" pre-linguistic layer of experience, since any account is "always already" enfolded in language. Hence any new account will be only an inflection of linguistic practices that "go all the way down." (p. 8)

The authors – surprisingly, because at least two have articulated appreciatively the insights of Derrida – suggest that their book is not for those who are "utterly convinced hermeneuts or Derrideans" (p. 8). I do recognize and bring out in my analyses that *praxis* works the way it does because of what practitioners make available to each other (most of which is not salient in and to consciousness at the moment). But the very aspects of life that make us do what we do, the source of intentionality among the most important once, are in themselves not visible –. We do engage in something i.e. the writing of this chapter, the learning experiments and an investigation of lived experiences but the origin and source of the intention is invisible.

As Depraz et al., I think that there is no reason to stop investigating because something is invisible. The investigation of the foreign/strange [*das Fremde*], the future and non-anticipatable knowledge, would be impossible if we were interested only in the known and in that which we can capture as familiar (Waldenfels, 2006). It is precisely the foreign/strange [*das Fremde*] that can teach us about *pathos*, being-affected, or that which cannot be willed [*das nicht Wollbare*] ahead of time: "That which affects me and to which I respond does not inherently make sense and does not follow a rule" (p. 50). I translate here as "making sense" an expression that normally might be translated as "to have meaning." This translation takes me to the heart of my question about learning. Learning is not about the *construction* of meaning for if the to-be-learned subject matter is really unknown, then students encounter it as the foreign/strange [*das Fremde*]. As such, it does not make sense (does not "have meaning") precisely because it is foreign/strange [*fremd*]. As soon as familiarity attempts to colonize *it* and as soon as we attach it to the world we know so well and practically understand, the foreign/strange [*das Fremde*] has already receded and withdrawn: "Pathos means that we are affected by *something*, and this in such a way that the whereby [*Wovon*] is neither grounded in a preceding what [*Was*] nor captured/kept [*aufgehoben*] in the a posteriori achieved what-for [*Wozu*]" (p. 43). This foreign/strange [*das Fremde*] "exceeds boundaries of any order of" (p. 34) and therefore the boundaries of linguistic order as well. "The resistance of the foreign/strange [*das Fremde*] derives from the fact that there is no equivalent, not even a moral one, for something that escapes from order. The foreign/strange [*das Fremde*] remains a foreign body for any order" (p. 33). How then should I understand the experience of the twin silos? Because I was in the process of experimenting, I am in fact awaiting what I could not anticipate. This awaiting allowed me to be surprised when it came. This cogeneration of awaiting and being surprised can be understood in terms of *auto-antecedence* (Depraz, 2010) or *self-previousness* (Depraz, 2008) (with a structure based on the phases of imminence, crisis, and aftermath). As part of the experiment, I readied myself and prepared the ground for an imminent event. The instant itself constitutes a crisis where the non-anticipatable affection (foreign/strange [*das Fremde*]) provokes a response with which it is one. The aftermath continues to this day. It constitutes the very possibility of a return to what happened (Depraz, 2008). At the pre-individual level, "if we are less prepared or completely unprepared for its [figure against a background in perception] perceptual appearance, we might feel disturbed or shocked" (p. 250). The perceptual appearance of the twin silos, the shock actually has a positive valence associated with a surprise that something has happened unexpectedly although I was attuned for the unexpected to happen. Thus, "affectivity is an intrinsic component of the phenomenon of surprise, varying only in the degree of its positive or negative value" (p. 250). It is a common structure of the experience of non-anticipatable events that they provoke an emotional shock.

It is precisely for these reason that there is a limit to interpretation and that we must acknowledge passibility as a fundamental condition of knowing and learning. This is what I miss in other works: a response to the challenge "How we can engage with the foreign/strange [*das Fremde*] without already neutralizing and betraying its effects, challenges, and demands by the way in which deal with it" (Waldenfels, 2006, p. 9). It is the third [*der Dritte*] – rules, order, or laws of any kind – that interferes with and contaminates the foreign/strange [*das Fremde*]. Thus, "foreign/strange [*fremd*] is precisely that which does not allow 'incorporation'" (p. 128). The foreign/strange [*das Fremde*] thereby resists colonization by the visible and remains forever invisible.

NOTES

[1] In this chapter, I draw on texts published in their original language. All translations are mine, even though I check, where possible, my translations against the official one. Rather than choosing one word to translate a corresponding word, I may use two words to bring the word into a semantic *field* similar to the one in the original language.

[2] It is Galileo Galilei rather than Descartes who introduces the reduction that separated knowledge derived from the senses (that is, based on the qualities of objects, and rational knowledge based on the figures and forms of extended bodies). This move, therefore, was the decisive step that led to the foundation of the modern (natural) sciences.

[3] The idea of the intentional construction, and an over-emphasis on "interpretation" as part of a specific epistemological ideology: "in philosophy, for a variety of reasons, the agency of one-sided theories of actions is the dominant theme to the present day" (Waldenfels, 2006, p. 53). We are subject to, subjected to, and undergo the passions: we do not construct them.

[4] The French term for understanding is "comprehension." Translating it as "understanding" does not do justice to the philosophical history of the term. Thus, for example, Bourdieu (1997) refers to a text of Blaise Pascal that makes thematic the relation between the world that comprises me ["me comprend"] and that I understand ["je comprends"]: "Le monde me comprend, comme une chose

parmi les choses, mais, chose pour qui il y a des choses, un monde, je comprends ce monde [The world comprises me, as a thing among things, but a thing for which there are things, a world, I understand this world]" (p. 157). The comprehension therefore operates in two directions: A material world that comprehends me, and my understanding that comprehends the world. It is only because of my material comprehension in the world that I can comprehend it.

5   "The fundamental property of writing, we have called ... spacing: diastem and becoming-space of time, also unfolding in an original locality ... of significations" (Derrida, 1967, p. 321).

6   I use the term "moment" as it is used in materialist dialectics, where it refers to one of the many manifestations of a unit – use-value and exchange-value for the unitary phenomenon of value or wave and particle for the unitary phenomenon of light. I use the term "instant" when referring to a point in time.

7   Classroom research conducted in the 1980s showed that teachers waited on the average only 0.7 seconds for a student to respond prior to moving on and asking another student or in some other form of pedagogy to somehow elicit the desired response. Research conducted in the area of conversation analysis similarly showed that the maximum sustained silence between two turns at talk – in phone conversations – was less than 1 second.

8   Dreyfus (1991) proposes the differentiation between Articulation [*Artikulation*], the telling of intelligibility, and articulation [*Gliederung*], the way in which the natural world appears as an assembly of things. The two terms are related to the double function of logos in *apophansis*: "Speech 'lets appear' π [apo] ... from itself what is spoken about" (Heidegger, 1927/1977, p. 32). Speech, as *apophansis*, manifests something other than itself and thereby makes this something available to others.

9   I do not see sufficient references to the fact that Heidegger's texts *resist* translation. They read very differently in English. They do not say in their official translations what they say in their native German. Since practical understanding is so central to phenomenology, I cannot be satisfied with this or that direct translation but also have to have a sense of what it means to read the texts in German. Friedrich Hölderlin, Walter Benjamin, Paul de Man, Paul Ricœur, and Jacques Derrida all have written about the impossible possibility of translation.

REFERENCES

Bourdieu, P. (1997). *Méditations pascaliennes*. Paris: Éditions du Seuil.

Depraz, N. (2008). The rainbow of emotions: At the crossroads of neurobiology and phenomenology. *Continental Philosophy Review, 41*, 237–259.

Depraz, N. (2010). Phenomenology of surprise: Lévinas and Merleau-Ponty in the light of Hans Jonas. In T. Neon and P. Blosser (Eds.), *Advancing phenomenology: Essays in honor of Lester Embree* (pp. 223–233). Dordrecht, The Netherlands: Springer.

Depraz, N., Varela, F., & Vermersch, P. (2002). *On becoming aware: Steps to a phenomenological pragmatics*. Amsterdam: Benjamins.

Derrida, J. (1962). *L'Origine de la géométrie de Husserl: Introduction et traduction*. Paris: Presses Universitaires de France.

Derrida, J. (1967). *L'Écriture et la différence*. Paris: Éditions du Seuil.

Derrida, J. (1972). *Marges de la philosophie*. Paris: Les Éditions de Minuit.

Derrida, J. (1988). *Limited inc*. Evanston, IL: Northwestern University Press.

Derrida, J. (2000). *Le toucher, Jean-Luc Nancy*. Paris: Galilée.

Dreyfus, H. (1991). *Being-in-the-world: A commentary on Heidegger's* Being and Time, *Dvision I*. Cambridge, MA: MIT Press.

Franck, D. (1981). *Chair et corps: Sur la phénoménologie de Husserl*. Paris: Les Éditions de Minuit.

Friesen, N. (2009). *Re-thinking e-learning research: Foundations, methods, and practices*. New York: Peter Lang.

Heidegger, M. (1977a). *Gesamtausgabe I. Abteilung: Veröffentlichte Schriften 1914–1970. Band 5: Holzwege*. Frankfurt/Main: Vittorio Klostermann.

Heidegger, M. (1977b). *Sein und Zeit*. Tübingen: Max Niemeyer. (First published in 1927)

Heidegger, M. (1982). *Gesamtausgabe II. Abteilung: Vorlesungen 1923–1944. Band 54: Parmenides*. Frankfurt/Main: Vittorio Klostermann.

Heidegger, M. (2000). *Gesamtausgabe I. Abteilung: Veröffentlichte Schriften 1910–1976. Band 7: Vorträge und Aufsätze*. Frankfurt/Main: Vittorio Klostermann.

Henriksson, C. (2008). *Living away from blessings*. London, Ontario: Althouse Press.

Henry, M. (1988). *Voir l'invisible: Sur Kandinsky*. Paris: Presses Universitaires de France.

Henry, M. (2000). *Incarnation: Une philosophie de la chaire*. Paris: Éditions du Seuil.

Henry, M. (2004). *Phénoménologie matérielle*. Paris: Éditions du Seuil.

Husserl, E. (1939). Die Frage nach dem Ursprung der Geometrie als intentional-historisches Problem. *Revue internationale de philosophie, 1*, 203–225.

Husserl, E. (1980). *Vorlesungen zur Phänomenologie des inneren Zeitbewusstseins*. Tübingen: Max Niemeyer.

Ihde, D. (1986). *Experimental phenomenology: An introduction*. Albany, NY: State University of New York Press.

Leontyev, A. N. (1981). *Problems of the development of the mind*. Moscow: Progress.

Levinas, E. (1978). *Autrement qu'être ou au-delà de l'essence*. La Haye: Martinus Nijhoff.

Maine de Biran, P. (1859). *Œuvres inédites: Tome I & II*. Paris: Dezobry et Magdeleine.

Maine de Biran, P. (2006). *Influence de l'habitude sur la faculté de penser*. Paris: L'Harmattan.

Marion, J.-L. (1996). *La croisée du visible*. Paris: Presses Universitaires de France.

Marion, J.-L. (1997). *Étant donnée: Essaie d'une phénoménologie de la donation*. Paris: Presses Universitaires de France.

Merleau-Ponty, M. (1945). *Phénoménologie de la perception*. Paris: Gallimard.

Ricœur, P. (1986). *Du texte à l'action: Essais d'herméneutique II*. Paris: Éditions du Seuil.

Roth, W.-M. (2007). Emotion at work: A contribution to third-generation cultural historical activity theory. *Mind, Culture and Activity, 14*, 40–63.

Roth, W.-M. (2010a). Incarnation: Radicalizing the embodiment of mathematics. *For the Learning of Mathematics, 30*(2), 2–9.

Roth, W.-M. (2010b). *Language, learning, context: Talking the talk*. London: Routledge

Roth, W.-M. (2011a). *Geometry as objective science in elementary classrooms: Mathematics in the flesh*. New York: Routledge.

Roth, W.-M. (2011b). *Passibility: At the limits of the constructivist metaphor*. Dordrecht, The Netherlands: Springer.

Roth, W.-M. (2011c). Researching living/lived mathematical work. *FQS: Forum Qualitative Sozialforschung / Qualitative Social Research, 12*(1). Accessed May 5, 2011 at http://www.qualitative-research.net/index.php/fqs/article/view/1604.

Roth, W.-M., & Tobin, K. (2010). Solidarity and conflict: Aligned and misaligned prosody as a transactional resource in intra- and intercultural communication involving power differences. *Cultural Studies of Science Education, 5*, 805–847.

Sheets-Johnstone, M. (2009). *The corporeal turn: An interdisciplinary reader*. Exeter, England: Imprint Academic.

van Manen, M. (2007). Phenomenology of practice. *Phenomenology & Practice, 1*, 11–30.

Varela, F. J. (1996). Neurophenomenology: A methodological remedy for the hard problem. *Journal of Consciousness Studies, 3*, 330–350.

Varela, F. J. (1999a). A dimly perceived horizon: The complex meeting ground between physical and inner time. *Annals of the New York Academy of Science, 879*, 143–153.

Varela, F. J. (1999b). The specious present: The neurophenomenology of time consciousness. In J. Petitot, F. J. Varela, B. Pachoud & J. M. Roy (Eds.), *Naturalizing phenomenology* (pp. 266–314). Stanford, CA: Stanford University Press.

Varela, F. J., & Depraz, N. (2005). At the source of time: Valence and the constitutional dynamics of affect. *Journal of Consciousness Studies, 12,* 61–81.

Varela, F. J., & Shear, J. (1999). *The view from within: First-person approaches to the study of consciousness.* Thorverton, UK: Imprint Academic.

Vygotskij, L. S. (2005). *Мышление и речь.* Moscow: Изд-во Смысл; Эксмо.

Waldenfels, B. (1999). *Sinnesschwellen: Studien zur Phänomenologie des Fremden 3.* Frankfurt/Main: Suhrkamp.

Waldenfels, B. (2006). *Grundmotive einer Phänomenologie des Fremden.* Frankfurt/Main: Suhrkamp.

PART II

Hermeneutic Phenomenology:
Reflection and Practice

KATHLEEN GALVIN AND LES TODRES

6. THE CREATIVITY OF 'UNSPECIALIZATION'

A Contemplative Direction for Integrative Scholarly Practice

INTRODUCTION

In this chapter we wish to contribute to an emerging debate about what scholarship means in a changing world where domains of knowledge have become exceedingly complex, in that knowledge is increasingly specialized and raises significant challenges for how these different discourses relate to one another in both theory and practice. Such complexity is particularly highlighted in caring professions such as nursing, midwifery, medicine, psychology, social work and other professions allied to medicine, where immersion in practice has exposed a deep inseparability between knowledge, ethics and action.

Boyer (1990) put forward a model of scholarship that emphasized the integration of a number of scholarly domains including research, teaching and application. In 1999, the American Association of Colleges of Nursing (AACN, 1999) adopted a position statement on scholarship that built on Boyer's work. Riley et al. (2002) took this further and proposed that such scholarship is setting-related but not setting-dependent, that it is holistic and fluid, and that it combines knowledge, experience, rigour and a service base. In a wide-ranging article, they consider some of the complexities of knowledge-in-action and knowledge-for-action, in which the sources of knowing are intimately intertwined with experience and practice. In this way, Riley et al. (2002) refer to how a very local and situated engagement is relevant to knowledge production: "The intimacy of the relationship is essential; because it provides important information and it is the therapeutic vehicle for applying knowledge" (p. 386).

These ideas draw on a tradition of thought that focuses on forms of applied knowledge (e.g. Carper, 1978; Schon, 1983; Benner et al., 1996; van Manen, 1999). By emphasizing action, service orientation and immersion in practice, this tradition integrates knowing and being (epistemology and ontology), and includes the ethical dimension of the 'good.'

In this chapter, we meditate further on the integration of knowledge, ethics and action and pursue the following goals:

– Locating the separation of the domains of knowledge, ethics and action within a historical context;

N. Friesen et al. (eds.), Hermeneutic Phenomenology in Education, 107–118.
© 2012 *Sense Publishers. All rights reserved.*

- Considering the nature of '*phronesis*' – the kind of knowledge that is already not separate from ethics and action;
- Formulating 'scholarship' as a 'seamless' way of being, rather than the integration of separate domains of knowledge, ethics and action;
- Indicating some directions for promoting a scholarship that draws on more contemplative directions, which open up creative, 'unspecialized' possibilities for feeling, thinking and doing. The term 'unspecialized' is developed in relation to Heidegger's thought and expresses a fundamentally human way of being that cannot be objectified and as such is a deep source of creativity.

We conclude by considering whether the creativity of "unspecialization" can be practiced, and draw on Heidegger and Gendlin as helpful guides.

A CONCEPTUAL EXPLORATION OF SCHOLARSHIP FOR CARING PRACTICES

Historical context: the 'dignity' and 'disaster' of modernity

In this section we would like to briefly offer one perspective on the gradual specialization of knowledge. Although there are many accounts of the fragmentation of knowledge domains (e.g., see Weber, 1963; Taylor, 1985; Habermas, 1990), we offer a brief historical analysis that draws on Wilber's (1995) discussion of the post-modern separation of science, art and morality. Understanding modernity and postmodernity as historical phenomena, the first of these can be identified with the project of the enlightenment in which the progress of natural science became a primary source of knowledge, value and justice. Postmodernity correspondingly refers to a certain disillusionment with the hopes that scientific progress would bring, both epistemologically and ethically. (We acknowledge that particular strands of postmodern thought have been accused of certain excesses of relativism and even narcissism but also acknowledge other strands within this discourse that emphasize respect for diversity in terms of values and culture as well as the validity of heterogeneous ways of knowing.)

It is within this distinction between modernity and postmodernity as a historical phenomenon that Wilber (1995) brings together a historical analysis of the sociology of knowledge that began with Weber (1963), and was pursued further by Taylor (1985) and Habermas (1990). Central to this analysis are the developments of modernity that heralded the differentiation of science, art and morality. This differentiation allowed much progress to take place in the spheres of the sciences, the arts, and justice, because each could pursue its activities without having to be too contaminated by the concerns of the other. Science was less constrained by aesthetic or ethical concerns, which allowed it to concentrate on the pursuit of knowledge in the objective world. This heralded technological progress in attempts to control the environment. Art, too, became much less classically wedded to morality or to an accurate and knowing portrayal of reality. What Wilber calls the "dignity of modernity" refers to the positive value of modernity, the advantages of creating the space for specialization, where welcome progress could be made within each domain's own terms and in accordance with their own logic:

> By the end of the eighteenth century, science, morality and art were even institutionally *differentiated* as realms of activity in which questions of truth (science), of justice (morals), and of taste (art) were autonomously elaborated, that is, each of these *spheres of knowing* [was pursued] under its own specific aspect of validity. (Habermas, 1990, p. 19)

Such differentiation, however, poses the question that has become increasingly apparent in our times: how can these different domains become re-integrated? According to Wilber, the disaster of modernity is that these domains, through their specialized paths, have become dissociated from one another: "... if the *dignity* of modernity was the differentiation of the Big Three, the *disaster* of modernity would be that it had not yet found a way to *integrate* them" (Wilber, 1995, p. 416).

Habermas (1990) has been strident in his criticism of what he called the 'colonisation of the lifeworld' by social engineering, technical approaches to practical life and subjectivity, and the increasing control by 'experts' of political and social life. All this constituted a 'commodification;' to turn the values of life into mere commodities. Habermas (1990) elaborated on how the differentiation of the domains of science, art and morality created a situation of uneven development in these spheres and how a healing of such dissociation is needed. We are currently scrambling to address the ethics and justice of scientific progress, the art of applied knowledge and the boundaries of art and the scientific and aesthetic dimensions of law. A metaphorical way to express Wilber's question about integration would be: how does the head (knowing), the heart (ethics) and the hand (the art of action) function as one body? What is this way of being and what are its implications for the meaning of scholarship?

In postmodern times, we cannot simply turn back to a form of simplistic holism in a way that denies specialization and diversity. However, in honouring differentiation, we can, nevertheless, pursue such differentiated domains through an understanding of the fundamental non-separation of science, morality and the art of action in the way that life *moves*. We may need to make this background much clearer when considering scholarship and so we refer to Aristotle's notion of a way of being in which knowing, doing and valuing are fundamentally inseparable.

The nature of 'phronesis': The kind of knowledge that is already not separate from ethics and action

Polkinghorne (2004) advocates an expanded notion of rationality that can accommodate living situations that are highly specific to their context, that involve the unpredictability of the human realm, and where exceptions to rules often apply: "Effective practices of care require that practitioner actions are decided by their situated and timely judgements" (p. 2). Furthermore:

> Practical choices in situations calling for actions to bring about the human good require a kind of thought that can deal with complex and competing goals and take into account the timing and context of the action, as well as the uniqueness and particular characteristics of the situation and person for whom the action is undertaken. (p. 21)

In this view, scholarship is tested by the "... situations in which we run out of rules" (Brown, 1988, p. 139). So what kind of knowing and way of being is adequate for this task? Polkinghorne refers back to ancient Greece, before the differentiation of the value spheres had taken place, to Aristotle.

Aristotle distinguished between the kind of deliberations that were appropriate for making things (techne) and those that were appropriate for acting in the human realm. He used the term '*phronesis*' to mean a practical wisdom that can address a plurality of values.

> The most characteristic function of a man of practical wisdom is to deliberate well: no one deliberates about things that cannot be other than they are, nor about things that cannot be directed to some end, an end that is a good attainable by action. In an unqualified sense, that man is good at deliberating who, by reasoning, can aim at and hit the best thing attainable to man by action. (Aristotle, 1141b 9-14)

The complexity of living situations means that such plurality often results in conflict between values. Conflicts such as the good of an individual versus the good of the collective, or conflicts that surround the inherent risks of acting versus not acting when certainty of outcome cannot be guaranteed. The sources of understanding and knowing that are drawn on in such situations are multiple and are already based on an interwoven fabric of knowing, morality and the art of applied action. Such interwoven 'fabric' is only separated into categories by means of reflection – it is originally a seamless way of being and moving. Polkinghorne sees such a way of being as an expansion of the traditional understanding of rationality; it is intelligent in that it varies with situations, is receptive to particulars, and has the quality of improvisation. Polkinghorne links Aristotle's notion of *phronesis* to a number of current developments in philosophy and psychology that articulate a broader understanding of rationality. We merely wish to indicate these developments in order to acknowledge that there are currently a number of ways to develop a kind of practical wisdom that emphasizes the way human beings are embedded in their world.

This broader understanding of rational thinking includes Epstein's (1994) 'experiential thinking,' Lakoff and Johnson's (1999) 'embodied rationality' and Gendlin's (1992) notion of the 'felt sense.' These notions resonate deeply with Aristotle's *phronesis*. However, in this chapter, we would like to highlight 'empathic imagination' as a kind of practical wisdom of particular relevance to caring practices.

First of all, empathic imagination involves imaginative thinking. Murray (1986) draws on Heidegger to show how this is not simply an imaginary experience, such as imagining 'being able to fly like Peter Pan.' Imaginative thinking is more directed in that it may be used to solve complex problems. It is also a participative form of knowing in that you imaginatively put yourself in a series of scenarios so as to be open to the possibilities of those scenarios. Such thinking is particularly relevant when a unique situation asks you to dwell with the specific complexities of that situation. Imaginatively we see what is *there* and what is *not there* and move forward in time to imagine outcomes and possibilities. In that way, we participatively and imaginatively move in many directions, in a 'rhizomatic' manner, just as a rhizome is a plant with an intricacy of interconnections. In imaginative thinking there is the interconnection between past and future, feeling, thought and situation; a multiplicity of felt connections. Emphasizing the difference between generality and particularity, Nussbaum (1990) indicates the complexity of such interconnected, imaginative presence:

> Instead of ascending from the particular to the general, deliberative imagination links particulars without dispensing with their particularity. It would involve, for example, the ability to recall past experiences as one with, as relevant to, the case at hand, while still conceiving of both with rich and vivid concreteness. (p. 78)

As one kind of deliberative imagination, empathic imagination goes further. It brings in an interpersonal focus whereby the world of another person is imagined. The phenomenological tradition has been helpful in articulating an approach to understanding others by trying to suspend our own preconceptions and 'taking a walk in another person's shoes.' Developmental psychologists such as Kohlberg (1981) have shown how moral development requires the ability to shift from an egocentric position to one that can see something from another's point of view. Empathic imagination is thus already an interwoven fabric of thought, ethics and action in that an individual is fundamentally engaged in *being with* and, in some cases, *being for* another as a source of knowledge and action. The meaning of caring is founded on this possibility, with its imagination of what another's world may be like. It provides rich, detailed and context-specific possibilities for knowing and acting. It is consequently a form of *phronesis* (practical wisdom) that may be centrally important when considering the meaning of scholarship for caring practices.

Scholarship as a seamless way of being rather than the integration of separate domains of knowledge, ethics and action

Our consideration of the kind of scholarship that is central to caring practices has so far emphasized a kind of integration of knowledge ethics and action that intimately work together as a coherent movement. For caring practices we have emphasized how this kind of integration is centrally informed by an empathic sensibility that underpins such integration. We would like, however, to consider further the nature of this kind of integration.

There is a danger in any analysis of 'integration' that integration of knowing, ethics and action is achieved by actively *doing* such integration. This often serves to increase the feeling that we are 'in over our heads' (Kegan, 1994), scrambling to increase our professional life-loads by becoming everything: researchers, teachers, business-fellows and internet junkies perusing the latest evidence. The feeling quality of this is often impending fragmentation rather than coherence. But the question is: what gets 'dropped out' in all this increased doing?

An alternative view of integration that is more contemplative and less strident is provided by Heidegger (1960), and is essentially contained in his image of a clearing in the forest. Once such a clearing has been attained within this image, integration does not have to be actively strived for because what was thought of as requiring integration (as separate domains) is found to already be there, 'together.' This view of integration suggests an uncovering of what can obscure it rather than an active search to put things together, as if this needs to be achieved through ardor and artifice. Such uncovering requires a more contemplative direction and draws on a critique by Heidegger of the spirit of technology, and how this can obscure integrative possibilities as a way of being.

In the 1920s, Heidegger (1926/1962) was already facing fundamental questions about the relationship between the spirit of technology and more foundational issues of being human. He wasn't against technological progress but wanted to strike a note of caution about how the essence of technology is such that it is defining not only the world around us, but also ourselves as objects. Furthermore, he was concerned that as we became increasingly capable of objectifying ourselves in this way, something very important would become obscured – namely our unspecialized capacity of being. Such unspecialized capacity is the place where knowing, ethics and action were never separate. It is rather 'one song' (Todres, 2000) or a movement that is always unfinished because it is open to the new and is already an interconnection of head, hand and heart; it is the realm of possibility. In this view, integration has always been happening and we only become excessively concerned with integration if it is blocked or if we wish to overly control its direction.

Nurturing the space for such being-possibilities does not mean that nothing is happening. Applying this to a kind of scholarship that is a seamless movement of head, hand and heart would mean that the ongoing learning and opportunities within our professional and personal lives could 'settle.' The importance of 'settling' as a kind of clearing that allows integration to be, does not eradicate the value of pursuing specialized developments or the activity of relating these developments to one another. Rather, it offers some relief that striving in a specialized way is not the only path to productivity – that our unspecialized capacities for being can be productive. As touched on earlier in this chapter, this is the place from where integration is already vitally tasted. The question then changes from how to 'effortfully' achieve a scholarly integration of knowledge, ethics and action, to how to bring specialized activities into the spaciousness of being where integration is already 'humming.' Approaching the question in this way may raise particular challenges for how we support this possibility. The kind of scholarship that attempts to accommodate such a *how* may be best conceptualized as a way of being that needs a different kind of support and permission by our learning and institutional contexts. The challenge is then to recognize such times of settling as a creative resource for seamless knowing-valuing-acting. The feeling-quality of such settling and connecting with this natural integrity may be one of vitality. There may be a certain sense of excitement and coherence as we begin to give space to and trust these possibilities of being. Such a sense of vitality and coherence may also mitigate a feeling of burnout. We consider later how a more contemplative scholarly path can be given permission and supported with reference to Gendlin's philosophy of entry into the implicit. But first we would like to consider the path of contemplation as a way of being that is relevant to scholarship for caring practices.

A contemplative scholarship: can unspecialization be practiced?

Turner (1994), Van Manen (1999) and others have indicated the complexity of the notion of 'practice' in relation to pedagogy. In this view, practice is not merely instrumental in the sense of applying pre-determined methodologies, but is rather embedded in ways of being that are pre-reflective and often spontaneous. Does this mean that such practice 'just happens' or is there a way that we can take more conscious responsibility for it? Van Manen, drawing on Turner, indicates how such practice is nevertheless a certain kind of activity that can be cultivated: "... in spite of this intangibility, the concept of practice must include the connotation of something transferable, teachable, transmittable, or reproducible" (Van Manen, 1999).

Van Manen is writing about the practice of teaching. However, for the purposes of this chapter, we wish to consider practice in relation to the question of whether the integrative development (in terms of head, heart and hand) of the scholar can be actively cultivated, and in what sense an opening to the creativity of unspecialization can be practiced.

This direction has been pursued by several writers under different rubrics and in different contexts. This includes Bachelard's (1964) notion of 'reverie,' Gadamer's (1986/1994) concept of 'play' and various mytho-poetic directions for education (MacDonald, 1981; Willis, 2005). In particular, Heidegger (1959/1966), in his writings on contemplative thinking, gives us some helpful directions about the sense in which such an opening to *being* can be 'practiced.' His argument is associated with a long-standing tradition of what Keats has called 'negative capability.' Negative capability means the natural 'generativity' that arises, not by positively seeking integration in a goal-directed way, but by allowing integration 'to be.' This occurs during periods of 'letting go,' 'lying fallow' or having space and time for what has been called 'blue skies thinking' (see, for example, Claxton, 1997, for a fuller discussion of this logic).

In an essay entitled 'The Age of the World Picture,' Heidegger (1977) cautioned against the tendency to secure the precedence of *methodology* over *presence* as a way of *opening to understanding*. He was concerned that the way science was being organized and practiced resulted in the 'scholar' disappearing and the 'research worker' becoming a technologist whose specialising concerns prematurely close down the creativity of unspecialization in a self-referenced and self-reifying way:

The human becomes that being upon which all that is, is grounded as regards the manner of its Being and its truth. The human becomes the relational centre of that which is as such. (Heidegger, 1977, p. 128; translation adapted based on the original German)

Such a self-referencing, specialized perspective forms the foundation of what Heidegger called calculative thinking. It is characterised by a thinking that is preoccupied with existing patterns in the way we organise, categorise and particularize phenomena.

Heidegger distinguished contemplative thinking from calculative thinking. Our argument proposes that it is contemplative thinking that is centrally relevant to the question of whether the creativity of unspecialization can be practiced. Contemplative thinking is about how one can think in a receptive way that is open to the excess of being beyond oneself (being-in-the-world) and not the more calculative type of thinking that is 'always on the move' and merely 'doing' an existing pattern of organized thought.

This does not mean that such presence and openness to 'being-in-the-world' is passive. There *is* a certain 'waiting' in it; but that waiting is a form of actively practicing a 'negative capability' that keeps at bay the kind of possessive 'willing' that prematurely grasps at what is already known. In this way, contemplative thinking can be said to be actively practised in the sense that it holds open the possibility of not knowing, and so allows a release into the openness and creativity of a more unspecialized realm: "We must develop the art of waiting, releasing our hold…" (Hixon, 1989, p. 4). And this is not far away. It is very near; nearer than our habitual ways of thinking. In releasing ourselves from our more habitual thinking, a less specialized presence is possible, one that is open to profiles of the world that are at the edge of the known, where novelty occurs. "Openness is not due to any specific point of view but is rather the absence of single-perspective perceiving and thinking" (Hixon, 1989, p. 9).

In relation to an integrative vision of scholarship, we thus wish to include the creativity of unspecialization. Heidegger has provided us with clues for a more contemplative direction in this pursuit; one that is receptive, but that can nevertheless be practised by actively becoming aware of an alternative to calculative thinking. But we would like to take this one step further and propose some directions for such practice based on Eugene Gendlin's philosophy of 'entry into the implicit' (Gendlin 1991). Gendlin's notion of 'the implicit' refers to the place where unspecialized possibilities have their life. Entry into the implicit then involves an experiential movement that allows the aliveness of the implicit to be sensed and to function as an ongoing creative source of possible new meanings. As such, Gendlin provides one possible practice that can serve scholarly integration through the remembrance to discipline our specialized concerns and thus give way to the 'letting be' of our more unspecialized possibilities.

In his philosophy of entry into the implicit, Gendlin sets out a relational ontology in which contemplative thinking can be practiced by attending to ones own lived body and, as such, opens up the excesses of being-in-the-world beyond pre-existing patterns.

GENDLIN'S PHILOSOPHY AS A PRACTICE OF OPENING THE CREATIVITY OF UNSPECIALIZATION

Gendlin's philosophy of entry into the implicit (Gendlin, 1991) builds on the thoughts of Heidegger and Merleau-Ponty. It focuses on how the lived body can open profiles of the world beyond pre-patterned thought. The phrase 'entry into the implicit' means that words, thoughts and representations are formulated and come from an experiential practice based on attending to the lived body's sense of felt meaning in any moment. Two practices arise out of this philosophy. One is called 'focusing,' the other, 'thinking at the edge.'

Focusing

Focusing describes an experiential practice of attending to the relationship between language and the aliveness or excess of what language is trying to point to, by grounding such aliveness in the lived body's *felt* sense. Through a felt sense, meaning is apprehended in a holistic way that is more than its formulation in language and already-patterned thought. The felt sense is full of the excess of the life-world – its fleshly textures and abundances of meanings. The felt-sense is "… implicitly intricate in a way that is more than what is already formed or distinguished" (Gendlin, 1992). The practice of focusing is then a body-based hermeneutics that goes back and forth between this 'more than' of the lifeworld, and the many ways of patterning the lifeworld, as it comes to form in language and thought.

Thinking at the edge

Thinking at the edge is a stepped process that uses focusing but builds theory from the freshness of the focusing process. In such a way, it aims "…to think and speak about our world and our selves by generating terms from a felt sense. Such terms formulate experiential intricacy rather than turning everything we think about into externally viewed objects" (Gendlin, 2004).

Opening up unspecialized possibilities

Both these practices may provide direction for how to open unspecialized possibilities through an embodied contemplative approach. In order to illustrate this in a concrete way, let us refer to an illustration that Gendlin provides (the use of (...) in the following passage refers to the 'more than words can say' of the felt sense (the many ellipses are in the original):

> An artist stands before an unfinished picture, pondering it, seeing, feeling, bodily sensing it, having a … Suppose the artist's … is one of some dissatisfaction. Is that an emotional reaction, simply a feeling-tone? No indeed. Implicit in the … is the artist's training, experience with many designs, and much else. But more: the … is also the implying of the next line, which has not yet come. The artist ponders 'what it needs.' It needs some line, some erasure, something moved over, something …. The artist

tries this and that, and something else, and erases it again each time. The ... is quite demanding. It recognizes the failure of each attempt. It seems to know precisely what it wants and it knows that those attempts are not it. Rather than accepting those, a good artist prefers to leave a design unfinished, sometimes for years. (Gendlin, 1992)

This illustration shows how the lived body is an important gate to the alive and implicit 'more' where unspecialized possibilities can be touched. So, in answer to our earlier question of whether unspecialization can be practiced, we suggest that it can and that Gendlin offers important understandings and practices that, although active in a certain sense, can honour the kind of contemplative attitude that is hospitable to being addressed by new meanings from 'the more' as we pursue scholarly enquiry.

In relation to contemplative scholarly practice relevant to care, we can imagine the following vignette. Sarah a nurse has been struggling on the ward with a deep sense of discomfort she experienced in a case conference. This discomfort is highly complex but implicitly 'there' in the 'more' of her felt sense. 'In it' is the 'head,' 'hand' and 'heart' as already together. But as she settles and lets go of her specialized concern to be a competent staff nurse and even her specialized concern to be professional, scholarly and caring, she attends to what wants to come from her felt sense of the whole of everything together there. Her discomfort carries a number of different dimensions: how she had recently read a scholarly work on Levinas that led her to think about the nature of respect, how certain experiences in her past professional and personal life had impressed upon her the importance of being careful not to assume what another needs, and how all this and some other things gave her a sense of possible directions of action that were consistent with the uncomfortable feeling of what was missing in terms of the kind of respectful care that she would like to offer in this particular situation. In this situation she thus actively made space for a more contemplative approach to the integration of head , hand and heart that was implicit in the 'pre-formed' unspecialization of her felt sense. Yet this was productive. A clear understanding and possible action did come, that was ultimately supported in a way that included what could be called an integrated scholarly way of being as articulated in this chapter.

CONCLUSION

We have tried to set out the idea of a more contemplative scholarship, one that draws on a natural movement in 'being' to embody and live in a knowing, valuing and action-oriented way. We looked at historical evidence before the 'doing' of integration became such a dilemma and highlighted virtue inhering in our unspecialized possibilities of being, while at the same time questioning how our specialized engagements can be held more vitally within these unspecialized movements. In particular, in relation to scholarship for caring practices, we noted how empathic imagination is a central faculty for integrating the head, hand and heart.

So why are contemplative practices important for the kind of scholarship that acknowledges an integration of head, hand and heart? In an increasingly specialized and even fragmented world, the humming integration of head, hand and heart that naturally occurs becomes easily obscured by the excessive compartmentalisation of attention to specialized tasks. The essence of creativity requires the kind of space that only comes with a slowing down, an in-breath, that for a moment, releases a relentless hold. The kind of integrative focus offered in this chapter may suggest some interesting directions for consideration as to how contemplative orientations for scholarly practice can be supported, guarded and nurtured.

REFERENCES

American Association of Colleges in Nursing (AACN). (1999). *Hallmarks of scholarly nursing practice*. Washington DC: Author.

Aristotle. (1983). *Nichomachean ethics*. Indianapolis: Hackett Publishing Company.

Bachelard, G. (1964). *The poetics of space*. Boston: Beacon.

Benner, P., Tanner, C. & Chesla, C. (1996). *Expertise in nursing practice: Caring, clinical judgment and ethics*. New York: Springer.

Boyer, E.L. (1990). *Scholarship reconsidered: Priorities of the professoriate*. Princeton: Carnegie Endowment for the Advancement of Teaching.

Brown, H.I. (1988). *Rationality*. New York: Routledge.

Carper, B.A. (1978). Fundamental patterns of knowing in nursing. *Advances in Nursing Science*, 1(6), 13-23.

Cahoone, L.E. (Ed.) (1996) *From modernism to postmodernism*. An anthology. Oxford: Blackwell.

Claxton, G. (1997). *Hare brain, tortoise mind: Why intelligence increases when you think less*. London: Fourth Estate.

Epstein, S. (1994). Integration of the cognitive and the psychodynamic unconscious. *American Psychologist*, 49(8), 709-724.

Gadamer, H-G. (1986/1994). *Truth and method* (2nd rev. ed.). New York: Seabury Press.

Gendlin, E.T. (1962). *Experiencing and the creation of meaning*. Glencoe: Free Press.

Gendlin, E.T. (1991). *Thinking beyond patterns: body, language and situations*. Retrieved October 15th, 2006 from www.focusing.org/tbp.html.

Gendlin, E.T. (1992). The primacy of the body, not the primacy of perception: how the body knows the situation and philosophy. *Man and World*, 25(3-4), 341-353. Retrieved October 15th, 2006 from http://www.focusing.org/pdf/primacy_excerpt.pdf.

Gendlin, E.T. (2004). Introduction to 'Thinking at the edge.' *The Folio. Thinking at the Edge: A new Philosophical Practice*, 19(1), 1-10. Retrieved October 15th, 2006 from www.focusing.org/tae-intro.html.

Habermas, J. (1990) *The philosophical discourse of modernity*. Cambridge: MIT Press.

Heidegger, M. (1962). *Being and time*. Oxford: Blackwell.

Heidegger M. (1960). The origin of the work of art. In *Poetry, language and thought* (pp. 17-87). New York: Harper and Row.

Heidegger, M. (1966). *Discourse on thinking*. New York: Harper & Row.

Heidegger, M. (1977). The Age of the world picture. In: *The question concerning technology and other essays* (pp. 115-154). New York: Harper & Row,

Hixon, L. (1989) *Coming home: The experience of enlightenment in sacred traditions*. Los Angeles: Tarcher/Perigee.

Kegan, R. (1994). *In over our heads: The mental demands of modern life*. London: Harvard University Press.

Kohlberg, L. (1981). *Essays on moral development* (Vol. 1). San Francisco: Harper.

Lakoff, G. & Johnson, M. (1999). *Philosophy in the flesh: The embodied mind and its challenge to western thought*. New York: Basic Books.

MacDonald, J.B. (1981). Theory, practice and the hermeneutic circle. *Journal of Curriculum Theorizing, 3*(2), 130-138.

Murray, E.L. (1986). *Imaginative thinking and human existence*. Pittsburgh, PA: Duquesne University Press.

Nussbaum, M.C. (1990). *Love's knowledge: Essays on philosophy and literature*. Oxford: Oxford University Press.

Polkinghorne, D. (2004). *Practice and the human sciences: The case for a judgement based practice of care*. Albany, NY: SUNY.

Riley, J.M., Beal, J., Levi, O., & McCausland, M.P. (2002). Revisioning nursing scholarship. *Journal of nursing Scholarship, 34*(4), 383-389.

Schon, D. (1983). *The reflective practitioner*. New York: Basic Books.

Taylor, C. (1985). *Philosophy and the human sciences – Philosophical papers 2*. Cambridge: Cambridge University Press.

Todres, L. (2000). Embracing ambiguity: transpersonal development and the phenomenological tradition. *Religion and Health, 39*(3), 227-237.

Turner, S. (1994). *The social theory of practices*. Chicago: University of Chicago Press.

Van Manen, M. (1999). *The practice of practice*. Retrieved October 15th, 2006 from http://www.phenomenologyonline.com/max/articles/practice.html.

Weber, M. (1963). *The sociology of religion*. Boston: Beacon.

Wilber, K. (1995). *Sex, ecology, spirituality: The spirit of evolution*. London: Shambhala.

Willis, P. (2005). Mythopoetic communities of practice in postgraduate Educational Research. In: T. Stehlik & P. Carden (Eds.), *Beyond communities of practice: Theory as experience* (pp. 47-66). Brisbane: Post Press.

CARINA HENRIKSSON

7. HERMENEUTIC PHENOMENOLOGY AND PEDAGOGICAL PRACTICE

INTRODUCTION

Ki mai koe ki a au,
he aha te mea nui tenei ao:
He tangata, he tangata, he tangata.

If you should ask me what is
the greatest thing in the world,
the answer would be:
It's people, it's people, it's people.

(Maori song)

The Swedish scholar, Oscar Öquist (1992), once complained that everything he loves about people – our complexity, our vagueness, our irrationality, and our insecurity, in other words, our humanness – is being persecuted and demeaned by technology's distant and logical ideals. The values we cherish today – such as efficiency, assessment, and productivity – leave no room for softer, human qualities such as intuition, emotions, imagination, and creativity. They are denigrated as feminine, childish, or immature. And yet we implicitly know how important these qualities are for human growth and development.

Schools are places where human beings, people, meet and spend a lot of time together. Does research in pedagogy mirror the conviction that people in school are "the greatest thing in the world"?

One could question what significance pedagogical research has for teachers and students in a classroom. Do research reports reach the schools and the teachers at all? If so, do the teachers find them useful; do they make a difference for their pedagogical practice? Teachers often discard academic knowledge about teaching as theoretical nonsense; it is simply of little use in the classroom. Teachers often express the opinion that theoretical knowledge does not help them cope in their every day mission. Furthermore, it seems as if the research

N. Friesen et al. (eds.), Hermeneutic Phenomenology in Education, 119–137.

questions that academics dwell upon have little to do with the urgent questions, which arise in everyday pedagogical practice.

To be a child or a young person in school is to be situated in a world engineered and planned by adults. And these adults no doubt have ideological and political reasons for their decisions. Schools, educational policy, and curricula aim foremost at producing citizens who are productive from a societal perspective. A lot of effort is put into designing curricula and syllabi which serve society's current political interests. Even though most educational policy documents include some paragraphs about values and ethics, they seldom put focus on the growth of human beings. As Pinar (2006) points out, "the academic field of education is so very reluctant to abandon social engineering" (p. 109). It also seems as if teachers themselves rely too heavily on the technical-instructional side of education:

> If only we can find the right technique, the right modification of classroom organization (small groups, collaborative learning, dialogue), if only we teach according to "best practices," if only we have students self-reflect or if only we develop "standards" or conduct "scientific" research, then students will learn what we teach them. If only we test regularly, "no child" will be "left behind." (Pinar, 2006, p. 109)

At the same time, teachers know that being in a classroom with students cannot be reduced to a technical or an intellectual endeavor. It involves an intuitive sense of a world, a state of mind and a way of feeling and acting.

In order to make pedagogic research useful for pedagogic practice, methods which prompt a pathic, reflective understanding – rather than an objectifying, gnostic knowledge – have been developed (cf. van Manen, 1990/1997; Halling, 2008; Todres, 2007). Furthermore, research questions of great importance for pedagogic practice need to be addressed and communicated in a language accessible to everyone who has an interest in pedagogical matters. In other words: *How* we speak about pedagogy is equally important as *what* we speak of. Gadamer (2002) elucidates a fundamental aspect of the intrinsic relationship between language and life when he says:

> The word becomes binding, as it were: it binds one human being with another. This occurs whenever we speak to one another and really enter into genuine dialogue with another. (p. 106)

Language discloses the world and how we co-exist and orient ourselves in this world. If the language of scientific reports does not disclose a world that teachers recognize, if it talks about things alien to pedagogical practice, are we then surprised that teacher are reluctant to read them? If teachers do not feel that the words used bind them with their students or their practice, can we blame teachers for not getting any further than the first few pages of pedagogical books?

There is unquestionably a close link between language, our worldview, and our attitude towards fellow human beings; they shape and modify each other. Phenomenology is an attitude towards life, or as Merleau-Ponty (2001) puts it: "phenomenology can be practiced and identified as a manner or style of thinking, that existed as a movement before arriving at complete awareness of itself as a philosophy" (p. viii). Hermeneutic phenomenology aims to elucidate lived meanings; "it attempts to describe *and* interpret these meanings to a certain degree of depth and richness" (van Manen, 1990, p. 11, italics added). Hermeneutic phenomenology draws upon subjective experience, that is true, but the description and interpretation that are central to its method are also prerequisites in everyday communication. We regularly share stories about our experiences: Phenomenology is thus also a matter of intersubjectivity and interaction.

No doubt, many contemporary phenomenological researchers are willing to attest to Merleau-Ponty's (2001) statement that phenomenology "has given a number of present-day readers the impression on reading Husserl or Heidegger, not so much of encountering a new philosophy as of recognizing what they had been waiting for" (p. viii). It is not just the philosophers, Husserl and Heidegger, who makes us feel "at home"; we feel evocatively addressed by the writings of contemporary researchers. It is through the works of pedagogues such as Bollnow, Langeveld, van Manen, and those who build upon their works that we recognize what we had been waiting for. It is through well-written hermeneutic phenomenological texts that we learn and understand by example.

The same seems to be true for teachers and educational researchers who wish to explore and better understand pedagogical practice. Phenomenology gives us a different kind of knowledge, knowledge that is relevant for pedagogical practice and classroom interaction. It is my experience that in-service teachers, when they encounter hermeneutic phenomenology, rather immediately recognize their own practice, their classrooms, and their students. This recognition is not just a feeling of "homecoming," of recognizing their pedagogical practice. Embedded in this recognition is a feeling of relief; the world is recognizable. Perhaps most important of all: hermeneutic phenomenology takes the concrete minutiae of pedagogy and classroom interaction seriously; it acknowledges the embodied, ethical knowledge possessed by teachers, but which is rarely the subject for research. One remarkable feature of hermeneutic phenomenology is that it does not just politely affirm teachers' tacit knowledge so that they can comfortably dwell in it. Paradoxically, phenomenology is "uncomfortable" since it challenges taken-for-granted attitudes, as language makes these both visible and audible. So, Merleau-Ponty's "what they had been waiting for" holds a promise of both proximity and distance, of the familiar and the alien, the known and the not-yet known.

What is it that teachers have been waiting for? There are aspects of pedagogical practice, which teachers are confronted with on a daily basis; aspects which do not lend themselves to quantification, intellectual reasoning, or theorizing. So, what do teachers know about pedagogy and classroom interaction that educational researchers tend to miss? Some of these aspects are discussed in this chapter.

"WALKING THE DOG"

I am halfway through my lecture on hermeneutic phenomenology. For the last ten minutes I have been talking about the reduction, how we need to bracket our preunderstandings and how phenomenology can make us question what we take for granted. While I talk, I notice that one of the students seems restless, as if she finds it hard to sit still. I expect her to raise her hand and ask something, but she does not. I keep on talking, giving examples and then, suddenly, the student says out loud, "But, oh, this sounds so tedious! Are you saying that whenever we see something, we need to think that maybe it is the other way around, that I cannot trust what I see? That things are not what they seem to be? For instance, if I see a woman walking her dog, do I think, 'Hey, maybe it is the dog walking the woman'?" I let her question hang in the air for a moment; waiting for what I hope will come. It does not take long before another student says,

"Well, you know, it does sometimes look as if the dog is walking the person, because often the dog is the one which goes first." Suddenly the classroom is filled with comments.

"Usually it is my dog that tells me when he needs to go out."

"Yes, so does mine. And sometimes you stand there waiting for the dog to sniff something, and sometimes you yank the collar, because otherwise you'd be standing on the same spot for ages."

"So, how can you tell who is leading and who is following?" one of the students says.

We had good discussions that day, about teaching and about what it means for a teacher to lead his or her students. When the class was over, the student who raised the question about walking the dog came up and asked, "Do you feel like a better person, now that you have found phenomenology?"

"Do you feel like a better person, now that you have found phenomenology?" A question with religious nuances. But phenomenology does not look towards divinity or mysticism; it looks towards human lived experiences in the realm of the mundane, in our professional lives, in our private lives, in our social lives. Luijpen (1960) expressed phenomenology's orientation towards the world colorfully when he wrote:

> What is the meaning of speaking about the world if this world is not the world in which the girls are so sweet and the boys so manly and generous, if it is not the world in which there is a difference between a deceased and a murdered individual, in which there is a difference between the red of an apple, the red of lips, and that of blood? (p. 88)

Even though the wording bears witness to the fifty years that have passed since these thoughts were written down, I think we all understand the gist of Luijpen's statement. But does turning towards the world that Luijpen describes make us better teachers? If better means more thoughtful, more willing to question the taken-for-granted, more open to others' experiences, then yes, phenomenology makes us better persons and probably also better teachers.

Returning to the classroom and the walking of the dog, what does it mean for a teacher to lead his or her students?

Leading means going first, and in going first you can trust me, for I have tested the ice. I have lived. I now know something of the rewards as well as the trappings of growing towards adulthood and making a world for yourself. Although my going first is no guarantee of success for you (because the world is not without risks and dangers), in the pedagogical relationship there is a more fundamental guarantee: No matter what, I am here. And you can count on me. (Van Manen, 1991/1993, p. 38)

Judging from the conversation I had with my students, being a teacher who leads is more complicated than just being the one who holds the leash. The asymmetrical and vulnerable relation between teacher and child cannot be reduced to a "leader-follower" relation. Van Manen, of course, knows this and in a thoughtful and sensuous passage he says:

The adult who is oriented to the child's vulnerability or need may experience a strange sensation – the true authority in this encounter rests in the child and not in the adult. We might say that the child's presence becomes for the adult an experience of being confronted with a demand for his or her pedagogical responsiveness. So the child's weakness turns into a curious strength that the child has over the adult. (Van Manen, 1991/1993, p. 70)

When van Manen turns the table and suggests that it is the child who has the power over the adult, he illustrates what hermeneutic phenomenological methodology urges us to do: to suspend our taken-for-granted attitudes and ask ourselves: "What if it is the other way around?" In doing so, we move from what Husserl (1983) calls our natural attitude towards a phenomenological attitude. The word attitude has its origin in the Latin, *aptitudinem*, meaning "a posture of the body supposed to imply some mental state"(Online Etymology Dictionary, 2011). So, shifting from a natural attitude to a phenomenological attitude implies a change of mental state; we shift from one way of seeing reality to another. This alteration in attitude, the *epoché*, is often misunderstood as a suspension of reality, but Zahavi (2003) explains the concept and its relevance for methodology and research:

We do not effect it [the *epoché*] in order to deny, doubt, neglect, abandon, or exclude reality from our research but simply in order to suspend or neutralize a certain dogmatic *attitude* toward reality, that is, in order to be able to focus more narrowly and directly on the phenomenological given – the objects just as they appear. (p. 45)

Transferred to the classroom, the *epoché* asks that teachers, for a moment, suspend the natural attitude and question the taken-for granted. This does not mean that teachers, when reflecting upon their everyday work, should deny what they see, hear, or understand, but question the explanations that might first come to mind.

Hermeneutic phenomenology has the potential to create a sense of wonder, openness, change, and readiness to reflect on pedagogical matters. It has the power to create a pedagogical attunement, bringing pedagogical research into harmony with everyday pedagogical practice. If well written or well conducted, hermeneutic phenomenology and reflection can awaken a forgotten attunement to teaching and to life itself. Hermeneutic phenomenology nurture the budding practitioner who deeply and sincerely reflects on "who is walking the dog?"

PEDAGOGICAL EYES

There is a Malay saying: "Keep a green tree in your heart and perhaps a singing bird will come." The gist of the saying is beautifully captured in Dorit Riley's painting *For You.*[1] It depicts an asymmetric but also sensitive relationship set in a peaceful atmosphere.

When Bollnow (1989) talks about *the pedagogical atmosphere*, he takes it to mean "all those fundamental emotional conditions and sentient human qualities that exist between the educator and the child and which form the basis for every pedagogical relationship" (p. 5). Bollnow himself was a bit reluctant to use the term *atmosphere,* since it conjures up emotional and sentimental undertones. However, when he explores the notion, there is nothing sentimental about it. On the contrary, Bollnow describes basic human needs as being the prerequisites for bringing up children in a manner that is pedagogically responsible. Some of the notions he explores are for instance security, trust, hope, cheerfulness, joy, love, confidence, serenity, and goodness. These are all qualities and knowledge which a teacher, as a human being, needs to possess – and radiate – in a cultivated classroom.

As teachers, we have a very special relationship to cultivate, the one between teacher and student. In the best of worlds, a classroom is a garden where children and teenagers can grow and flourish – intellectually, emotionally, and socially. In such a classroom, the teacher has special eyes, pedagogical eyes. These eyes need to see what the child has to offer, who the child is, and how the teacher can make each unique child grow. In the classroom, most of the time, the teacher interact with his or her students verbally, but behind the words hides a moral message mediated through the teacher's body language, facial expression, or simply by the teacher's look – or non-look.

> My peers are almost done with the assignments, but I am not. I cannot just dig into the examples to be worked out. I need time to think about how to solve the problems. I also want to keep my books neat and tidy, and so before I start I use the ruler to draw lines vertical and horizontal lines. I am particular with how I write; I want the digits to look, you know, nice. I use the eraser a lot. Besides, I need time to go through, in my mind,the rules, and methods. I repeat the multiplication table. My teacher snaps at me:

"Anna, stop fiddling about and get started." He thinks that I am avoiding the assignment, that I am lazy. But I am not! I am not lazy. I am not thick. I am just slow. Besides, when I ask for help my teacher ignores me. You know, it's like: "a student who needs special support in several subjects ... oh, well ... leave her to draw lines and digits."

How are we to understand Anna's "fiddling about"? Does she spend most of her lessons drawing lines? If that is so, one might also suspect that what was once a wish to keep her notebooks tidy, has developed into a conscious strategy to avoid facing difficult work. Nonetheless, it might be exactly what Anna says it is, her way of approaching the assignment, that she simply needs time. Regardless of how we understand Anna's behaviour, a modified outline of the pattern described by Jackson, Boostrom and Hansen (1993) seems to be in operation here. The teacher uses both verbal and non-verbal signs to comment on Anna's improper behaviour, i.e. she does not work fast enough. Anna tries but fails to comply, and accordingly she does not get her teacher's approval.

What knowledge does Anna gain during math lessons? Apparently, she does not learn much geometry or algebra. What she *does* learn was that she is always behind, that she does not work and understand fast enough. That is, fast enough for the teacher's "assumption of worthwhileness" (Jackson, Boostrom, & Hansen, 1993, p. 24). She also learns that she will never get a "pass" no matter how hard she tries. The crucial knowledge Anna gains is that she recognizes her position; she has been weighed and found wanting. The positioning made here, both by the teacher and Anna herself is no secret. On the contrary, it takes place in the open and is visible for all to see. Anna's peers will inevitably notice what goes on, other teachers will probably learn about Anna's failure in staff meetings, and her parents will likely also be informed, in one way or another. In fact, anyone who might have an interest in Anna's school career is welcome to have a look at her school reports.[2] On the surface, everyone in Anna's surroundings are forming their own *understanding* of what Anna is like. Going deeper, these experiences are uniquely Anna's, for her to *live*. She learns that "slow" and "stupid" are synonyms in the teacher's mind, she learns that she is stupid and not worth the teacher's time and effort. In the eyes of the teacher, she becomes not only insignificant but also in a way invisible:

When they approach me they see only my surroundings themselves, or figments of their imagination – indeed, everything, and anything except me. That invisibility to which I refer occurs because of a peculiar disposition of the eyes of those with whom I come in contact. A matter of the construction of their *inner* eyes, those eyes with which they look through their physical eyes upon reality (Ellison, 1947/1972, p. 7)

When Piaget (1951) raises the question about children's conceptions of internal and external vision, he shares with us a childhood recollection from one of his collaborators.

When I was a little girl I used to wonder how it was that when two looks met they did not somewhere hit one another. I used to imagine the point to be half-way between the two people. I used also to wonder why it was one did not feel someone else's look, on the cheek for instance if they were looking at one's cheek (p. 48).

The image of looks meeting halfway between two people is both an intriguing and a striking description of intersubjectivity, and relationality. Authentic pedagogy begins with the meeting of looks, an encounter between the eye of the teacher and the eye of the child, thus creating a place and grounding for the child's growth. When we are engaged face-to-face in what Buber (1958) calls an I-Thou-relation in which we strive for mutual understanding, a We-relationship can be said to be created. This We-relation constitutes an empathic participation in each other's lives, even if for a limited period. The meeting-point for the look of the thoughtful teacher and the anticipating child would constitute such a we-relation. At best, there are pedagogical moments when such a relation rises like a soap bubble, almost tangible, between child and teacher. In reality, numerous children never get to experience such a We-relation with their teachers. These children feel the teacher's look as an arrow passing over or beside them.

Oddly enough, the passing look of the teacher could also be an arrow straight into the child's being. For Anna, the distressing experience during her math lessons is not simply that her teacher ignores her. The look of the teacher, which says that Anna is not worth his time and effort, goes straight into Anna's being. Indeed, the look does not remain on the surface of her cheek, it penetrates the skin. The skin becomes transparent. In fact, Anna becomes transparent, defenceless to the teacher's penetrating arrow, vulnerable to the teacher's judgement.

Hermeneutic phenomenology teaches us to reflect on students' experiences as well as our own experiences in the classroom. In that way, a hermeneutic phenomenological attitude can offer deeper understanding of our pedagogical practice. It offers knowledge, which creates teachers with "green trees" in their hearts where "singing birds" can dwell and grow.

WALKING ALONG OR LEADING?

The Dutch scholar van den Berg (1961) holds that the relationship between adults and children appears to him to be "the first and most important subject of pedagogy" (p. 20). One could, of course, argue that what van den Berg says is quite trivial in it obviousness; teacher and student are thrown into a relationship, willingly or not. However, the *nature* of that relationship needs to be examined and explored.

As tradition has it in Sweden, we are seated in church to celebrate graduation day. The first eight pews are reserved for our ninth graders. There they are, class by class. They are unusually quiet today. Perhaps they are tired after yesterday's trip to the amusement park, or perhaps they feel like I do, that the surrounding atmosphere creates an inner stillness. After the sermon, hymns, and the headmaster's speech it is time to hand over the diplomas. In alphabetical order, the classes together with their head teachers are called to the altar rails. As they are all waiting in line, I watch my colleague, Thomas. Tall, muscular and with shaved head, a former UN soldier. He joined the teaching staff last autumn and within a year he has created stability in a class, which for several years was known as unruly. Now his last task is to hand over the diplomas and with a handshake send his students into the world. As he hands over the diplomas, Thomas smiles, tousles their hair, or simply puts his hand on their shoulder. Most of his students hug him, totally indifferent to how that intimate act is perceived by others in the church. Some of the girls sob and even the boys, who have a reputation of being wild, look decisively moved when they face Thomas. When the class and Thomas return to their pews, I see how Thomas bends his head and swiftly wipes his eyes.

How can we understand what happened between the teacher and his students in the church? What kind of relationship do they have and by whom has it been created? Was the students' affectionate goodbye to Thomas a sign of thankfulness for having learned the German prepositions or how to use English adverbs correctly? Obviously not: It is more likely to be about something that we have difficulties to put words to.

When Bollnow (1989) stresses the importance of mood and feeling, he follows in the steps of Heidegger (1962), who claimed that mood is the fundamental ground from which life develops. Embedded in the overall responsibilities of teaching, to carefully guide the child through childhood into adolescence and adulthood, rests the responsibility to cultivate an atmosphere of *trust*. This sense of trust and security is created, primarily, in the home. Parents are the first persons to create a sheltered domain, in which the child can safely grow. As the child gradually moves from this shelter, and reaches out for the larger world outside home, parents rely on the teachers to safeguard their child. If parents and teachers provide a safe haven, then, what was once the child's trust in one specific person will almost certainly develop into a generalized trust in life. The child's trust in the teacher – and later in the world – is, however, reciprocal. That is, the teacher must concurrently have trust in the child and his or her abilities to learn and develop. By highlighting the reciprocal relationship, Bollnow distinguishes *trust* from *confidence*. Confidence, he argues, is one-sided and relates to specific, mostly cognitive abilities. For instance the teacher – or the child – may be confident that certain assignments will be satisfyingly accomplished. Trust, on the other hand, is relational and demands a response and refers to the emotional bond between teacher and child. Both trust and confidence is crucial to the feeling of *belief*. "The belief of the educator strengthens the positive faculties which he or she presumes present in the child" (Bollnow, 1989, p. 25).

Even though, the pedagogical relationship is a reciprocal one, it is at the same time an asymmetrical relationship, in which the teacher is responsible for the student's intellectual and emotional growth. In many curricula, the notion *responsibility* has a wide denotation, from a general attitude towards pupils to more mundane and practical matters. Teachers can, indeed, learn what their responsibilities are, but to *learn about* responsibility is not equivalent to *exercising* responsibility, and it is something quite different from *living* it. To exercise and to live responsibility is to embody nurturing in such a way that each child under the teacher's care experience respecting and honoring recognition:

> Good pedagogy is mutual identification but from asymmetric, or unequal positions. Good pedagogy always indicates a movement towards suspension of these conditions, towards exceeding of borders. Passion and motivation do not arise in such relationships. They *are* passion and motivation. (Börjeson, 2000, p. 37, *my translation*)

In an earlier study on lived experiences of school failure (Henriksson, 2008), the students showed that they were highly aware of the pedagogical relationship between themselves and their teachers. However, they did not articulate any frustration over an asymmetrical relationship. Quite the contrary. They – more or less explicitly – expressed irritation over a too symmetrical relationship. They had repeatedly encountered teachers, who tried hard to become their friends; who did not take on responsibility, and teachers, who were more lost and bewildered in the classroom than the students. But students did not want teachers to be their friends, but they *did* want them to be friendly; students did not want teachers to take care of every aspect of their lives, but they *did* want them to be caring; students did not expect teachers to understand everything, but they *did* want them to be understanding. To be friendly, caring and understanding are some of the teacher qualities which we cannot plan for the same way we plan the content of a lesson, nor can we teach it to our students as an instructional object.

Some teachers, however, seem to have an intuitive understanding for how and when to bond with students:

> Although Tommy learned how to read and write by using the computer, his patience did not last long. He needed to move about. This particular day we were walking down a country road, which was popular among riders. As we strolled along, Tommy discovered a huge amount of dung beetles, which was busy munching on horse manure. Tommy stopped, bent down and picked up one of the beetles, while he carefully examined its bluish-black, blazing wing sheaths. Being a teacher, I took the opportunity to give Tommy a spoonful of information – biological as well as historical – about the lives of dung beetles. To Tommy, my chatting was probably like background radio music – nice company, but nothing to pay attention to. I was deep into Egyptian religion and myths when Tommy said: "Listen!" Somewhat annoyed I stopped talking and wondered what this was all about. "Listen," he said again and then by letting air out between his teeth he made a faint sigh. He held the beetle next to our faces, which by now were close together. He made a faint sigh again and waited. Suddenly the beetle answered with an almost similar sigh! Tommy sighed again and the beetle answered. Beneath its blue wing sheaths, the dung beetle moved its wings and produced the same singular sound, that Tommy had used to call to it. Time stopped, and an entrance to another life suddenly became visible. For a moment, an innate happiness and exaltation filled us. We talked to several dung beetles, and laughed at our discovery. I felt as if we were the first humans to communicate with extraterrestrials. I have often thought of this incident in relation to my pedagogical mission. There I was, trying to teach Tommy about dung beetles while the child walks next to me talking to the beetle. By coincidence, maybe due to a pure and open childlike mind, Tommy did – to my knowledge – what no one had done before him.

"How do you find knowledge and insights? Is there a better teacher than life itself?" this teacher asks himself.

When Moustakas (1994) introduces his phenomenological orientation, called heuristic[3] research, he says:

> It refers to a process of internal search through which one discovers the nature and meaning of experience and develops methods and procedures for further investigation and analysis. The self of the researcher is present throughout the process and, while understanding the phenomenon with increasing depth, the researcher also experiences growing self-awareness and self-knowledge. Heuristic processes incorporate creative self-processes and self-discoveries. (p. 17)

Moustakas illustrates the intrinsic link between pedagogical research and everyday-pedagogical practice. Not only in research do we need to take a heuristic stance to the subject of our inquiry; to an even higher degree, we need a heuristic attitude to gain a deeper understanding of pedagogical practice. To understand the nature of pedagogy and to experience self-awareness and self-knowledge means to let go of taken-for-granted attitudes, to honestly see students and listen to their experiences, and to let yourself be a part of life as it unfolds.

"FROM THE OUTSIDE OR THE INSIDE?"

It is said that when the Greek god Zeus was suckled by the horn of a goat, Amalthaea, the horn broke off and instead of milk, it was filled with fruit or whatever the owner of the horn desired – riches in abundance. Some teachers *are* owners of horns of plenty, horns brimming with different fruits for each unique child. Unfortunately, there are also teachers, whose horns have gone dry; teachers who feel that neither they nor their students have anything to offer.

Although I finished my teacher training almost thirty years ago, I remember the focus on method (anything from how to make nice, multiple-layer overheads to strategies for teaching literature). I also remember our lectures on pedagogy and how they dealt exclusively with children's psychological and mental development (Piaget, Kohlberg, Maslow, etc.). On one occasion our professor retold a story from a second grade classroom: The teacher had asked the class to draw a picture of a human face. When one boy raised his hand and asked: "Should I paint it from the outside or from the inside?" he was scolded by his teacher: "Don't ask stupid questions, Marcus. From the outside, of course!" I vaguely recall that our professor thought that the boy's question was a nice example of some stage in a child's mental development. What I vividly recall is how odd and excluded I felt when I could not join my fellow student teachers in their laughter. For me the story was not a laughing matter. To me, the boy's question posed some important pedagogical questions but it also touched the fundamentals of ontology and epistemology. "From the outside or from the inside?" Obviously, Marcus was addressed by the task to draw a face; the face being a thing "thinging" (Heidegger, 2000) – when allowed to emerge as itself before one ...." The abundance of that question! How could a teacher hear this question without welcoming the world hidden within this "gift"? Why did the teacher not experience "a sense of something *happening*, something *arriving*, something starting to open up, something stirring, becoming enlivened, lively" (Jardine et al., 2006, p. 40)? How did this child encounter the task of drawing a human head? What images came before him? What space did he and the thing dwell in and what did he experience when the thing was "thinging"? In thinging, Heidegger (2001) says, "the thing stays the united four, earth and sky, divinities and mortals in the simple onefold of their self-unified fourfold (pp. 175-176), "the fouring presences as the wordling of world" (p. 178). Heidegger goes on to describe that within these united four are fruits, water, rock, plant and animal; here we find the sun's path, the course of the moon, the glitter of the stars, the year's seasons, and the blue depth of the ether. For Marcus, who was addressed by the face, the thing was "thinging"; it had not been fixed, locked in, determined. It was also not reducible to a particular developmental stage or genetic epistemology. The teacher, on the other hand seems to be deaf to the "thinging" of the thing; it is already been made definite, nicely wrapped in scarcity. When the teacher sneered at Marcus' question, was he aware of the world he denied the young boy to dwell in?

While this may, for some teachers, be nothing but a nice teacher story that educators love to tell each other; it may for other teachers be an epiphany experienced as a call to act upon the question. In the hands of a sensitive pedagogue, the anecdote transgresses the boundaries of an amusing story and imposes an ethical demand, brought forward by a question from a child. We could thus argue that in pedagogical practice when teachers are unexpectedly confronted ("From the outside or the inside?") they are forced to respond to this calling on the spur of the moment. The response may be wise; it may be in the best interest of the child but it may just as well be unwise, unreflected, and – at worst – harmful. Now, on the surface, the question posed by the boy is nothing more than a question of how to draw or a way for the boy to check that he has understood the task. But there is so much more at stake here:

> By our very attitude to one another we help to shape one another's world. By our attitude to the other person we help to determine the scope and hue of his world; we make it large or small, bright or drab, rich or dull, threatening or secure. We help to shape his world not by theories and views but by our very attitude toward him. Herein lies the unarticulated and one might say anonymous demand that we take care of the life which trust has placed in our hands. (Løgstrup, 1971, p. 19)

By scolding the boy for asking a stupid question, his teacher did indeed make the boy's world small, drab, and dull. No space for "adventure of inquiry ... rejoicing in the abundance and intricacy of the world, entering into its living questions, living debates, living inheritances" (Jardine et al, 2006, p. 101). We can only imagine how many ways of the world were left uncovered, unexplored in the teachers "Don't ask stupid questions, Marcus. From the outside, of course!"

Today's – and even more so, tomorrow's – world needs people, who are not just trained for a specific profession. We need human beings who are innovative, creative, open-minded, and caring human beings, who take responsibility for our world and see fellow human beings as equals. For that, school has no subject, teachers no curricula, governments no educational policy. The only way we can foster and educate the younger generation is for teacher education to foster and educate teachers, who are what Buber (1993) calls *whole human beings*. Whole human beings, who would love to see a head from the inside, who do not find any questions stupid, who do not make children's world small, drab, and dull, and who create space for adventures of inquiry.

As a philosophy, as well as a research orientation, hermeneutic phenomenology teaches us to open our minds to wonder; to appreciate the unexpected; to keep an open mind and to begin to cherish what is unique in every human being.

CAPS AND BREASTS

The ethical responsibility, discussed here is two-fold: First is the assumption that a teacher should think, act, and embody morally sound values. Second, that it is the teacher's task to instill values that are equally sound in his or her students. Students' possible cognitive shortcomings are hardly ever the main source for teachers' anger. What seems to ignite the teachers' anger is the students' non-compliancy to school rules and regulations. "The teacher's wrath, in other words, is more frequently triggered by violations of institutional regulations and routines, than by signs of his students' intellectual deficiencies" (Jackson, 1968, p. 35). In order to maintain order in the classroom, teachers – often together with their pupils – decide on what rules to have in school. In spite of the rules agreed upon, teachers often find themselves in dilemmas:

> I let my eyes wander up and down the rows of desks, so I can jot down who's absent.
>
> As I do so, much to my surprise, I notice that Martin, a quiet and very compliant boy has decided to break the "no-caps-in-the-classroom" rule. Although puzzled, I decide to ignore it and instead start the lesson. Once I have put the students to work, I go down to Martin, lean forward and quietly ask: "Why the cap, Martin? You know it's against the rules." He looks up, blushes, and quietly says: "Sir, I did not have time to wash my hair this morning." As he offers his explanation, he glances towards the desk where Molly sits. Yes, I have noticed that something is "going on" between Martin and Molly. I have a few seconds to decide what to do. As I look at Martin, I am unexpectedly transported back in time. I remember the wonderful – and painful – feeling of being a teenager in love and I simply cannot find it in my heart to force him to take off his cap. Instead I say: "Next time, get up earlier!"

From the moment he spots the cap on Martin's head, the teacher has at least two options. He can follow the rules strictly, and loudly demand: "Take off your cap, Martin!" Or he can simply ignore it. But instead he seems to "choose" a middle road. Regardless of which road he takes, his action gives rise to a plethora of ethical questions about what is appropriate for Martin, for the class, and for his own goals as a teacher. For now, I will leave these questions open, with the hope that this anecdote will be food for thought.

Sometimes, school rules seem to have less to do with the students' moral growth than with adults' own interests. They are often "meant to make daily decisions easier for the teacher by regulating how issues are to be solved to maintain order" (Colnerud, 1995, p. 126). Rules, which pervade and surround the classroom, are also likely to be general or even self-evident: "Raise your hand, if you want to speak," "Do not scribble on the white board," "No talking when the teacher talks," etc. However, I have yet to encounter a classroom rule which says: "Do not grab girls' breasts":

> Our ward is mixed; we have both girls and boys, who are at a point in life when hormones take over common sense. Lucas – charming and witty but hyperactive boy – often has mood swings which are difficult to predict. He also moves very quickly and he has no impulse control whatsoever. One day while we were visiting the public library, his emotions got the better of him and he sneaked up behind one of the girls and grabbed her breasts. I was so surprised that I could not even react. The girl, however, found the incident rather pleasant. Once I had recovered and managed to get him off the girl, I took him aside and told him that what he just did was completely unacceptable. I tried to explain how disrespectful his behavior was and that he could not treat girls like that. He did not listen, just kept wandering about in the library. Back at the institution, I informed the staff of the incident. Their first question was: "How much did you deduct?" The policy on our ward is to deduct money from their allowance when they behave badly; for instance five dollars for swearing, ten dollars for getting up late, etc. I was so surprised at the response that I could hardly believe what I heard. The question: "How much did you deduct?" translates: "How much does it cost to grab a girl's breasts?"My answer was that I did not deduct anything. Frankly, I did not know the going rate for grabbing girls' breasts! I did not dare put a price on his action. What if he thinks that it is worth it?

Lucas gives the notion *worthwhileness* a somewhat new twist. While Jackson, Boostrom, and Hansen (1993) refers to *worthwhileness* as teachers' and students' deliberation on whether something is worth learning or not, Lucas might, as his teacher fears, ponder whether he can afford to grab a girl's breasts. How much is it worth in money and effort?

Would a written rule forbidding boys (or girls, for that matter) from grabbing girls' breasts have stopped Lucas? I seriously doubt it. Will the teacher's verbal correction stop him from repeating his action? That too, I doubt.

Dewey (1909/1975) argues that training

> is pathological when stress is laid upon correcting wrong-doing instead of upon forming habits of positive service. Too often the teacher's concern with the moral life of pupils takes the form of alertness for failures to conform to school rules and routines. (p. 15)

Would agreeing with Dewey's argument help the teacher to stop Lucas from grabbing girls' breasts? Again, I doubt it. So, how, then, can teachers guide their students into desired and accepted ethical behaviour – without simply relying on allowance deductions, on written rules, or on the direct application of theoretical knowledge?

Buber (1993) holds that it is a fatal mistake for a teacher to *teach* morality, since the student perceives what the teacher says as a sort of marketable knowledge currency. Morality would then be treated as a commodity, subject to the laws of commerce, and as such impossible as a foundation for character building.

> The single thing that may influence the student as a whole being is the teacher himself or herself as a whole being. The pedagogue does not have to be a moral genius to foster character but he has to communicate with his fellow beings in a direct way; his vitality beams towards them and has its strongest and purest influence precisely when he is not explicitly thinking about influencing them. (Buber, 1993, p. 108, my translation)

We often assume that teachers act in morally appropriate ways, that teachers recognize that they stand in relations of influence to the children they teach, that teachers act in the best interests of the child. But teachers do not automatically become noble moral models just because they work with children. When discussing man as moral being, Kant (2000) brings into play the notions *value*, *price* and *dignity*. Speaking exclusively in terms of value and price, every individual has a basic value. Accordingly, and depending on the utility of a person's skills and abilities, one person could be said to have a higher value than another. And this value can change according to the demand for his or her skills and abilities. A person thus becomes a commodity, useful for a certain purpose, and of greater or lesser value depending on the market. However, Kant says:

> /.../ a human being regarded as a *person*, that is, as the subject of a morally practical reason, is exalted above any price; for as a person (*homo noumenon*) he is not to be valued merely as a means to the ends of others or even to his own ends, but as an end in himself, that is, he possesses a *dignity* (an absolute inner worth) by which he exacts *respect* for himself from all other rational beings in the world (p. 186).

Hansen (1986) draws a pedagogical parallel from Kant's definition of man as a moral being. Education may have a price, a pure instrumental value, based on utilitarian principles, and as such it serves one or another externally defined end. Through the demands that society imposes on their citizens, and consequently school on their students, this utilitarian approach has become dominant: Education is seen as adding value to human capital (i.e. students), and this value is then realized, assessed, and revalued according to market conditions. This results, in turn in a discourse of consequences, which judge moral worth or moral action based on consequences. In this sense, "teaching becomes a moral endeavour solely with respect to its consequences" (p. 830). But education, Hansen continues, is more than an end since it is "a moral practice that partakes in the idea of dignity" (p. 830).

Not all morally inappropriate behaviour is as blatant as Lucas'. Much of what goes on in classrooms is subtle, invisible, inaudible and often not even intended – escaping the attention of the teacher. If actions do not receive the teacher's attention, the students' lived experiences are bound to remain silent.

The narrative about Lucas in the library was the result of an assignment that I gave to a group of teachers at juvenile institutions in Sweden. My specific request was: "Write a story about one moment when you experienced an ethical dilemma."

Did the teacher who shared her experience think, act, and embody moral soundness? I think we can agree that she did. Did she also instill equally sound values in Lucas? That we do not know. Judging from the narrative, we have good reason to doubt it. What I do know, is that the teacher, by sharing her experience with her colleagues initiated a pedagogical discussion of what it means for a teacher to be a moral model. I also know that the question of ethics and what is morally good had been a subject of reflection and discussion among the teachers in this school for a long period. Hermeneutic phenomenology had given them the tools and the language to do so.

WHAT WE HAVE BEEN WAITING FOR

It is time to recapitulate the connection between hermeneutic phenomenolog as research method and pedagogical practice. Why do I hold that this is what teachers have been waiting for?

Hermeneutic phenomenology could be described as a "reality check." It gives us the tools to discover what goes on, moment-by-moment, in different corners of the classroom. As Dewey (1964) says:

> It is sometimes supposed that it is the business of the philosophy of education to tell what education *should* be. But the only way of deciding what education should be, at least, the only way which does not lead us into the clouds, is discovery of what actually takes place when education really occurs. (p. 3)

Hermeneutic phenomenology is interested in lived experiences; it takes human experiences seriously; it takes a bottom-up perspective on pedagogical issues and as such is a democratic way of doing research. Simultaneously, a hermeneutic phenomenological perspective on pedagogy can promote ethical action in the classroom.

Hermeneutic phenomenology can also be described as the "missing link" between theory and practice, between governmental edicts and their demands for results on the one hand, and every-day classroom interaction on the other. Long before teachers are forced – by curricula and school bureaucracy – to reduce students and their action to theoretical concepts and medical diagnoses, they see and encounter children and teenagers in different circumstances, with different needs, dreams, problems. Hermeneutic phenomenology lets researchers and teachers alike see the unique person as a living, breathing subject. The student, who wonders who is walking the dog; the teenager, who talks with dung beetles; the child, who wants to paint the head from the inside; even the impulsive pubescent, grabbing the breasts of a nearby girl. They all teach us to think, feel and act with circumspection in the duration of the moment.

Hermeneutic phenomenology works against compartmentalizing: It is neither simply subjective nor objective, it does not seek to derive the particular from the universal nor does it work to isolate our private life from our professional life. Its interest is in our lifeworld is a whole. Its ideal, as Galvin and Todres (2007) says, "a seamless way of being" (p. 33), in which the head (thinking), hand (doing), and heart (feeling) come together in harmony. Teachers, who are asked to embody this seamless way of being, most probably also agree with the Maori song, that people are "the greatest thing in the world."

Hermeneutic phenomenology advocates a language which is expressive and which resembles the language we use. Language, simultaneously, needs to be innovative and lead us back to forgotten meanings. Language (even) in academic articles – hermeneutic phenomenological or otherwise – needs to have *verve*, i.e. it must show energy and enthusiasm in its expression of ideas; it has to show vitality and liveliness; it needs to have a sparkle.

In hermeneutic phenomenology students' and teachers' lived experience descriptions – if well written – inevitably invoke a feeling of "rightness"; they give us a sense of recognition that is not a matter of one-to-one correspondence, but that involves a kind of transposition of the mind. However, experiential accounts do not "prove" anything, no matter how much *verve* they have. They do not *point out* the right method, the best technique, the most desirable ethics – or *the* truth, but they *point to*[4] something. "The real phenomenologist must make it a point to be systematically modest" (Bachelard, 1994, p. xxv).

The Jain wisdom of *Anekant* or Many-Sidedness is a complex idea, which avers that truth has multiple facets, and depends on the position of the seeker and their assumptions and world-views, explicit or implicit. This is not the same as relativism, where there is no objective truth, but neither is it purely rational, or purely spiritual or purely emotional. The Jains allow all these perspectives to cohere and in their philosophy of "maybe-ism," *Syadvada*, show that truth can be tentative but that it must be sincere, non-violent, and respectful of all living beings and their rights to co-exist.

It can be transformative to recognize what one has been waiting for. A phenomenological attitude or attunement has the potential to show us what we earlier did not see or understand. Jenner (2000) uses a metaphor to describe how life can be brought to a sudden standstill, when the unforeseen happens:

> A man who lives by a waterfall does not "hear" the fall; it is such a familiar sound that it goes unnoticed. Yet, he notices the cry of the wild geese in the sky above when they fly through the autumn night. But let's say that the waterfall should freeze to ice over night – then he notices the difference in an instant. (p. 38, my translation)

Low key as it is, hermeneutic phenomenology has the potential of being a "freezer of waterfalls." It can silence the rush and roar in our everyday environment, and allow us to suddenly see our students and ourselves with new eyes, or perhaps just see and start to question what we take for granted.

NOTES

[1] The painting was not made to illustrate the Malay saying but when I saw it the first time, I immediately thought of the pedagogical relation between teacher and student – and the Malay saying. For more paintings by Dorit Riley, go to: www.doritriley.com.

[2] In Sweden, school reports are public documents.

[3] From the Greek word *heuriskein* meaning to discover or to find.

⁴ *Point out* and *point to* are notions, which Gadamer (2002) employs to differentiate between interpretation and understanding.

REFERENCES

Bachelard, G. (1994). *The poetics of space. The classic look at how we experience intimate places.* (M. Jolas, Trans.) Boston, MA: Beacon Press. (Original work published 1958).

Bollnow, O.F. (1989). Preliminary exploration of the notion of a pedagogical atmosphere (M. van Manen and P. Mueller, Trans.). *Phenomenology + Pedagogy*, 7, 5-63. (Original work published 1962.)

Buber, M. (1958). *I and thou* (W. Kaufman, Trans.). Edinburgh: T. & T. Clark. (Original work published 1923.)

Buber, M. (1993). *Om uppfostran* (Lars W. Freij, Trans.) Ludvika: Dualis. (Original work published 1953.)

Börjeson, B. (2000). *Om lusten och viljan att lära – några reflektioner.* SOU 2000:19.

Colnerud. G. (1995). *Etik och praktik i läraryrket. En empirisk studie av lärares yrkesetiska konflikter i grundskolan.* Stockholm: HLS.

Dewey, J. (1909/1975). *Moral principles in education.* Carbondale: Southern Illinois University Press.

Dewey, J. (1964). The need for a philosophy of education. In R. Archambault (1974), *John Dewey on education.* Chicago: University of Chicago Press.

Ellison, R. (1947/1972). *Invisible man.* Harmondsworth: Penguin.

Gadamer, H.-G. (2002). *The relevance of the beautiful and other essays.* (N. Walker, Trans.). Cambridge: Cambridge University Press. (Original work published 1977).

Galvin, K. & Todres, L. (2007). The Creativity of 'Unspecialization:' A Contemplative Direction for Integrative Scholarly Practice. In *Phenomenology & Practice*, Volume 1, (2007), No. 1, pp. 31–46.

Hansen, D.T. (1986). Teaching as a moral activity. In Richardson, V. (1986). (Ed.). *Handbook of research on teaching.* Chicago: Chicago University Press.

Heidegger, M. (1962). *Being and time.* (J. Macquarrie and E. Robinson, Trans.) New York: Harper and Row. (Original work published 1926).

Heidegger, M. (2001). *Poetry, language, thought.* (A. Hofstadter, Trans.). New York: Harper & Row. (Original work published 1971).

Heidegger, M. (2000). *Introduction to metaphysics.* (R. Manheim, Trans.). New Haven & London: Yale University Press. (Original work published 1953).

Henriksson, C. (2008). *Living away from blessings. School failure as lived experience.* London, Ontario: The Althouse Press.

Halling, S. (2008). *Intimacy, transcendence, and psychology: closeness and openness in everyday life.* New York: Palgrave Macmillan.

Husserl, E. (1983). *Ideas pertaining to a pure phenomenology and to a phenomenological philosophy. First book* (F. Kersten, Trans.). The Hague: Martinus Nijhoff. (Original work published 1913).

Jackson, P.W. (1990). *Life in classrooms.* New York: Teachers College Press.

Jackson, P.W., Boostrom, R.E., & Hansen, D.T. (1993). *The moral life of schools.* San Francisco: Jossey-Bass.

Jardine, D.W., Friesen, S., & Clifford, P. (2006). *Curriculum in abundance.* New Jersey: Lawrence Erlbaum.

Jenner, H. (2000). *Se oss i berättelsen.* Vaxholm: Bjurner & Bruno.

Kant, E. (2000). *The metaphysics of morals.* (M. Gregor, Trans.). Cambridge: Cambridge University Press. (Original work published 1785.)

Luijpen, W.A. (1960). *Existential phenomenology.* Pittsburgh: Duquesne University Press.

Løgstrup, K.E. (1971). *The ethical demand* (T.I. Jensen, Trans.). Philadelphia: Fortress Press. (Original work published 1969.)

Merleau-Ponty, M. (2001). *Phenomenology of perception* (C. Smith, Trans.). London: Routledge. (Original work published 1962).

Moustakas, C. (1994). *Phenomenological research methods*. London: Sage

Online Etymology Dictionary (2011). www.etymonline.com.

Piaget, J. (1951). *The child's conception of the world* (J. and A. Tomlinson, Trans.). Lanham, MD: Littlefield Adams. (Original work published 1927)

Pinar, W.F. (2006). *The synoptic text today and other essays. Curriculum development after the reconceptualization*. New York: Peter Lang.

Todres, L. (2007). *Embodied enquiry: phenomenological touchstones for research, psychotherapy and spirituality*. Basingstoke, Hampshire: Palgrave Macmillan.

Van den Berg, J. H. (1961). *The changing nature of man. Introduction to a historical psychology*. (H. F. Croes, Trans.). New York: Dell Publishing. (Original work published 1956.)

Van Manen, M. (1990/1997). *Researching lived experience. Human science for an action sensitive pedagogy*. Ontario: Althouse Press.

Van Manen, M. (1991/1993). *The tact of teaching*. Ontario: Althouse Press.

Zahavi, D. (2003). *Husserl's phenomenology*. Stanford: Stanford University Press.

Öquist, O. (1992). *Tyst erfarenhet*. Stockholm: Carlssons.

PART III

A "Science of Examples":
Illustration and Adaptations

ANNA KIROVA AND MICHAEL EMME

8. IMMIGRANT CHILDREN'S BODILY ENGAGEMENT IN ACCESSING THEIR LIVED EXPERIENCES OF IMMIGRATION

Creating Poly-Media Descriptive Texts

INTRODUCTION

The phenomenological understanding of the body, which Merleau-Ponty (1963) calls the "living envelope of our actions" (p. 188), is central to the human lifeworld, and thus central to phenomenological method. For him, the body and behavior are bearers of meaning that are known immediately as well as reflectively by the body. "The body is the basis for reflection and there is no possibility of pure reflection" (Merleau-Ponty, 1962, p. 62). Shapiro (1985) points out that the study of language and the development of linguistic methods in the past few decades have influenced all fields including phenomenology and have resulted in an "assertion of the primary and pervasive influence of language in experience" (p. xiv). He argues against the exclusive use of language-centered reflection as the core of the phenomenological method of inquiry. Instead, his work attempts to show how an "investigator can avail himself or herself of reflective modes and moves that are largely explicable in terms of a phenomenology of the body" (p. xvii), which he defines as the embodiment of our consciousness.

In this chapter, we too acknowledge that reflective practices grounded predominantly in language present phenomenology with a dilemma; human phenomena are lived through our bodies, but are typically described through language, which in turn is supposed to invoke an embodied response as part of the process of understanding. We explore the role of the lived body in meaningful understanding beyond linguistic conceptualization in phenomenologically oriented inquiries. In this exploration, we consider the role of visuality (i.e., still photography) and enactment (i.e., tableau) as possibilities for accessing meaning beyond language-bound descriptions of the phenomenon of moving childhoods – that is, children's lived experiences of immigration. We present an example of a method that bridges hermeneutic phenomenology and arts-based research methodology (i.e., fotonovela), which was developed specifically to engage immigrant children bodily in accessing their lived experiences of their first day of school in the host country and in the development of a multimedia text *showing* these experiences.

We want to stress here that this fotonovela method represents only one phase of phenomenological inquiry – gathering experiential accounts or lived experience descriptions in investigating childhood phenomena. The focus on this phase of a phenomenologically oriented inquiry is based on our work with young children over the years. This work has shown that commonly used methods of collecting

N. Friesen et al. (eds.), Hermeneutic Phenomenology in Education, 141–162.

experiential accounts based on oral or written descriptions of lived experiences is limiting as children rarely produce "thick descriptions" of their lived experiences if they rely solely on language to do so. As van Manen (1994) puts it, "Especially with young children this [writing] is a handicap. Often educational researchers like to ask children to write about their experiences or to keep a log or diary, and they end up being somewhat disappointed with the material they were able to generate from children this way" (p. 64). Although in general "it is easier to talk than to write about personal experience" (p. 67), this is not the case for children who are still learning the language of their host country, and with whom researchers do not share a common language. We argue that fotonovela is a particularly suitable method for engaging children in developing polymedia descriptive texts about their lived experiences.

SITUATING THE QUESTION OF THE BODY

Of particular interest and relevance to the method of inquiry presented here is Shapiro's (1985) explanation of how any situation invites a person to take a certain course of action, to move in a certain way with respect to it (e.g., playing a game, going through a door, using a computer, etc.) that also has a bodily aspect. This movement does not mean that a person is always aware in an analytical or language-based way of how a situation requires a bodily response or what this bodily response may look like. Quite the opposite, it is my body that is always with me; I am in it first and then in the world of objects around me that I may or may not know, but could encounter through my body. Gendlin (1997a) says, "The body knows the situation directly .... A living body knows its environment by being in it" (p. 27). This is the taken-for-granted level at which humans act and experience before attaching language to their actions or experiences.

Yet some life experiences change the pre-reflective, lived familiarity with the world or the potential for action that one's body had in a known world and bring the experience of the body into the realm of consciousness. To use Shapiro's (1985) words, some situations "invite a person" to take a certain course of action with which he or she is not familiar so the body's movement is changed with effort, and thus involves some level of nonverbal conscious participation. In this chapter we argue that immigration is one such experience – an experience that interrupts the familiarity of the lifeworld that we associate with the feelings of "normal" in the "home-world" (Steinbock, 1995) and brings to the forefront the "abnormality" of the "alien-world," the unfamiliar or even the phenomenon of non-recognition. We argue that this experience brings immigrant children's awareness of their bodies to a conscious level as they encounter the impossibility of trusting the outcomes of their otherwise familiar actions. These actions and unexpected outcomes might include, for example, the experience of approaching others and expecting to join them in an ongoing game, or simply speaking of achieving a particular goal. By not being able to count on the outcome of acts and of speaking in these kinds of situations we are referring not only to the fact that immigrant children initially speak a language that no one outside the home understands,

142

resulting in incomprehension or misapprehension. Rather, we refer also to the embodied, performative nature of such communication – and the fact that such embodied performances, despite their sometimes self-evident significance, are also put into question. We fully agree with Gendlin (1997b) that speaking is a "special case of body interaction" (p. 28), and that the interactional body provides a crucial grounding to language. A bodily sensed situation in relation to words "gives the words a new life" (Gendlin, 1997a, p. 8) by elevating meaning from the two-dimensionality of code and narrative to the multiple dimensions of embodied experience lived through time and space.

The following is a personal experience that illustrates the above statements about the act of speaking and the role of embodied language in understanding:

As an immigrant and adult learner of English, I am seen by many as an example of success. Not only do I make myself understood, but I am also a proficient reader and writer of English. I give public presentations and lecture at the university. Yet upon receiving a set of student evaluations a few years ago, I became aware of a strange phenomenon: I was profoundly ineffective in communicating my true intentions in my interactions with some of my students in class. It became clear to me that it was not what I said that offended the students, but how I said it. The What of the English language had to do with the accessibility of the factual meaning of the words, which regardless of my accent, was not perceived as problematic by the students. The How of my English language, that is, my tone of voice, speech rhythm, accompanying gestures, proximity to the students, movement around the room, pauses after a statement, or facial expression while listening and responding to questions, however, was not consistent with the conventions of the English language that the students expected. Thus the intended meaning of my words was lost.

When I was in the beginning stage of learning English, speaking was hard work: I first composed a simple sentence in my mother tongue and then painfully rushed though my "stored" vocabulary in English to find the words that were most appropriate or closest in meaning to use in the sentence that I held in my mind. It seemed like it took a lifetime to be able to do this, yet people were patient, polite, understanding, and accommodating. No one laughed at me. On the contrary, people filled in my half sentences trying hard to make sense of my desperate gesturing; they smiled or nodded enthusiastically and supportively. With time and practice, composing sentences became less work, and I was able to express myself with less effort. Paradoxically, however, the more fluent my spoken language became, the less accurately some native speakers understood me. I was faced with a contradiction that seemed irresolvable: my increased facility with the spoken language increased my difficulty in conveying the intended meaning. In other words, I was speaking a language fluently that I did not embody fluently. I realized that in the how of my spoken English, I remained a Bulgarian.

From this moment on, I became painfully aware of my body every time I spoke English, which is now more than 90 per cent of the day. I am trying to "see" myself speaking and trying to match my gestures and my tone of voice to what I have observed native speakers doing when they express meaning similar to what I wish to express. It is hard work again, and I am not sure that it works any better. I am always unsure of the outcome of my spoken communication in English. People who have seen me speak my mother tongue have commented that I am a "different person" when I speak it. And I certainly am. I now think mostly in English and have to spend some time thinking what words to use in Bulgarian when I talk to my mother, for example, but I do not have to think about not being Bulgarian- enough in my body language. My body is in my native language as much as the language is in my body. (Emme, Kirova, Kamau, & Kosanovich, 2006, pp.161-162)

We wonder if immigrant children have similar experiences of the how and what of the language they learn in their host country. The following recollection of a childhood experience provided by a foreign-born graduate student who was "angry at her mouth" for not being able to speak English like her classmates is a powerful example that children, too, are not only aware of the what but also the how of the new language.

I remember clearly spending long hours in our bathroom looking at myself in the mirror while trying to say the few English words I knew then. I even used my fingers to move my mouth in a different direction from the one it would normally take when forming the sounds with the hope that this time the word would come out right. I did not care that I looked ridiculous with my fingers in my mouth; the only thing I wanted was to be able to say the words like everyone else. At the beginning my mother was not worried, but when I started spending way too much time in the bathroom and used to come out of it with my mouth bright red and my eyes filled with tears, she stepped in. I was no longer allowed to close the door when I was in there. I was angry at myself, no, I was angry at my mouth and at my mother. (Personal communication, 2004)

A description provided by a child when he was 5 years old about his experience of learning English as a second language in the first few months after immigrating, shows clearly that young children are aware of their bodies as they speak another/new language, not only upon reflection on their childhood experiences, but also close to the time when the experience was lived.

It was like I couldn't control what was going to come out of my mouth. It was in my head, I could hear the appropriate sounds but when I opened my mouth, the sounds were very different from the ones I thought they would be. I was really embarrassed and didn't want to talk at all. It was like I couldn't trust myself anymore. I felt so stupid. (Kirova, 2001, p. 263)

Based on the above descriptions gathered as part of previous studies, we wonder, in the context of this study, what other circumstances make immigrant children acutely aware of their bodies. What situations invite bodily responses that require conscious efforts? A close examination of the above descriptions also made us aware of the difference in the "think-ness" of descriptions provided by adults and by young children. From a methodological point of view, then, we began to wonder how these bodily experiences can be understood. The main question we explore in this chapter is: What methods of inquiry can be used to access more directly the "embodied understanding" and, in particular, the lifeworlds of immigrant children as they leave the familiar "home world" and enter the "alien world" of a new school?

In exploring this question, we build on Gadamer's (1993) notion of understanding as the linguistic "happening" of tradition – that is, the embodied knowing of home, body, community, and meaning, but also a happening that exceeds tradition and lives it forward. We also build on Heidegger's (cited in Todres, 2007) understanding of the relationship between language and being as mysterious, for "the 'unsaid' lives always exceedingly as that which the said is about" (p. 19); being in the world always transcends its forms and intrinsically exceeds linguistic capture. Heidegger's "unsaid" is similar to Gendlin's (1997a) "mores" – that is, our bodily relational understandings exceed any precisely formulated, languaged, or other patterned ways of describing it. Thus as Gendlin (1997b) puts it, "in an embodied way, understanding is rather a procedure which includes the invitation to experience more" (p. 1).

EMBODIED INQUIRY AND PHENOMENOLOGY

The phenomenological method aims at establishing "what is typical of the phenomenon and expressing such typicality in an insightful and integrated manner" (Todres, 2007, p. 8). Based on individual experiences, phenomenology strives to describe "how the elements of a phenomenon function constitutively; how they are interrelated to form unity of the experience" (Reed, 1987, p. 102). This level of generality is known as *structure*, which once achieved is in danger of losing the individuality and particularity of each experience. The tension between the particular and the general is ongoing in phenomenological inquiry. How this tension is resolved in phenomenological descriptions affects a reader's sense of the phenomenon and, thus, of his or her understanding of it based on the description. The notion that there is always more to the experience than what is captured in its language-based description is central to the role of the lived body in understanding a phenomenon.

> Merleau-Ponty's (1962) work on the phenomenology of perception is explicit in describing how the human body is intimately present not only in all human experiences, but also in any act of understanding the structure of experiences that "are lived rather than known and therefore can never be apprehended passively; but only by living them, assuming them and discovering their immanent significance" (p. 158).

In the preface of his book *Bodily Reflective Modes: A Phenomenological Method for Psychology*, Shapiro (1985) gives a powerful example of the experience of watching a mime (in this case, the now well-known French mime Marcel Marceau), whose portrayal of a prisoner behind a prison wall evoked comprehension of the experience based on one's bodily sense of the phenomenon performed on stage. Based on the experience of seeing Marcel Marceau's performances, Shapiro suggests that our bodily knowledge of a phenomenon enables us virtually to enact a particular phenomenon. In other words, it allows us to create the space of that experience, and the relationships and world implied in it even without seeing it bodily performed. He argues that "enactment is a critical step in the explication of any given phenomenon" (p. xviii). The importance of "re-enact-ment" in understanding is also pointed by Dilthey (as cited in Todres, 2007) for whom to understand any experience, either our own or others,' is to be able "to bring it into light of one's own possibilities – and thus to re-enact it" (p. 10). Thus, the ultimate task of phenomenologically oriented inquirers is to evoke the presence of a lived experience. The question faced by researchers becomes, if there is always *more* to a phenomenon than words can capture, how else can we seek to show its presence?

We note here that in doing phenomenologically oriented research, we looked for concrete ways to apply Dilthey's (Todres, 2007) notion of "bringing to light" one's (bodily) possibilities as well as Dilthey's and Shapiro's (1985) notions of "re-enact-ing" these possibilities as a way of understanding a phenomenon. Applying these notions allowed us to attempt to show the *more* of a phenomenon – more than children, and sometimes even adults, could describe in words. In the following section, we explore the controversy surrounding the use of photography – the Greek combination of the two words, *photos* (light) and *graphein* (to draw) (Chan-fai, 2004) – in phenomenologically oriented research as a means of capturing the *more* of a phenomenon. We revisit the notion of "en-act-ment" below, by providing an example of our own work in which we used a technique borrowed from performative research – that is, tableau – to engage children in enacting their lived experiences of their first day in school.

As a performative art form, tableau is a non-language-dependent medium that "transcends the customary limits of discursive language, making coherent the knowledge and the understanding that students may not be able, at first, to express in spoken language but that, once embodied in movement, can be translated into spoken and written language" (Salvio, 1990, p. 272). In the study described here, children used their bodies – through hand gesture, facial expression, body posture, and body positioning relative to others (Wilson, 2003) – to show emotion and action. Bruner (1986) identifies action as one of the two landscapes of story. Narrative, he says "deals with the vicissitudes of human intentions" (p. 16), and to understand these intentions means to understand life. Through the use of performative gestures, which build on the natural gestures used in communication (Wilson, 2003), as well as through culturally established gestures, the children showed a range of emotions related to situations involving peers. In drama, as in play, children had to negotiate with each other to create a single vision of the meaning of a gesture or any other visual sign – "*this* stands for *that*" – in the context of the visual narrative. As an effective means for helping children create meaning and deepen their understanding of the peer relationship aspect of their school life, the process of playful dramatization was invaluable. It allowed children to be "launched on a voyage toward a truth beyond mere facts" (Wagner, 1998, p. 33).

PHOTOGRAPHY AND PHENOMENOLOGY

Ziller and Smith (1977) present a phenomenological approach that is extended to the medium of photography. They define the photograph as "a non-verbal projective technique" (p. 177), and a "unique medium which frees subject from some of the constraints of language" (p. 182), but they also acknowledge that there are similarities between verbal reports and photographs as both are "mediational" (p. 172). They point to advantages inherent in the use of photography as opposed to verbal self-reports as a phenomenological technique. "The most significant perhaps, is that the camera documents the subject's perceptual orientation with a minimum of training and without the disadvantages of the usual verbal report techniques. Thus the 'training' does not obtrude between the subject and [his] report of the phenomenon" (p. 173).

Not surprisingly, Shapiro dismisses the notion of the unproblematic objectivity of photography in phenomenological investigations. In this sense, according to Shapiro (1985), the photograph can only provide the researcher with "'pseudo-presence' of the thing itself" (p. 27). If read naturalistically, photographs can be seen as evidence for the existence of objects as they really are. Shapiro sees no value in using photography in phenomenological research. He states:

> What might appear at first glance to provide a "technology for phenomenology" (Ziller & Smith, 1977, pp. 172-182), a way of returning to and staying with a version of the thing itself by carrying away its direct impress, is yet another brand of externality. The photographic posture toward things is an imposition of self and tool that typically fails to recognize the constitutive level of that implication. Rather, as a photographer, I believe that that which is evidently "out there," separate from me and unrelated to me or to my approach, is now duplicated by an image, recorded. The imposition so denied is one that makes "having an experience identical with making a photograph of it" (Sontag, 1977, p. 24). As a habituated posture, photographing knows only its own way of living, a particular aestheticizing, passivating, and disengaged from of exteriority. (Shapiro, 1985, p. 28)

Photography as an objective tool for providing evidence of the existence of things is not supported by Hüsserl's (1960) definition of evidence either. "Evidence is, in an extremely broad sense, an'experiencing' of something that is, and is thus; it is precisely a mental seeing of something itself" (p. 52). In order for the *seeing subject* or the transcendental ego to *experience* something however, he or she must be abstracted from the world, "not aiming confusedly at something, with an empty expectant intention, but being with it itself, viewing, seeing, having insight into, it itself" (p. 93). Both Ziller and Smith (1977) and Shapiro (1985) position photography on one or the other side of the immanence-transcendence divide (Sjöholm, 2000) that has troubled philosophical inquirers generally and phenomenologists in particular. Each positioning implies a division between the embodied and the known that both Merleau-Ponty (1968) and later Irigaray (1992) contest. By focusing on the photograph as an evidentiary artifact to the exclusion of the photographic performances of subject, photographer, and viewer, Ziller and Smith as well as Shapiro lock themselves into the narrowing consideration of "a photograph as truthful representation." More broadly considered, the photographic performance can be understood as a disturbance that resonates between participants. Fully understood, drawing with light invites viewers and photographers to engage the optical and the tactile in the context of meaningful experience without consolidating each into the other. As explored in Oliver's (2001) response to Vasseleau's (1998) reading of Merleau-Ponty and Irigaray,

> If vision involves touching light, then we are touched by and touching everything around us even as we see the distance between ourselves and the world or other people in the world. The texture or fabric of vision is even more tightly woven than Merleau-Ponty's reversible flesh. It is not just that the fabric of vision is reversible between subject and object, invisible and visible, ideal and material; rather the texture of vision is the result of an interweaving of elements both distinct and intimately connected in their sensuous contact. The texture of light is what is between us and other people in the world. We are both connected and made distinct by the texture of light that wraps us in the luxury and excesses of the world. (p. 107)

In his discussion of photography in the 21st century, Flusser (2000) traces a three-millennial shift in the social construction of meaning. Flusser describes each age as committing to conventions of meaning. He sees these as moving from a stage of contestation, through entrenchment, into a stage that he describes as "magical thinking" (p. 8). From Flusser's perspective, the social contestation of meaning is vital; when the meaning of a convention slips into the realm of faith, it poses a vital problem. He focuses on the "technical image" (p. 13), with its blending of the spectacle (from a still earlier millennium) and the technical, as an important response to what he has described as "textolatry" (p. 85). By linking to, but also calling into question the code, distribution, and accessibility of language as well as the presence, open-endedness, and tactility of embodied experience, digital images as part of the photographic process represent an important site for renewing the contestation of meaning.

Photography, then, is interesting because its imperfection makes us conscious of both seeing and not seeing, of touching and not touching. What is framed out in the performance of photography is at least as interesting as what is framed in. However, more significant still is the littoral in-between space that serves as a constant reminder of the excess of experience, or the *more* for both the photographer and the viewer of a photograph. It is the promise of experience hindered by the need to negotiate the grammar of the frame that places a photograph somewhere between language and experience. Like an intertidal zone, the photographic process sheds compellingly incomplete artifacts that draw the subject, photographer, and viewer into an embodied exchange. It is in this experience of exchange that the phenomenological richness of the photographic process resides.

> We have argued elsewhere (Kirova & Emme, 2006) that photographic seeing is similar to phenomenological seeing, in that it involves "the art of showing" by drawing light onto a given object. It is the photographer's relational orientation to a given object, or a phenomenon that allows him or her to be in touch with it, and thus to evoke an embodied understanding in the reader or viewer. Thus, the notion of an image or a photograph as a visual representation of truth is no longer tolerable, and it is now replaced by a new sense of the place of visuality in meaning (Levin, 1985; Rose, 2001; Stafford, 1996).

Nevertheless, does this photographic/phenomenological *seeing* apply to one's own body? Unlike all other objects, my body is "something I *live*, and only secondarily *know*" (Moss, 1989, p. 68, emphasis in original). However, my body is not fully accessible to my visual perception, as I do not see my whole body. I have an image of my body, but it is not a matter of reflective knowledge of my body that I acquire. As Merleau-Ponty (1963) explains, before reflecting about the body, one already has familiarity with one's body that is acquired at the pre-reflective level. The process of knowing one's body begins in childhood when children reflectively appropriate their body images during the "mirror stage" (Merleau-Ponty, 1962, 1963) by recognizing, labeling, and owning it in the context of close relationships with their families. In this context, the child acquires the physical image of his or her own body through "seeing him- or herself in the others' eyes" (Moss, 1989, p. 67). The ability to recognize himself or herself in the mirror, and the experience of being recognized and identified by his or her family supports the child's formation of a solid body image and identity.

Wawrzycka's (1995) analysis of Barthes (1981) describes a focus on the concept of *punctum*, the sharp point or prick of recognition that touches us when we look at some photographs in which we can find:

> the genius of Photography and its horror: a photograph simultaneously testifies to the presence of a thing at a certain past moment and to its absolute pastness, its death. By attesting that what we see had indeed existed, Photography partakes in the economy of "Death and Resurrection." (p. 94)

Looking at an image of one's self as part of the photographic process makes both the space and the vitality between self and sign explicit. In extending Barthes' (1981) thinking to children's participation in phenomenological inquiry through fotonovela described below, our focus was on sensitivity to the child's sense of embodied recognition as experienced through a combination of tableau, photography, and digital manipulation. These significant layers of playful inquiry became an opportunity for the children to discover stories in their experience and create a hybrid language of image, body, and sometimes word for that story.

RETURNING TO THE PHENOMENON: ENGAGING THE BODY

In order to show a phenomenon as lived, a phenomenologically oriented researcher gathers experiential accounts from individuals who have experienced the phenomenon of interest, or accesses participants' written descriptions or even fictional narrative. Gathering relevant experiential accounts is only the first step toward describing the structure of the phenomenon, as others can understand it. "It is best to think of the basic method of phenomenology as the taking up a certain attitude and practicing attentive awareness to the things of the world as we live them rather than as we conceptualize them" (van Manen, 2000, p. 460). This attitude indicates a relation, an orientation to the phenomenon that allows a *return to things* as lived. The return to things that phenomenologists of all schools call for involves accessing the phenomenon, being in touch with it.

149

When I take part in the phenomenon that I am seeking to understand and show, I am not simply taking on what is simply given in it. Instead, as Shapiro (1985) explains, in "one moment of the same act, I impart to it. My participation is coconstitutive of the moment, situation, or phenomenon" (p. 36). Of a particular interest to the method presented below is Shapiro's explanation of the coconstitutive reentry and the role the abstractive act – for example, in phenomenological descriptions of the structure of phenomena – as "an embodied act that participate[s] in the immediate engaged moment of lived experience" (p. 31). As part of a phenomenologically oriented method that we called fotonovela, we invited the immigrant children with whom we were working to select "telling moments" of their experiences of their first day in school, and enact them as tableau that eventually became images. In this case, a fotonovela was a form of storytelling that combined the familiar framing devices, sequencing, and text balloons of the comic book with posed or candid photographs of the participants in place of pen-and-ink sketches, which we have described elsewhere (Kirova & Emme, 2006; Emme & Kirova, 2005). Whereas performance is generally accepted as a means that allows participants to depict and examine their real-life "performances," thus "providing insight into their lived experiences and their cultural world" (Conrad, 2004, p. 10), we explored enactment – a performance of tableau – both as a form of reliving the phenomenon of the first day at school in a new country, and as an abstractive act that originated in the relived phenomenon.

According to Shapiro (1985), the task of the phenomenologist is to make the "implicit structure of a phenomenon explicit by enacting it" (p. 140). For him, enactment is possible through reflection as a bodily mode that involves both the virtual feel of the bodily experience of the phenomenon and virtual conduct that leads to apprehension of the structure of the phenomenon achieved through a mode of abstraction. Shapiro refers to this virtual experience as *forming*.

> Forming is a virtual rather than an actual behavior, and its enactment occurs in abstract rather than a concrete space .... [However,] forming does not occur in the mind's eye. It is a bodily mode, a kind of doing, a virtual movement, not a species of imagination. (p. 134)

In the development of the fotonovela as a phenomenologically oriented research method, we considered children both as participants and as coresearchers; they were to provide the experiential accounts as well as create (visual) texts that captured the structure of their lived experiences of the first day in school. In other words, we intended the method to gain access to immigrant children's experiences in general – and their first day of school in particular – in a way that was not restricted to the English language. This arose as a special concern due to some of the children's limited proficiency, and because as researchers we did not share a common language with most of the children (Kirova & Emme, 2006). At the same time, we intended the method to help children reflect on their lived experiences, share these experiences among themselves in the process of performance, and, finally, share their experience with a new group of children/readers as a visual narrative based on a performance. We argue that the children's unique position in the process of inquiry allowed us to conceive enactment in a more literal sense than those described by Shapiro (1985). In fact, the conceptualization of enactment that we employed in the development of fotonovela as a research method was closer to Merleau-Ponty's (1962) and van den Berg's (1955) notions of engaging in a *return* to the phenomenon by "inhabiting" it or "being" in it.

ENACTING "BEING AT THE DOOR"

In reference to a point by Shapiro (1985) cited above about the role of situations in inviting a particular body action, we clarify here that we consider the structure of a school building itself as able to create a particular type of situation. Like a cathedral or any other public building, a school building is "a living body" (p. 115) that represents special kinds of relationships which require certain types of behaviors. Although the living relations that a school building embodies are implicitly present in everything experienced in it, it is impossible to know what the experiences are before one lives them. For example, encountering the relationships embodied in the dynamics between hallway and classroom, and the varied behaviors expected by a child while in each, can be a challenge for a refugee or immigrant child who has not experienced being in a school building. This does not mean that children lose a sense of their body as a vehicle for action – that is, a vehicle for relating to the physical world of objects through the body. Rather, the lived moment of being at the door of a classroom for the first time in an unfamiliar school building is one that invites a body action that is far from habitual and thus brings the body to the child's consciousness. Our work with the participating immigrant and refugee children over two years (Kirova & Emme, 2006) pointed to the importance of this moment in children's recollections of their first day of school. Yet the children knew more about that particular lived moment than they could tell. By inviting them to relive the phenomenon through a re-enactment of the moment of being at the door of their new classroom, we hoped that the children's bodies would remember their original experiences. We also hoped that through this enactment, they would be able to abstract some commonalities from their individual experiences, and that these would represent certain general aspects of the structure of the phenomenon that we were attempting to show.

The actual performance or act of reliving the experience of being at the door of an unknown classroom took place in the participating children's home classroom, where we offered them photographic experiences as members of the photo club. We asked the children to remember the first day of school and the moment when they came to the door of the classroom. The following questions facilitated the children's recollection of that particular moment. Were you by yourself? If not, who came with you? Was the door open? What was the first thing you remember seeing? Were there other people in the classroom, and what were they doing?

It is worth noting here that while children were bodily engaged in enacting their past experiences of being at the classroom's door, they also had the task of reflecting bodily on the experience by selecting a "telling moment," a moment that is intended to show the essence of this particular moment as they (individually) lived it. This selection of a telling moment, in turn, allowed the moment to be photographed as tableau – as "a still, silent performance that involves three dimensional representation" (Wilson, 2003, p. 375). A further description of tableau as a still image in structuring drama work clarifies that in the process, either "groups devise an image using their own bodies to crystallize a moment, idea, or theme, or an individual acts as sculptor to a group" (Neelands, 1998, p. 19). We used both the above approaches in our particular case.

As a group, the children participated bodily in the development of the moment of being at the door, and each child acted as a "sculptor" of the group, shaping his or her particular individual experience, including the assignment of roles to each of us. Thus enactment – as an element of the phenomenologically oriented fotonovela method – allowed the children both to reside bodily in the lived moment (as a return to the phenomenon) and to distance themselves from it (as an abstractive act, enabling reflection on the structure of the phenomenon). In the process, however, we did not lose sight of the fact that we were working with young children and that we needed to maintain the playful nature of performance if we wanted the children to participate in the process.

CREATING VISUAL TEXT

Comic book artist and visual theorist McCloud (1994) articulated many of the formal qualities of what Eisner (1985) called "sequential art" (cited in McCloud, 1994, p. 5). In discussing the invitation to meaning in images as they are affected by framing and text layered together, particularly when such images are sequenced with others, McCloud describes an enormously complex and flexible resource. A gesture as simple as putting two images beside each other, or changing a speech bubble to a thought bubble, can fundamentally shift the meaning. As described elsewhere (Emme, Kirova, & Cambre, 2006; Kirova & Emme, 2008), we offered immigrant children a variety of approaches to fotonovela as a way of playfully embodying their experiences as new students in a Canadian school. With children engaged in building fotonovela, the photographic and tableau processes described above were sequenced and adjusted by each child. Whether self-consciously edited or incorporated into playful creation, the visual elements were susceptible to any embodied nuance that the children brought to their engagement.

Shapiro (1985) defines a phenomenon as "the theme in the variations on a theme" (p. 53). In looking at these images from a phenomenological point of view, we suggest that they show more than variable appearances of the phenomenon; we gain a feel of the phenomenon. This general feel of the phenomenon, known as *texture,* is what affects the reader bodily and is recognized by the reader as a plausible (human) experience. "Every phenomenon intends a world … [that] has a general atmosphere or ambience or tone or style or way or physiognomy" (p. 53). In this sense, it is the *texture* that allows the reader to enact the phenomenon in the virtual, empathic sense indicated by Dilthey (as cited in Todres, 2007) and Shapiro. We suggest that the use of fotonovela, both as a performance of the lived experience and as a process of creating an image of that experience, allowed for a richer description of the phenomenon than could have been accomplished by relying on children's oral recollections alone. However, although the structure of the phenomenon of being at the door of a new classroom may be less explicit in the visual texts presented, which may in fact be enhanced by the use of language, the texture or feel of the phenomenon is communicated fully by the visual texts. Singly, and as a varied group, these nuanced choices by the children have texture.

WRITING THE TEXT/READING THE TEXT: THE ROLE OF LANGUAGE

While looking at the visual texts presented below, a phenomenologist may ask: Are they sufficiently descriptive of the phenomenon of being at the door of a new classroom? All of the children worked hard to "sculpt" the moment as they lived it, and yet do we have a sense of what they were thinking or feeling as they stopped at the door and looked in, or derived enough courage from their mother's hand on their shoulder to walk into the classroom? The structure of the building (the hallways on each floor with doors to separate rooms), as well as the situation (being in that school for the first time), invited a particular body response presented in each image. However, can we tell by looking at the images how children's previous experiences coloured that lived moment? "My body can carry the significance of an earlier moment and in that my behavior can find similarities in different objects, through them I can embody, enact, and in those cases, express metaphors" (Shapiro, 1985, p. 157). If metaphor is a "carrying over of the sense or meaning of one reality to another" (Romanyshyn, as cited in Shapiro, p, 157) then language in the form of metaphor, or another figure of speech, is a necessary step in the journey toward returning to the phenomenon as lived. However, as Todres (2007) puts it, "Even though language and experience are implicated in one another, they cannot be reduced to one another nor replace one another in the ongoing aliveness that is understanding" (p. 23). He further explains that they "both require one another as partners in a conversation, and both phases (embodying and languaging) constitute both limits and freedom in this conversation" (p. 34).

In the development of fotonovela as a research method, our next step was to ask the children to insert in their photograph a thought balloon – a common device used in comic books to indicate what a character is thinking – that captured their overall feeling as they were at the door of the new classroom. This is what the five children wrote; the children's words and punctuation are presented verbatim.

Ooooo …!!! They stare at me to death!!! I want to go HOME!!

Don't hit me teacher!

Uh oh! What are these people like?
What if they laugh at me that I don't know English?!

What scary people. Why they [sic] staring at me. I am so nervous.
Don't make fun of me people.

What can I do from today?

The *unsaid* in the Heideggerian sense is always more in the Gendlinian sense than the *said*. Yet as the above examples of the *said* show, the *said* has the power to give meaning or even change the *more*. Although the implicit remains in the *unsaid* (in our case the visual), the *said* allows itself to be thematized and is thus given meaning through language. However, we argue that it is the combination of the two that presents the lived moment of being at the door as a whole.

Along with the overall feeling of fear and uncertainty, in this case the *said* revealed the children's bodily awareness as they felt others looking at them and were fearful of being laughed at because of their English. In fact, the lived sense of being looked at was so dominant in the next experiential moment that all the children agreed to have one central photograph representing the moment when they were in the classroom and everyone stopped their work to look at the new kid (Kirova & Emme, 2006). For the purposes of this chapter, however, we focus only on the first frame of the three-frame fotonovela.

We argue that fotonovela both as a process and as a product creates a space for a new relationship between the visual and the linguistic that enables us to artfully capture the phenomenon of being at the door of a new school. We wondered, however, if readers could feel the phenomenon, and if the visual was the only aspect of the description of the phenomenon to which they would have access. To elicit responses from readers, we gave one version of the three-frame fotonovela to 14 Grade 5 children who were not part of the performance of the tableau or the production of the fotonovelas. Twelve of these children were themselves first-generation immigrants to the country, and some had recently arrived from their countries of origin. The children were given the fotonovela with the first two frames titled "My First Day in this School" and a sheet of blank speech/thought balloons to cut out and glue onto the pictures as they saw as appropriate to the story.

The last frame was left blank so that the children could personalize the story in accordance with their own experiences of the first day in school. They could choose either to take a photograph or to draw a picture of what happened when they were introduced to the class.

Most of the children related to the visual text as intended by its authors. The following are these children's responses to the first frame of the fotonovela, the one addressing the experience of being at the door.

- I am scared. (two children)
- I am scared. What if they make fun of me?
- This class looks dangerous.

- Uh! Oh! I am gona [sic] die!
- I think that I am going to faint!
- What if they don't like me?
- I think that I am going to pee my pants.
- I am really shy.

Other children expressed less fear of the unknown "hiding" behind the door of the classroom and were even optimistic about what they encountered. These are their responses:

- I am shy. Wonder if I don't get any friends but now I know I will.
- Holly [sic] that's a lot of kids. Maybe I can say hello my name is Michelle.
- Well this looks fun.
- Today is my first day I am happy.
- C'mon be nice at least say "hi" to your new classmates. Gulp! (clears throat)

Based on the work of Ricoeur (1987), we have argued elsewhere that the reader/viewer is the imaginary *me* created by art as a playful representation of a world (Emme & Kirova, 2010). "It is a question of entering into an alien work, of divesting oneself of the earlier 'me' in order to receive, as in play, the self conferred by the work itself" (Ricoeur, 1987, p. 190). In viewing or reading photography, the meanings intended by the image-maker and those envisaged by the viewer partly converge in their shared experience of the photograph. By emphasizing playfulness in both the production of the visual narratives and their reading/viewing by readers, we wish to emphasize that there is no representational truth in either the visual or the linguistic descriptions of the phenomenon, and so there is always a complex sense-making of the lived experiences based on the tension between languaging and embodying. As we demonstrate here, the "phenomenological nod" is a result of readers' engagement in their own experiences of the phenomenon as *shown* through words in the text. Thus, we suggest that a visual narrative as in fotonovelas has similar evocative power.

DISCUSSION

In this chapter, we explore the role of the lived body in meaningful understanding beyond linguistic conceptualization in phenomenologically oriented inquiries through the question, what methods of inquiry can be used to access more directly the "embodied understanding" and, in particular, the lifeworlds of immigrant children as they leave the familiar "home world" and enter the "alien world" of a new school? We believe that the phenomenologically oriented method that we call fotonovela provided an example of how the process of engaging the body and visuality in the process of phenomenological inquiry provided space for each of the immigrant children who participated in the project to recall and relive his or her experiences of being at the door of a new classroom and to reflect on it. In this sense, it enabled these children "to cast back light, to give back or show an image" (Random House Webster Dictionary, 1990, p. 1132), and to share this experience with others in a format that had evocative power similar to that of a phenomenological text. We have argued elsewhere that as a research method characterized by collaboration between researchers and participants, fotonovela "changes both the way of seeing and readers' self-understanding" (Kirova & Emme, 2008, p. 52), and thus it is qualitatively different from other methods employed in research with children that are still "prompted, designed, analyzed and disseminated by adults" (Greene & Hill, 2005, p. 12). In this particular chapter, we extend these arguments even further by explicating the contributions of our method to accessing and understanding embodied experiences and the complex relationships between body, language, and image in this understanding. The notion that there is more to the experience than can be captured by language-based descriptions inspired our exploration of the possibilities offered by arts-based research method – derived from the performative and visual arts – in developing a collage method of inquiry (Kirova & Emme, 2006). This method is one that invited young children to be fully included in the process of making meaning of their lived experiences, and it simultaneously affirmed the embodied nature of understanding. We suggest here that the method discussed in this chapter and elsewhere does not favor image over text or body over language. Rather, we argue that by exploring the complex interplay of all of the above, what is described elsewhere as "poly-media" (Emme & Kirova, in press), adds to the ongoing conversation in the human sciences about the questioning of "what it means to know." We believe that the examples of children's exploration of their fotonovelas depicting the first day of school and our discussion of this process demonstrate that we see knowing as understanding that is non-consensual, ever evolving, and relational. We also believe that these examples show how the knowledge children gain through such a process of understanding can be shared in a multimodal text that evokes, in turn, embodied responses as part of children-as-readers' understanding. From this perspective the fundamental ethical question in research, "Knowledge for whom?" takes on a new meaning.

NOTES

[1] "Poly-Media" is a term chosen to create a distinction from "Multi-Media." As described by Alsop (2007), poly- media art making is understood as a collaborative system in which all collaborators, such as composers, video artists, choreographers, actors and writers contribute to the final product by interacting collaboratively throughout the development process to the eventual presentation of the work. This system is distinct from a "multi-media" approach where the different aspects may be developed independently and then marshaled towards the end of the development process.

REFERENCES

Alsop, R. (2007). Compositional Processes in Developing Poly-Media Performance Works. Retrieved from http://people.smartchat.net.au/~rogeralsop/Compositional_Processes_R_Alsop.doc

Barthes, R. (1981). *Camera lucida: Reflections on photography* (R. Howard, Trans.). New York: Hill & Wang.

Bruner, J. S. (1986). *Actual minds, possible worlds*. Cambridge, MA: Harvard University Press.

Chan-fai, C. (2004). Separation and connection: Phenomenology of door and window. In D. Carr & C. Chan-fai (Eds.), *Space, time, and culture* (pp. 253-262). Dordrecht: Kluwer Academic.

Conrad, D. (2004). Exploring risky youth experiences: Popular theatre as a participatory, performative research method. *International Journal of Qualitative Methods, 3*(1). Retrieved from http://www.ualberta.ca/~iiqm

Eisner, W. (1985). *Comics and sequential art. Principles and practices of the world's most popular artform.* Tamarac, FL: Poorhouse Press.

Emme, M., & Kirova, A. (2005). Fotonovela. *Canadian Art Teacher, 4*(1), 24-27.

Emme, M, Kirova, A., & Cambre, C. (2006). Fotonovela and collaborative storytelling: Researching the spaces between image, text and body. *Exposure, 39*(2), 45-51.

Emme, M., & Kirova, A. (2010) Body/Image/Text: Fotonovela, digital technology and poly-media narratives. In C. Mullen & J. Rahn (Eds.), *View finding: Perspectives on new media curriculum in the arts.* New York: Peter Lang

Emme, M., Kirova, A., Kamau, O., & Kosanovich, S. (2006). Ensemble research: A means for immigrant children to explore peer relationships through fotonovela. *Alberta Journal of Educational Research, Theme Issue: Researching With Children and Youth, 52,* 160-182.

Flusser, V. (2000). *Towards a philosophy of photography* (A. Matthews, Trans.). Suffolk, England: Reaktion Books.

Foucault, Michel. (1983). *This is not a pipe.* With illustrations and letters by René Magritte (J. Harkness, Trans. & Ed.). Berkeley: University of California Press.

Gadamer, H.-G. (1993). *Truth and method* (2nd ed.). (J. Weinsheimer & D. G. Marshal, Trans.). New York: Continuum.

Gendlin, E.T. (1997a). *Experiencing and the creation of meaning.* Evanston, Springfield, IL: Northwestern University Press.

Gendlin, E.T. (1997b). How philosophy cannot appeal to reason and how it can. In D.M. Levin (Ed.), *Language beyond postmodernism: Saying and thinking in Gendlin's philosophy* (pp. 3-41). Evanston, IL: Northwestern University Press.

Greene, S., & Hill, M. (2005). Researching children's experiences: Methods and methodological issues. In S. Greene & D. Hogan (Eds.), *Researching children's experiences: Approaches and methods* (pp. 1-21). Thousand Oaks, CA: Sage.

Hüsserl, E. (1960). *Cartesian meditations* (D. Cairns, Trans.). The Hague: Nijhoff.

Irigaray, L. (1992). *Elemental passions.* In J. Collie & J. Still (Eds.), London: Athlone Press.

Kirova, A. (2001). Loneliness in immigrant children: Implications for classroom practice. *Childhood Education, 77*(5), 260-268.

Kirova, A., & Emme, M. (2006). Using photography as a means of phenomenological seeing: "Doing phenomenology" with immigrant children. *Indo-Pacific Journal of Phenomenology Special Edition: Methodology, 6*(1), 1-12. Retrieved from http://www.ipjp.org

Kirova, A., & Emme, M. (2008). Fotonovela as a research tool in image-based participatory research with immigrant children. *International Journal for Qualitative Methodologies, 7*(2), 35-57.

Levin, D.M. (1985) *The body's recollection of being: Phenomenological psychology and the deconstruction of nihilism.* London: Routledge & Kegan Paul.

Levin, D. M. (1990). *The body's recollection of being.* London: Routledge & Kegan Paul.

McCloud, S. (1994). *Understanding comics: The invisible art.* New York: Harper.

Merleau-Ponty, M. (1962). *Phenomenology of perception.* London: Routledge & Kegan Paul.

Merleau-Ponty, M. (1963). *The structure of behavior.* Boston, MA: Beacon Press.

Merleau-Ponty, M. (1968). *The visible and the invisible.* In A. Lingis (Ed.). Evanston, IL: Northwestern University Press.

Moss, D. (1989). Brain, body, and world: Body image and the psychology of the body. In R.S. Valle & S. Halling (Eds.), *Existential-phenomenological perspectives in psychology: Exploring the breadth of human experience* (pp. 63-82). New York: Plenum Press.

Neelands, J. (Ed.). (1998). Structuring drama work: A handbook of available forms in theatre and drama. Cambridge, UK: Cambridge University Press.

Oliver, K. (2001). Review of textures of light. *Hypatia, 16*(1), 106-108. Retrieved from http://muse.jhu.edu/journals/hypatia [10.11.09].

Random House Webster's College Dictionary (1995). New York: Random House.

Reed, D.I. (1987). An empirical phenomenological approach to dream research. In F. van Zuuren, F. J. Wertz, & B. Mook (Eds.), *Advances in qualitative psychology* (pp. 96-116). Berwyn, PA: Sweet and Zeitlinger.

Ricoeur, P. (1987). *Hermeneutics and the human sciences.* Cambridge, UK: Cambridge University Press.

Rose, G. (2001). *Visual methodologies: An introduction to the interpretation of visual materials.* Thousand Oaks, CA: Sage.

Salvio, P.M. (1990). The world, the text, and the reader. In A. A. Lunsford, H. Moglen, & J. Slevin (Eds.), *The right to literacy* (pp. 269-275). New York: Modern Language Association.

Shapiro, K.J. (1985). *Bodily reflective modes: A phenomenological method for psychology.* Durham, NC: Duke University Press.

Sjöholm, C. (2000). Crossing lovers: Luce Irigaray's elemental passions. *Hypatia, 15*(3), 92-112.

Sontag, S. (1977). *On photography.* New York: Farrar, Straus & Giroux.

Stafford, B. (1996). *Good looking: Essays on the virtue of images.* Cambridge, Massachussetts: MIT Press.

Steinbock, A. (1995). *Home and beyond: Generative phenomenology after Husserl.* Evanston, IL: Northwestern University Press.

Todres, L. (2007). Embodied enquiry: Phenomenological touchstones for research, psychotherapy and spirituality. New York: Palgrave Macmillan.

Van den Berg, J. H. (1955). *The Phenomenological Approach to Psychiatry.* In: Charles C. Thomas.

Van Manen, M. (1994). *Researching lived experience: Human science for an action sensitive pedagogy.* London, ON: The Althouse Press.

Van Manen, M. (2000). Professional practice and 'doing phenomenology.' In S.K. Toombs (Ed.), *Handbook of phenomenology and medicine* (pp. 457-474). London: Kluwer Academic Publishers.

Vasseleau, C. (1998). *Textures of light: Vision and touch in Irigaray, Levinas and Merleau-Ponty. Warwick studies in European philosophy.* New York: Routledge.

Wagner, B.J. (1998). *Educational drama and language arts: What research shows.* Portsmouth,NH: Heinemann.

Wawrzycka, J. (1995). Photographeme: Mythologizing in *camera lucida.* In J. Rabaté (Ed.), *Writing the image: After Roland Barthes* (pp. 90-99). Philadelphia, PA: University of Pennsylvania Press.

Wilson, P. (2003). Supporting young children's thinking through tableau. *Language Arts, 80*(5), 375-383.

Ziller, R.C. & Smith, D.E. (1977). A phenomenological utilization of photographs. *Journal of Phenomenological Psychology, 7*(2), 172-182.

CHARLOTTE SVENDLER NIELSEN

9. CHILDREN'S EMBODIED VOICES

Approaching Children's Experiences through Multi-Modal Interviewing

INTRODUCTION

We constantly experience and express ourselves through our bodies, and children use their bodies to communicate even before they develop a verbal language. The body is central in our efforts to create meaning and make sense of our experiences. For example, when children develop concepts of wet and dry, wet means *wetter than my body* (Egan, 1997, p. 40). It is through our bodies that we translate our perceptions to actions and vice versa – actions also colour our perceptions. According to Kieran Egan (1997), curriculum should involve the somatic[1] dimension to a much higher degree and ensure that this dimension is a continuous part of children's education and development. But how do we develop tools to focus on the somatic dimension? How do children experience their bodies in movement? And how can they express their embodied experiences? In this chapter, I wish to dig deeper into these questions through presenting a multi-modal approach which I have developed for interviewing children about their embodied experiences. The multi-modal approach could also be applied as a pedagogic tool that would help cast light on the questions highlighted above regarding the teaching of movement and dance in schools. As such, the multi-modal interview approach is the focus of the chapter, but the development of the approach is attuned to discussions of relationships between body, movement and language, and somatic approaches in teaching.

The multi-modal interview approach emphasizes the non-verbal, giving children an opportunity to focus on "the felt sense" (Gendlin, 1978), and to express their experiences in a variety of forms and through the use of metaphors (Egan, 1997; Gendlin, 1978, 1997). Inspired by Arnold Mindell's (1985) work on shifting channels in our ways of experiencing the world, this chapter works with an adaptation of Eugene T. Gendlin's "focusing technique" – one that significantly expands Gendlin's repertoire of modalities by using drawing, colours, words, sound, music and movement. Narratives have been created using children's voices and expressions. The chapter includes an example of a narrative that illustrates how the approach has helped children express their movement experiences. The narrative is analysed by means of a hermeneutic phenomenological approach (van

N. Friesen et al. (eds.), Hermeneutic Phenomenology in Education, 163–176.

Manen, 1990), through which themes/lived meanings of the child's experiences are elucidated.

THEORETICAL BACKGROUND

An important methodological question in relation to exploring children's experiences and expressions in movement is *how* to create knowledge about their embodied experiences. This is a question which I have explored by applying theories about the body's significance in learning and consciousness processes (Egan, 1997; Sheets-Johnstone, 1999), phenomenological theory and methods (Merleau-Ponty, 1962, 1968; Gendlin, 1978, 1997; van Manen, 1990), and somatic perspectives (Gendlin, 1997; Mindell, 1985). Overall the research presented here is based on an understanding of the body as both lived and expressed, and has its roots in Maurice Merleau-Ponty's (1962) phenomenological notion of embodiment (in French: "corporalité"), and in bodily approaches to investigating experiences and movement described by Eugene T. Gendlin (1997) and Arnold Mindell (1985, 1989). In this philosophical and psychological interpretative framework, embodiment is the "bodily being" understood as the physical body, the communicative expression, and the experienced "felt sense" of the body – all at once. The lived body is understood as "chiastic" (Merleau-Ponty, 1968): it is both seeing and seen, acting and acted upon, experiencing and experienced – by oneself and others. Metaphorically expressed, we are always entwined with one another and the world surrounding us. We influence and are influenced through our embodiment. Indeed, it is through our embodiment that we participate in the world at all.

CREATING KNOWLEDGE ABOUT CHILDREN'S EMBODIED EXPERIENCES

Now, I will ask you to join me in a lesson of a second-grade class in a public school in Copenhagen. The children are participants in my investigation of embodied experiences and expressions in dance and physical education, but here we are in their classroom. It is on the second floor, with big windows looking out on a green school yard filled with trees. Even though it is a rainy day in November, the room seems very light. It has been three months since I started following the class in their weekly physical education lessons and in their weekly dance lessons with a professional dance teacher who is running a project at the school. Today, the classroom teacher and I have agreed that I can spend a lesson giving an introduction to the individual interviews I will be carrying out during the coming months. Today we will do some introductory body awareness exercises all together that I will build on in the individual interviews. It is not easy to focus on embodied experiences or to verbalize them. I wonder how the children will react. Will they think that this is just too strange or will they enter the "game" with me?

The children usually sit grouped around round tables. We move the tables and chairs to the sides, and I ask the children to find a spot on the floor.

They all find a spot where they can stand and start looking interestedly in my direction. After I have explained to them what this lesson will be about I start by saying, "Shake your hands as much as you can while they are hanging in front of your bodies, then liiiift them up to the height of your shoulders, and let them stay there for a little while ..." The children start shaking their hands energetically, and slowly bring their arms up in tune with my voice. I continue, "Let's do it again. OK? Shake! All loose, all loose, all loose, all loose aaaaand let them move up to your shoulders and just staaand for a moment ..." I ask if they feel anything in their fingers.

"Yes!" some say.

"What do you feel?"

Viktor says, "It's tingling."

"It's tingling? Yes?"

Louise says, "It is really hard out in your arms when you have just been resting them."

Signe adds, "I think it is because when you have just done like this then your blood is rushing around."

We try once more. It is as if an angel is passing through the room when they very gently lift their arms up. Thomas interrupts the stillness and says "It's tingling."

Sabine adds, "You get all hot." And Signe says, "You also get all red out here on your nails and your fingertips."

I ask, "And why do you get red?" Many children raise their hands.

Signe herself answers, "Because the blood is running around out there."

Kristian says, "And then when you press your finger it gets white."

"Yes, it turns white because the blood disappears," I say and then continue, "We're doing these exercises so you can try out different ways to describe what you feel in your bodies." I ask the children to lie down on their backs. They all quickly lie down and squirm until they are comfortable. They lay spread out on the floor.

One child says, "You take up much more space when lying on the floor."

I answer, "Yes, because when you're standing it is really only your feet that take up space."

Signe says, "Now I feel that I am so heavy because my blood has rushed down."

I say, "Yes! And now we will close our eyes and try and lie for a while and just breathe so that you can feel it all the way down in your bellies." The lesson goes on with more body awareness exercises. I also ask the children to draw their bodily sensation, first a sketch and afterwards they decide whether other colours could better serve to express their experience.

Figure 1: Tom's drawing titled "Blood out in my fingers." (The monster on the right is the blood drawn with red colour and on his drawing of himself on the left he has marked the sensation of the blood with red lines).

GUIDE TO MULTI-MODAL INTERVIEWS

Neither children nor adults are often readily able to verbalize embodied experiences. But through multi-modal exercises and interviews, it is possible to practice feeling and expressing one's embodied experiences. Gendlin's "focusing technique" (1978) involves transforming experiences to verbal language so as to become more conscious of them, share them with others, and acquire tools to change or accept whatever it is that has occasioned the sensation – "the felt sense" (Gendlin, 1978). Some psychotherapists inspired by Gendlin also employ drawing as a method to investigate the felt sense (Lejissen, 1992; Rappaport, 1988; Stapert, 1997). As a part of the research presented here, I developed the *multi-modal interview approach* which puts the non-verbal in the forefront by giving children opportunities to focus on the felt sense and use their imagination as a way of opening up and expressing it through different modalities (Mindell, 1985). Inspired by Mindell's (1985) work on shifting channels in experiential modes, I have expanded Gendlin's focusing technique even further by providing the children with opportunities to express themselves in many modalities – through words and metaphors, colours, drawing, sound, music, and movement. *Choosing a "significant moment"(move headline up).*

The child chooses a significant moment[2] (an experience) or a movement. Either we begin talking about a drawing that the child has made beforehand showing a significant experience in dance or physical education, or I ask the child to choose a movement that he or she likes to do. I ask what the movement is, if the child would like to show it to me, and then we do the movement together.

The "immediate felt sense" of the movement/experience

When a drawing is the starting point, I begin by asking the child to tell me about the drawing. Then, I ask the child to find words that describe how it felt "in the body" to do the movement that has been drawn. In order to make the child focus on the felt sense of the moving body, I suggest that the child does the movement and tries to focus on how it feels to do it, and then we do it together. This lets me also experience how it feels to do the movement. That I involve myself bodily with the child helps to intensify our communication in the situation, because the children involve themselves even more than when I just sit and watch them. While we move together I ask the child what it feels like and I explain what I feel. This leads to a dialogue about our experiences. If the child finds it difficult to verbalize the experience, I give an example, "What feels good to me is that I feel that I am in a kind of rhythm. Do you also feel that?" Offering an example often works as a cue that makes the child enter the "game" and go on from there. Together we create some new insights into our movement experiences; the interviews become an embodied learning process – both for the children and for me.

"Clearing a space" and "the felt sense" again

I now tell the child that we are going to conduct a little experiment. I suggest that we close our eyes briefly and imagine how it feels to do the movement. I emphasize that closing their eyes is a choice, but not something that the child must do. Closing their eyes when they are alone with an adult who they do not know very well can, for some children, feel too intimidating (Stapert, 1997). However, all the children that I interviewed as part of this research closed their eyes without further ado and did not seem to feel uncomfortable. When we have focused on the experience for a little while, I ask if the child feels the sensation all over their body or in some specific body parts. And then I ask if she/he can find a word that describes the sensation. Some find this a very difficult task. If they do not say anything I suggest some ideas like "is it true to say that it feels, for example, bubbly or sharp?" Some children then find a word themselves, while others choose one of the words that I have mentioned.

"Channel shifting" and "attuning" (move sentence up?)

Depending upon how easy or difficult it seems to be for the child to understand my questions, I try different ways to help the child express the embodied experiences, either in language or through other modes of expression. I suggest communicating in other modalities by asking if the sensation can be described by for example a colour. If the child says "blue" in order to attune the experience, I ask if red could also be a possibility. If the child keeps to blue, I ask if it is a light or a dark blue, and what the difference between light and dark blue is. The children usually join "the game" and find it easy to relate the movement experience to a colour. For the interviews I also bring a variety of musical instruments (e.g., a drum, a triangle, and a tambourine) which the children can use to communicate the embodied experience through sound. But I also mention that they are welcome to find other sounds and instruments. Some choose to make a sound that simulates the sound of the movement (if the movement is to jump like a ball the sound can be drumbeats that sound like a jumping ball). If the child chooses a drum, I ask, for example, if the tambourine is also a possibility, in order to help to nuance and "attune" which auditory image best expresses the experience.

"Synthesizing" and "application"

I try to find out if the child can distinguish between the embodied sensation and the image that he or she has of the form of the movement. I ask the child to make a new drawing, a quick drawing of what *it looks like* to do the movement. After that I ask if the child would like to draw the *experience* of moving like he or she has explained (for example, the experience of running). The goal is to create an understanding of the difference of the sensations we have while moving in certain moments – in contrast to how the movements look from the outside.

"Closing" and "orientation ahead"

It is very important that the children leave the interview with a sense of success. I try to make sure that they feel that they have understood what the exercise was about and that they have participated in a good way. With some children, the dialogue becomes so intense that we have to "rise to the surface" again together before I can finish the interview. I cannot just stop and say, "Well, goodbye and thanks for coming." I try to discern whether we are both ready to finish the conversation by introducing some ordinary subjects and giving the child space and time to see if he or she comes forth with other issues that we need to talk about. Children are individuals with different experiences and interests. With each child I, therefore, use the presented guide in a different way. In each situation, I estimate how it would be constructive to start the focusing exercises and how deep I can go with the child. Gendlin (1978, p. 67) has "clearing a space" as the first part of his focusing method, but with many children I feel it works better to start the exercise by doing the movement that they have chosen to tell about, and to make some opening efforts to verbalize the experiences before going deeper into the focusing process.

AN EMBODIED RESEARCH PROCESS

Phenomenological research always begins "in the lifeworld" (van Manen, 1990, p. 7), and has as its aim to create deeper understandings of the meaning of experienced phenomena. The essence of a phenomenon can be "described through a study of the structure that governs the instances or particular manifestations of the essence of that phenomenon" (van Manen, p. 10). Hermeneutic phenomenological research (van Manen, 1990) is basically characterized by a research process that takes place in the production of texts. But when "text" is understood in a broader sense (i.e., "action as text"), as it is the case in the writings of hermeneutic philosopher Paul Ricoeur (1991, p.160), conceptualization can take place not only during the writing process, but also, for example, in the creation of visual narratives and film (e.g. Svendler Nielsen, 2009). During the focusing exercises, I encourage the children to use various modes of expression to describe their embodied experiences. Through their choice of words, the children show how they understand my questions regarding their embodied sensations, how they relate to movement activities and make meaning while expressing their experiences. I have collected their direct statements from the interviews, sentences from log books, and words and drawings that they have made about their experiences, and transformed them into narratives.

Moments of closeness and distance

As a researcher in the process of hermeneutic phenomenological analysis, I move between moments of closeness and moments of distance in relation to the phenomena and the children whose experiences and practices I am exploring (Todres, 2007, p. 58). The moments of closeness happen when I am involved in communicating the children's and my own experiences by bringing the essences of the experiences to a verbal form as first-person narratives. These narratives can help to get to the core of the phenomenon of embodied experience by making related special themes/lived meanings visible. The moments of distance happen when I seek to pull meanings forward from the texts through hermeneutic interpretations in which I constantly move between single sentences and the whole narrative in order to get to a deeper understanding of the meanings that are communicated about the phenomenon.

Experiences and expressions as "text"

A hermeneutic phenomenological approach (van Manen, 1990) highlights that the interpretation of a social situation is to treat the situation as a "text" and look for metaphors that appear in the text. In the analysis I therefore "feel into" what words, associations, and metaphors the children use to express themselves about their lived movement experiences and meanings. The interpretation process takes place both during the interview, in the transcription of the recordings, and in the analysis of the material.

The body as "method"

According to the Finnish dance researcher Jaana Parviainen (2002), a dance teacher makes use of her or his own embodied experiences and kinaesthetic empathy to understand the participants' experiences, and to help learners in their learning process. Phenomenologically speaking, empathy is "an act of knowing within others" (Stein, 1917, as cited in Parviainen, 2002). Parviainen claims that we can make sense of another person's kinaesthetic experience through verbal communication, or through empathic understanding. Former dancer and phenomenologist Maxine Sheets-Johnstone (1999, p. 57) highlights that "we can distinguish kinetic bodily feelings such as smoothness and clumsiness, swiftness and slowness (...) we make bodily-felt distinctions." To be able to conceptualize such nuances in movement requires sensitivity to differences in movement qualities. Moreover, in order to delve into and understand other people's movement experiences from their viewpoint we need embodied sensitivity (Parviainen, 2002, p. 148). This also applies to me as a researcher when I try to capture the children's embodied experiences. My own embodied experiences influence my investigation of experiences in the movement-education area. I seek to understand the children's experiences in an embodied way by watching and joining them in their movements. In the mimetic process (Ricoeur, 1990, pp. 52-87), my visual and kinesthetic senses work together to give me an embodied experience like the one the child is trying to communicate. In all phases of the project I strive to understand what the children express, and listen with my whole body through kinesthetic empathy, but also with an openness to other forms of expression. In order to analyse the children's experiences, perspectives, and ways of moving and making meaning through and about movement, I must accept and welcome plurality in forms of expression and interpretation by paying attention to how and what the children say and do, and by making space for their direct choice of words (their "voices").

The interview as a touching dialogue

From a phenomenological perspective, the living meeting that comprises an interview, is an existential situation for both the child and me, as a researcher. Once in a while, subjects arise during the interviews that I could explore if the purpose were therapeutic, but because I am in an educational context, I consciously focus on the learning process. But it is a delicate balance. A dialogue can be so deep that both parties are touched. The same applies in teaching situations when themes of a more personal nature arise, and as a teacher one has to consider what to delve into and what it might be better to talk to parents or other professionals about. As educators, we want to start processes of learning, and in those processes we cannot help touching upon personal aspects. But as an educational researcher, it is not my task to explore personal problems; on the other hand I cannot for ethical reasons reveal the more personal thoughts that children bring up in the atmosphere of trust that we have created. On a few occasions I became aware of something that an adult closer to the child should know about. I then talked to the class teacher without mentioning anything specific, but asked about the child's history in an open way. She could not discuss personal issues either, but I got the impression that my experiences with the children were no surprise. It may sound as if I have heard some terrible stories, but that is not the case. The personal issues are primarily about relationships, discussions of the social hierarchies in the class, about development of more positive self-images, and about children who have got more friends. The positive stories that can arise from being involved in a new subject, in this case the dance lessons; having the opportunity of being deeply bodily engaged; and having time to talk about those experiences as it happened during the interviews is also important knowledge to the adults closer to the children. In the following section, an example of one child's voice gives insights into what she experiences when performing movements that have made a certain impression on her, and how she expresses her embodied experiences.

ANDREA'S VOICE: FEELING ABSORBED IN AN IMAGE

Figure 2: Andrea's drawing titled "My dance as a fresh tree."

"I am standing on 'Dancescenen' [the Dance Stage] acting a fresh tree. We are all tree forms or tree sculptures that are standing, planted in a half circle and move in different ways. When it is our group's turn to dance we go to the middle and the other ones come out and are trees again. There are many who are watching us. My fresh tree is stretching itself a lot and is standing only on one leg. It is a nice feeling and it is like a little breeze is coming, just like it is breezy outside and it is sort of swinging, it swings from side to side, and the breeze… I can feel it in my whole body, also in my legs. It is a little like being close to a beach where you can hear the breeze and the water is all blue."

The significant movement experience that Andrea has chosen to talk about in the interview is from the children's performance on a professional dance stage which took place at the end of the dance project that I was following. Using Andrea's own words, I have developed this narrative in order to explicate the theme of "feeling absorbed in an image." This is the theme/lived meaning I find to be central through a "wholistic reading" (van Manen, 1990, p. 93) of the part of the interview when we talk about what a good movement experience is to her. Through a "selective reading" (van Manen, p. 93), I see that Andrea's bodily being in the narrative both shows that in her absorbedness she is aware of her body as both expressive and as sensuous. She explains how she, in the on-stage performance, creates the expression of stretching like a fresh tree, but is also very sensuously aware of the movement experience. The sensuous dimension is expressed through her use of metaphors which show an identification with nature and the elements. The metaphors give an idea of what she experiences through her metamorphosis to a bodily tree. "The fresh tree" is standing well-planted in the soil (*earth*). She is close to the sea (*water*), and the *air* is breezy. Her *body*, which according to Merleau-Ponty (1968, p. 139) is the fifth element, is a tree that stretches. In the dance she is using her imagination and experiences her body and the tree as something which is alive and able to be transformed into one another. The experience of stretching is kinesthetic, as is the swinging sensation she has when the tree sways from side to side. In her images of nature, Andrea relates to visual images and they facilitate the auditory and kinesthetic modes; she both hears and feels how it is to be close to the sea and the breeze. The colours (i.e., purple, green, and blue) in which Andrea chooses to draw her experience of moving like a fresh tree and the sounds and metaphors that she connects to the movement experience contribute to communicating the dynamic qualities she experiences when moving. In the analysis of the children's narratives, I elucidate how forms of movement merge with the sensing modes entered by the children via my guiding questions, and with the language they use to express themselves about the experience. The sensing, the movement, and the language that the children use to express their embodied experiences are dynamic and interwoven. The processes where the children connect to their experiences and express themselves about them take place in what Mindell (1985) calls "channels." Mindell (1989) distinguishes the following channels: the proprioceptive, the visual, the relational, the kinesthetic, the auditory, and the channel for "world phenomena." In my analysis of 25 children's narratives, channels of kinesthetic, visual, auditory, relational, and universal (world phenomena) character appear. But I also distinguish an emotional, a cultural, an existential, and a kinetic[3] channel, or mode, of expression. I see the word "channel" as a metaphor for the phenomenological understanding that highlights connections between body, mind, and the surrounding world (Merleau-Ponty, 1962; Sheets-Johnstone, 1999).

The children each experience their own bodies in movement, but the experiences are closely linked to experiences of their surroundings, to other children who are part of the situation they choose to tell about, or, as in the case of a girl who choseS to tell me about her experiences of running, to other people or situations in their lives. I primarily elicit kinesthetic expressions for the children's experiences and move to questions that open towards visual and auditory expressions. But once in a while the children themselves change mode of expression, through a phenomenon that Mindell (1985, p. 37) calls "switching channels." It happens when, for example, one suddenly changes focus from bodily sensations to images. For some of the children when I elicit their kinesthetic experiences, a multidimensional bodily sensation starts; the kinesthetic opens towards the relational. As in the case of the girl who tells about her running experiences, kinesthetic awareness invites memories in the "relational channel" (Mindell, 1989) as she suddenly remembers how it is to run holding her dad's hand.

THE METAPHOR AS AN EMBODIED TOOL OF UNDERSTANDING

Through hermeneutic phenomenological analysis of the children's narratives I distinguish many ways that they relate to experiences in movement and express them. Some see the embodied experiences primarily in images, some express their bodily-felt sense as a kinesthetic metaphor, while others describe or explain in more rational terms. The words that the children know in advance are not sufficient to express their embodied experiences verbally. That is why they invent metaphors that can help them communicate their experiences. "Ordinary words convey only what we know already; it is from metaphor that we can best get hold of something fresh" (Aristotle in Egan, 1997, p. 55). According to Egan (p. 58), "metaphor is one of our cognitive grappling tools; it enables us to see the world in multiple perspectives and to engage with the world flexibly." He also emphasizes that "metaphor is much more profoundly a feature of sense-making than the largely ornamental and redundant poetic trope some have taken it to be" (Egan, 1997, p. 58). Moreover, Egan (p. 54) mentions that young children are especially good at creating metaphors, and use them to get a handle on something new. To invent a metaphor for an experience shows a bodily felt understanding and the ability to translate this understanding to words or other expressions. The metaphor mediates between body, experience and language. In the children's narratives it appears that the metaphors that they invent during the focusing exercises indeed also are bodily tools of becoming aware, and that the metaphors can contribute to understanding how they make sense in the reflective processes about movement experiences.

THE MULTI- MODAL APPROACH AS A PEDAGOGICAL TOOL IN EDUCATION

With inspiration from Egan's theory of education (1997) and Sheets-Johnstone's (1999) phenomenology of movement, it can be argued that experiential and

173

creative bodily activities can contribute to further development of a child's "somatic thinking" and ways of learning. But Egan and Sheets-Johnstone only briefly touch upon how it is possible to work with a somatic approach in practice. In this chapter I have described my efforts to create connections between different modes of expression ("channels") in order to elucidate the children's embodied experiences. The multi-modal approach makes it possible to reveal how the body can be used to channel different forms of expression, and thereby provide a multidimensional, subtle sense of embodied experience and meaning-making. This approach has cast light on the ways that children can create connections to their embodied experiences and describe them in different "languages" and through the use of metaphors that they invent to suit the situation. The channels, or the ways of understanding and expressing embodied experiences, that I discern in the children's narratives probably also exist among other groups of children and young people. Their descriptions might be different and they might invent other metaphors, but presumably their ways of experiencing and expressing would lie within the same broad variations as suggested by Mindell (1989) and described in this chapter.

Although developed to explore children's embodied experiences in interview situations, the various ways of relating to body and movement that I have seen through the multi-modal approach could also be applied in dance and movement education in schools. Working with body awareness exercises and expressing experiences in various modes could also, in teaching situations, highlight an embodied perspective of learning in movement by expanding the children's consciousness in and about movement, emphasizing the lived body, the experiences and the connections between the children and their surrounding world. As a teacher, knowing that children respond to sensuous modalities in different ways, one can use different channels to raise awareness, help children focus on embodied experiences, and becoming good at expressing themselves about them. Such work will help answer the following questions:

– How can "focusing" and "switching channels" be used educationally?
– Can such approaches help to develop the children's embodied consciousness and expressive repertoire?
– Can attention on creating metaphors to communicate embodied experiences make the children more aware of their experiences?
– Does expression of embodied experiences enhance deeper experiences and learning, and how can this be a way to develop the movement-education field?

Children are good at entering "a bodily universe" – in fact, they are there all the time. But among the subjects taught in the Danish public schools, for example, physical education is the only one that focuses on bodily activities. Moreover, in practice the experiential and expressive opportunities of physical education are rarely at the forefront. If an educational system is to take seriously the fact that the body is an extremely important resource for learning and development, then children must learn to be aware of their own and others' experiences and to communicate what they sense, see, and feel in a bodily-based language. They can thereby develop greater consciousness in and about movement. Sheets-Johnstone

(1999) argues that movement is the basis for consciousness and cognition, but it is also the basis for sensing the body and other people, as emphasized by Merleau-Ponty (1962, 1968). As human beings, we are always influencing and influenced by one another through our embodiment (Merleau-Ponty, 1968). Understanding this relational dynamic of the lived body as "chiastic" could contribute significantly to developing awareness of our own and other's ways of being bodies, to developing tools for sensing and working with our bodies in many different ways, and enhancing the relationships between body, movement, and language in educational systems. An enhanced awareness rooted in the lived body could influence the ways children experience themselves and others and, therefore, also have a societal significance, as such awareness affects children's well-being, their relationships and quality of life.

NOTES

[1] Thomas Hanna defines "soma" as "the body experienced from within, where we experience mind/body integration." "Somatics" are practices that focus on the integration between body and mind (http://www.somaticsed.com/whatIs.html).

[2] Van Manen (1990, p.163) mentions that descriptions of "significant moments" are central when we want to understand human experience and lived meanings.

[3] The difference between the kinetic and the kineasthetic can with inspiration from Sheets-Johnstone (1999) be explained as differences between the actual doing of the movement – "I run," "I turn" etc. (kinetic) and the sensation of doing the movement (kinaesthetic).

REFERENCES

Egan, K. (1997). *The educated mind. How cognitive tools shape our understanding.* Chicago: The University of Chicago Press.

Gendlin, E.T. (1978). *Focusing.* New York: Bantam.

Gendlin, E.T. (1997). *Experiencing and the creation of meaning. A philosophical and psychological approach to the subjective.* Evanston: Northwestern University Press.

Lejissen, M. (1992). Experiential focusing through drawing. The Folio, Fall 1992. Retrieved from http://www.focusing.org/chfc/article_index.html [24-11-2003].

Merleau-Ponty, M. (1968/2000). *The visible and the invisible.* Evanston: Northwestern University Press.

Merleau-Ponty, M. (1962/2002). *Phenomenology of perception.* London: Routledge.

Mindell, A. (1985). *Working with the dreaming body.* London: Routledge & Kegan Paul.

Mindell, A. (1989). *Working with your self alone.* New York: Arkana..

Parviainen, J. (2002). Kinaesthesia and empathy as a knowing act. In A.M Fiskvik & E. Bakka (Eds.), *Dance knowledge – Dansekunnskap* (pp. 147-154), Proceedings of 6th NOFOD Cconference, Trondheim, 10-13 January 2002. Norges Teknisk-Naturvidenskabelige Universitet.

Rappaport, L. (1988). Focusing with art and creative movement: a method for stress management. In Reader from children's focusing corner. Retrieved from http://www.focusing.org/chfc/article_index.html [24-11-2003].

Ricoeur, P. (1991). The model of the text: Meaningful action considered as a text. In *From text to action: Essays in hermeneutics II* (pp. 144-169.) Evanston: Northwestern University Press.

Ricoeur, P. (1990). *Time and narrative,* Volume 1. Chicago: University of Chicago Press.

Sheets-Johnstone, M. (1999). *The primacy of movement*. Amsterdam: John Benjamins Publishing Company.

Stapert, M. (1997). Children focusing. Guiding and teaching children to focus. In Reader from children's focusing corner. Retrived from: http://www.focusing.org/chfc/articles/en/ stapert_f_children.htm [02-10-2004].

Svendler Nielsen, C. (2009). Ind i bevægelsen – Et performativt fænomenologisk feltstudie om kropslighed, mening og kreativitet i børns læreprocesser i bevægelsesundervisning i skolen. [Into the movement: A performative phenomenological field study about embodiment, meaning and creativity in children's learning processes in movement education in schools]. PhD Thesis. Copenhagen: Department of Exercise and Sport Sciences, University of Copenhagen.

Todres, L. (2007). *Embodied enquiry: phenomenological touchstones for research, psychotherapy and spirituality*. New York: Palgrave Macmillan.

Van Manen, M. (1990). *Researching lived experience: human science for an action sensitive pedagogy*. New York: State University of New York Press.

ANDREW FORAN AND MARGARET OLSON

10. SEEKING PEDAGOGICAL PLACES

INTRODUCTION: SEEKING PEDAGOGICAL PLACES

I realized pretty quick that you can't just beam your class outside, papers and all, expecting to do a more refreshing outdoor version of regular class. It's like tearing the roof and walls off the building and hoping the kids won't notice. Instead, I have to dream up missions – let's go collect some swampy water samples and bring them back inside where there are microscopes and desks, or let's go measure the angle of inclination to the top of the flagpole or the radio tower 5 kilometers away, then come back inside and draw up a trig problem about it on the board. The outdoors is a rich source of experience, but as far as regular school subjects go, teaching often seems easier inside. (Leslie, Geography teacher)

Leslie draws our awareness to the point that place matters, pedagogically, as she distinguishes appropriate places for engaging in different kinds of pedagogical activities with students, and that activities can be experienced as in-place or out-of-place. She reminds us that we cannot just replace one place or thing for or with another "hoping the kids won't notice" and that swampy water, flagpoles, and radio towers belong outdoors; microscopes, desks, and "the board" belong indoors. While we are now both university teacher educators, one of us (Andrew Foran) is a former outdoor educator of youth, mostly outdoors, and one of us (Margaret Olson) is a former kindergarten, elementary teacher, mostly indoors. Both of us are also curious about what underlies Leslie's and others' ability to seek appropriate pedagogical places as well as how they know when they have found one. What does it mean to be in the right place, pedagogically? What occurs in lived time, lived body, lived space, and lived relationships when the place becomes pedagogical? What tensions arise for students and teachers when it does not?

In this chapter, we explore the meaning of pedagogical place by focusing on the significance of relations between teachers, students, and the various places in which they appear to find pedagogical thoughtfulness. By pedagogy we refer to the relationship between teachers and students in a place that binds the adult and the child educatively. We are not discussing pedagogy as a science or technical craft, nor as an art in teaching. Our emphasis, instead, is on how a teacher "sees" (van Manen, 2002, p. 23) children during the teaching experience. We have noticed that this kind of *seeing* occurs in multiple locations. While the inside experience, especially the classroom, appears to be the dominant place set aside for pedagogy in schools worldwide, there are teachers, students, and curricular moments that have garnered pedagogical meanings by engendering and embracing relational moments removed from entrenched notions of classroom practice. The focus here

N. Friesen et al. (eds.), Hermeneutic Phenomenology in Education, 177–200.

is to question the pedagogical relationship between people and place – we do not see pedagogy being simply one or the other – so we ask, then, what it means to dwell pedagogically in a place. To bring this phenomenon into focus we were open to many possible pedagogical experiences conducted outside the typical classroom location. For instance, Leslie describes dwelling pedagogically as being absorbed, as being able to dwell authentically in a learning experience without interruption or the distractions often present within a classroom:

> The outside place for teaching can absorb you completely. Once I am out there I am lost to the world and my students as if these two items are reduced to the lowest common denominator: children and learning. I remember teaching a unit on soils. We spent our time making little individual piles of sand. There we were looming and screening under a blazing sun, oblivious to the goings on around us. I couldn't believe it when the kids were telling me that we had to go. I still do not know what happened to the allotted ninety minutes. I lost all track of the time, and from where we were I couldn't hear the bell. I loved it! No annoying reminders, interruptions, no schedule and no bells! Just me, my class, and piles of sifted soils, piles of glacial sand, the till of the past. We had time. (Leslie, Geography teacher)

The relationship between the students and Leslie was pedagogically focused as they became absorbed and drawn into the learning experience offered by this place. How might teachers open themselves more expansively to pedagogical possibilities with children by becoming more aware of their presupposed institutional confinements and moving into dwelling pedagogically both inside and outside of schools?

By opening up educational discourse to consider pedagogy beyond established notions of classroom practice, we invite readers to step outside perceived limits of classroom instruction. By considering other places where learning can occur we are creating an inquiry space that opens us to pedagogical possibilities. Where else might pedagogical moments occur? How might we know a pedagogical moment when we encounter one outside the classroom? When does a place become pedagogical?

METHODOLOGICAL BACKGROUND

A phenomenological lens enables us to address numerous questions we have posed regarding what it means to dwell pedagogically in a place. Our intention is to explore teachers' lived experience (van Manen, 1997), the concrete moment, of the teacher engaging children in learning. Our purpose is to move beyond theories, strategies, and debates that confront teachers daily. Orientating our practices pedagogically and our research phenomenologically allows us to challenge entrenched, taken-for-granted conceptions of formal education. Our phenomenological methodology aims to make connections with a "practical pedagogical orientation" (van Manen, 1988, p. 411) to the relational encounter through an examination of lived experiences and the showing of these experiences (Sokolowski, 2000) through a textual (re)presentation of the lived experience (van Manen, 1997).

Phenomenology provides descriptions of lived experiences and hermeneutics reveals an understanding of the moment through interpretation. This methodology can be harnessed to articulate the poignant insights of teachers' experiential pedagogical moments that enable the taken-for-granted-ness of teaching to eventually become visible and interpretable. Through layers of hermeneutic reflection, pre-understandings can disturb and break through the insulating surface of taken-for-granted assumptions that have been built up over time. Our hope is to *re-awaken* teachers pedagogically to the world by showing the experience of teaching in places other than classrooms. By actively reflecting on pedagogical encounters, we can learn about the richness of pedagogy and the *taken-for-granted-ness* of teaching.

Merleau-Ponty (1962) presents the complexity and simplicity of the phenomenological method as "a matter of describing, not of explaining or analyzing" (p. viii). Phenomenology is a process that brackets an experience (Husserl, 1989), and by the unique approach of the researcher, uses descriptive text and language to craft the lived experience. Influences that need bracketing, and that are of direct importance to this chapter, include a quagmire of theories of learning and ideas about teaching as a pedagogical act. In using the phenomenological method, we focus on what was present or absent in the teachers' pedagogical experiences. Dahlberg, Drew, and Nyström (2002) suggest that bracketing theoretical assumptions or pre-understandings in teaching methodology allows us to show, rather than argue about, the pedagogical experience of teachers. We can see the uniqueness of the experience, which allows for a more open investigation that remains true to the phenomena of pedagogical place. The vital experience here is the phenomena of the teacher engaged in pedagogical encounters with children as a lived experience.

Lived experiences: Lifeworld data

Phenomenology, philosophically rooted in the affirmation of human lived experiences, draws on concrete experiences, but also relies on a range of artistic, imaginary, and descriptive texts to show us the moment, the "phenomenological now" (Moran, 2001, p. 43). By using descriptive sources in the form of anecdotes, we resist the abstraction of philosophy, scientific empiricism, and argued explanation.

The crafting of anecdotes, written by teachers through reflective conversations, provides the data to support our inquiry. The anecdote is a portrayal of a concrete lived experience; it attempts to guard against "abstract theoretical thought" (van Manen, 1997, p. 119). Through these anecdotes we present the "here and now" (see Merleau-Ponty, 1962) of pedagogical moments in places outside the classroom. The use of anecdotes, within the phenomenological method, is not intended to validate science, prove theories, or establish factual-empirical quantification (van Manen, 1997); rather, it is essential in conducting reflective lifeworld research (Dahlberg, Drew, & Nyström, 2002). Each anecdotal description is based on actual experiences and not only provides an intimate link to past moments, but also, with

179

hermeneutical reflection, provides elements needed to inform pedagogical practices.

We focus on the lived experiences of teachers who seek pedagogical understanding in places where relational encounters occur within their practice. These teachers shared their lived-experience descriptions by crafting an anecdote that captures a specific pedagogical moment they experienced teaching outside the classroom. Through open-ended phenomenological–hermeneutic conversations with selected educators (and each other), pedagogical insights involving pedagogical place emerged. The anecdotes for this chapter were gathered from two sources: (1) open-ended phenomenological-hermeneutic conversations with teachers practicing in Nova Scotian schools, part of Foran's (2006) doctoral study; and (2) lived experience descriptions from Olson's recollections of her own experience as a Canadian elementary teacher and teacher educator.

The anecdotes in this chapter represent a careful blend of teacher reflections, researcher reflections, and significant literary sources. The result is a text of theory and practice: a lived praxis (see Smits, 1997) for teacher education. The research, therefore, is presented as reflective anecdotes grounded in their situated contexts.

SEEKING THE MEANING OF PEDAGOGICAL PLACES

Classrooms are often taken for granted as "natural" places for pedagogy to occur. That is their purpose. Mere mention of the word *school* is often enough to conjure nostalgic recollections among adults, drawing them back into memories of places they occupied as learners. The spectrum of words used to describe school experiences is vast, rich, and fraught with personal fears and delights. School stories tend to be associated with certain teachers, particular classrooms, personal hideouts, the gym, the office, hallways, lockers, the cafeteria, the playground, the back field, and even patches of woods used for play during recess. These places evoke individual memories about *school life*, pedagogical moments not limited to classrooms. Yet such memories also describe ways in which people have felt bound, perhaps even coerced or frustrated by the intent of school. Schools, like other buildings, "are spatially about social knowledge – that is taken-for-granted-knowledge…Social knowledge is about the unconscious organizing principles for the description of society. Often a building is a concretization of these principles" (Hillier & Hanson, 1984, p. 183). Teachers and children, then, not only bring their varying intentions for learning to school, but also are aware of the non-pedagogical intentions, or purpose of this place. At times, students and teachers intentions coincide with taken-for-granted intentions of school and of each other; at times they do not. We believe that examining places where pedagogical moments are experienced and where they are not can help us uncover lost dimensions of pedagogical place. We realize that meanings that emerge from dwelling with children in a place have been covered over by artificially imposed presuppositions that for many have taken on dimensions of permanence as rigid as the buildings we have learned to associate with school itself. In our work and in this chapter, we hope to illuminate some of the qualities of pedagogical places both inside and outside of school.

When is a classroom not a classroom?

Hallways are taken-for-granted places where school members congregate daily as part of a scheduled routine on their way to learning sites – the classrooms (see Figure 10.1).

Figure 10.1. Typical school hallway. Hallway space comprises an integral amount of overall school space. Photograph by A. Foran.

These passageways lead teachers and students into or out of school. The atmosphere of the hallway speaks volumes. By walking the school hallway, one is swept into the arterial flow, the rhythm and pulse of the place. Each step takes one deeper into the heart of the school, and with each echo of the treading foot one can sense the spirit of place. It is within the hallway that the intent of the place, the school, can be felt, even before entering the classrooms. Yet hallways have come to be thought of as non-pedagogical places not intended for instructional endeavors. What happens for teachers and students when learning and teaching occurs in this in-between place? What draws their attention? What is placed in tension?

Shoes

> I had dismissed my kindergarten students and, once everyone was out of the classroom, coats not needed on this warm Spring day, I headed down the hall to the doorway to ensure all the children had managed to put on their outside shoes and had made it safely outside for the 15 minute recess. I fully expected to find one or two students needing assistance with the complex task of putting on and tying or buckling their shoes. As I watched the crowd of children from several classrooms dissipate, I noticed Liza and Brianne, two of my students, seated facing each other in the hallway, heads and bodies intently focused on the task at hand. As I started to approach them, Liza's voice stopped me in my tracks. "You need to poosh, poosh hard … Harder … That's it … You are doing it … Keep trying … You just need to keep doing it … Keep pooshing … Good girl … You are doing it … Just keep pooshing … I know it is very very hard … You almost got it … There! It's on! Good girl! You did it! Now do the next one. I will watch you … You need to do it yourself." I could not interrupt this concerted effort but stood mesmerized by the process I had so fortuitously stumbled upon. "You got them both on all by yourself! See! You could do it yourself! Now you need to do the buckles. They are very hard. Your shoes are pretty. I like buckles, but they are very hard." Here a brief interlude while these two small girls took a moment to discuss the pleasures and difficulties of feminine dress. After this brief respite, Liza continued, "Just take your time … Ok … poot the strap in that hole … Right there … Ok, now pool it back … Pool it back really hard …Really really hard … Yes, you can do it … Just keep pooling … Now poot that in the little hole … Good girl … You are doing it … You are almost finished … Keep going … It's in! You did it … Now just poosh that part in there. Yes, you can do it… You need to keep trying… You can do it when you try… Just keep trying… See! You did it again. You did it all! You did it all by yourself!!!!" Up they jumped and off they ran out the door. (Olson, kindergarten teacher)

What had I just witnessed? Why did I choose to stay and watch when they certainly did not need me and I could have been thankful that I would have time to go to the staffroom for a cup of coffee rather than spend it yet again on the floor with more shoes? I was fascinated by how Liza, a student who had come to us from Poland the previous September, speaking no English, was giving such clear, specific, verbal instructions to Brianna, especially when it might have been so much easier to have said, "Let me do it for you." That would have taken much less effort on both Liza's and Brianna's parts. I was fascinated with the patience and perseverance they both demonstrated in what I saw as a pedagogical moment. A moment as profound as any that I have experienced in the classroom. Yet what strikes me is how significant this moment was for learning, removed from the lessons just beyond the wall separating the classroom from the hallway. If teaching is about learning and pedagogy is about the relational bond between teacher and learner what occurred in that hallway before recess?

Doubt

> I did not want to waste another minute inside. They followed me down the hallway laughing, scrambling; it was all so exciting. It was like they had never been outdoors before, or I, for that matter. When I reached the front door I froze. I could hear them

behind me and I could see the brightness, the sun forcing its way through the little square opening. I started to laugh inside, but I know it was a nervous laugh. Then I came face to face with the door. My spontaneity took a turn. Just what was I doing? Would this work? Am I allowed to do this? I think I was afraid, of what, I do not know. I was flooded with "what if" questions. I almost turned around and said, "Back to the class! This is not right!" But I didn't. I pushed the release bar and went straight out. As I looked around I remember whispering a line from Dr. Seuss, "It's opener there in the wide open air." And then they came pouring out behind me. For some reason I had this shadow of doubt hanging over my head despite the brilliant afternoon. (Jay, Career and Life Management teacher)

What taken-for-granted assumptions about school and learning stopped Jay in his tracks? What did Jay experience at that moment of hesitation as he looked out from the inside of the doorway? His hands would have been touching, feeling the cool aluminum release bar common to school doors. We are curious to understand the cause of his hesitation. The hesitation may be rooted in the idea that a class occurring outside is somehow unnatural to conventional instruction. Pedagogically, we find Jay's anecdote disturbing because somewhere, deep within his lived experience there is a quiet realization that the classroom seems to have power over the pedagogical.

Pedagogical Intent

Schools "arouse ... feelings alongside the associations" (Markus, 1993, p. 3). As previously noted, the mere mention of school immediately evokes meanings, memories, and stories about particular place experiences. What pedagogical implications are aroused when teachers abandon the accepted intentions expressed in the act of teaching indoors and embrace pedagogical possibilities in and of other places, and what happens to the relational associations of learning attached to the classroom in the physical sense?

From the two preceding anecdotes we can begin to tease out some pedagogical intentions. For Liza, perhaps because she was not yet old enough to have absorbed socially constructed conventions surrounding places in a school, the intensity she showed in teaching her friend was not disturbed by other conventions. Jay, however, was caught up short at the door as all of his pedagogical intentions were in tension with his presuppositions of what he should or could do in teaching his students. Liza's attention was drawn to Brianna's need to be able to get her shoes tied. The intention of going outside and the attention to the task of teaching Brianna how to tie her shoes in order to fulfill this intention were in harmony. They were, as Leslie introduced at the start of this chapter, dwelling authentically in a learning experience without interruption or distraction. Jay's attention, originally focused on the anticipation of going outside with his students, was abruptly interrupted and refocused on the door, which became for him, a silent reminder that he was leaving the sanctity of the school. For a moment his pedagogical intentions were in tension with his socially constructed, taken-for-granted assumptions about place with regard to his pedagogical relationships with his students.

Being pedagogical determines that something is to be learned. Historically, scholars secluded themselves by stepping out of the on-going nature of the world. These scholars wanted quiet, concentration, and discipline as can still be found with the Carthusian order of monks captured in Gröning's (2006) film documentary, *Into Great Silence*. Schools are busy places where the intent is for children to be quiet and productive – on task, a curricular focus similar to that of the monks. Tuan (1977) states:

> The building or architectural complex now stands as an environment capable of affecting the people who live in it …. [This] space can refine human feeling and perception…Architectural space – even a simple hut surrounded by cleared ground – can define such sensations and render them vivid. Another influence is this: the built environment clarifies social roles and relations. People know better who they are and how they ought to behave when the arena is humanly designed rather than nature's raw stage. Finally, architecture "teaches" …. In the absence of books and formal instruction, architecture is a key to comprehending reality. (p. 102)

The structure of the school itself has defined our roles as learners and teachers and the perception of where learning should take place. The building itself has the power to define (Markus, 1993). This causes us to wonder if classrooms may be at heart unnatural places for pedagogy to occur – present-day classrooms classify, segregate, isolate and institutionalize children according to a controlling system. Classrooms are imposed onto children and teachers as the only place where legitimate learning occurs. A classroom conditions their behaviors, their thinking, their feeling, and their relationships with others. In schools much of the teacher's role is management – not pedagogy. We often hear: "This is not the place for that." To question the sanctity of the classroom environment is to question the place of teaching. We contend that pedagogy should not be limited to a particular place; rather a quality relationship should exude an atmosphere and be felt in any place; in the classroom, a restaurant (see Olson & Craig, 2009) or outside (see Foran, 2006). In another Christian example, Jesus taught anywhere and everywhere, as his Sermon on the Mount attests. Crowds gathered. No bell rang. Sound pedagogical practice does more than simply cover given material indoors or outdoors. As teachers, we need to be free to develop our practice to include a variety of pedagogical places.

SEEING ONESELF AS PEDAGOGICALLY IN OR OUT OF PLACE

People's connections to place are developed over time and are informed by their relational understandings of their personal associations to a *physical place* and to *one another*. We understand the relational as a metaphorical, metaphysical place, no less influential than the physicality of the school building that typically shelters the relational connection between teachers and students. Relph (1993) notes the following:

> Belonging to a place, feeling part of it, gives many a positive sensation of security. Yet for others it may be oppressive and restrictive. Whether we know places with

deep affection or merely as stopping points in our passage through the world, they are set apart in time and space because they have distinctive meanings for us. (p. 28)

This connection to place is of crucial importance to how a teacher is able to foster the relational capacity with students. Di Leo and Jacobs (2004) suggest the following:

the *thisness* of the classroom is always already uniquely defined through the interrelation of its place with a particular set of individuals…as a site of interaction or struggle it is not generalizable .... It is a specific interaction between a place and individuals. (p. 3)

The following two anecdotes show pedagogical tensions when teachers felt out of place in the pedagogical relationships they believed they were expected to enact, bringing to consciousness deeply buried taken-for-granted assumptions of what they understood about their role and place as teachers.

Supervising in the hallway

"I don't think I am cut out to be a very good teacher," Shelly confided in me after her first visit to her first practicum placement. "What do you mean?" I asked Shelly, surprised by her comment, given that I had found her to be an excellent student in my university class. "The children wouldn't listen to me," Shelly continued. "I felt like I had no control." "What happened?" I asked. Shelly explained that her placement was with a grade 4 teacher. Shelly had been very excited and nervous about what she might be expected to do, wanted to learn all she could, but also wanted to figure out her place in this teacher's classroom. The details came out. "The teacher wanted the students to do their recorder exam one at a time in the classroom with her and she wanted me to supervise the rest of the class in the hallway while they each waited for their turn to go in and be tested. It took a long time and I couldn't keep them all quiet. It was awful!"

I was stunned. I assured Shelly that this was in no way any indication of her potential to become a good teacher. As I attempted to find the words to reassure her, I began to articulate to her and to myself why this seemed to me to be such a bizarre situation. I talked about the possible stress students were likely feeling due to the recorder test that was occurring in the classroom. Of how impossible it would be for them to stand silently when one of the things they needed to do most was ask anyone coming out of the room, "How was it? How did you do?" for the benefit of the student who emerged as well as for themselves. I also began to think out loud of hallways and how they are a different kind of place than classrooms and how classroom behaviors are not hallway behaviors. I talked about how hallways in schools are places through which students are encouraged to move quickly as they go from one place to another. In this sense a hallway is not "really" a "place" at all. Standing still in one feels out of place.

Shelly seemed on one hand to be a bit reassured, but now also seemed to be more aware of what she did not know, a place she did not find a comfortable fit as she tried to imagine herself as a teacher. (Olson, University Professor)

Perhaps this example points toward the impossibility of achieving outside the classroom what is inherent within the classroom for as teachers we "regard buildings as material classifying devices; they organize people, things, and ideas in space so as to make conceptual systems concrete" (Markus, 1993, p. 19). As Shelly suggests, when engaging pedagogically with children outside of the classroom, the experience may put our teaching practices into question. A pedagogical encounter outside the classroom seemingly erodes a teacher's sense of place and as a result many feel a pull, a call to return to the familiarity of a place where student-teacher relationships are intact as intended by a school. A building is a space shared with others and we do not doubt its tangibility as a place. A building implies and holds power; it has "form, function and space [and] each has meanings in the field of social relations, each is capable of signifying who we are, to ourselves, in society and in the cosmic scheme of things" (Markus, p. 30). One challenge confronted by educators is to understand the importance and structure of social relations as an organizing power that equals that of the school building.

Trespassing

It's hard to put my finger on it. It's like I didn't belong. I wanted to be outside with them, but was this really the best place for us? I kept thinking, "Is this not better than being inside? Am I not making the curricular experience more real?" I know the kids were enjoying it. I was too. Sometimes I feel as if the classroom smothers us. I know I came alive outside, in some way. We were imagining that we were the first explorers pushing into the interior of a vast land that became Canada. I was reading the account from Pierre Gaultier de Varennes, sieur de La Vérendrye. I was watching the faces of my students as I was reading the passage. They were staring at the wood's path and the glint of shimmering water of the lake off to our left. If it weren't for their faces I would have left. I now wonder if this feeling of belonging was what the explorers from years ago felt. What I want to know is why I feel so displaced when I take them out here. These woods are on school property, but I always feel like a trespasser. (Jody, History teacher)

During the *teaching moment* outside the classroom, numerous pedagogical questions emerge: What are they learning? Are these experiences outside school beneficial to their development? Why was this lesson so different from others taught before? These are just a few examples of questions that might surface once outside the classroom. Another concern from Jody is the issue of the *abundance of space* once outside the classroom – a kind of pedagogical agoraphobia. Jody's concern is summarized in the observation of feeling disconnected from the students and teaching in an outside place. Again, outside teaching occurs with a class of students, in a non-room, within an abundance of space. This becomes one of the challenges for teachers: to leave behind what is known, to venture into the unfamiliar, to hone a pedagogical practice that exists outside the norm of their established, pre-service training and their recollections of school as they experienced it. Regardless of Jody's uncertainty in an outside place, it was the relational encounter of pedagogy – the look on his students' faces – that held him in-place to explore the fullness of the pedagogical moment.

Place Realization

Outside the classroom, the teacher may be unsure of how to teach due to uncertainty about how to use the space. How does a teacher outside of the classroom, therefore, define a pedagogical practice? We find it interesting, almost puzzling, that a person can sense not belonging to a particular place that they normally inhabit. Shelly's developing image of her self as a teacher was brought into question when she found herself unable to "control" students, a role she implicitly understood as part of her responsibility as a teacher, one that appeared to preclude her pedagogical responsibilities. Jody, a more experienced teacher, seemed to have more pedagogical experience to draw upon as he attempted to make sense of how to relate with students in a place that seemed pedagogically unfamiliar, a space not naturally infused with pedagogical intent. Was Jody struggling to see this outside space as a pedagogical place? Did his sense of being a trespasser come from a presupposition that this outside space really was a place with its own particular meanings that were in tension with his pedagogical intent? Jody may have realized that indoor teacher intentions may not have belonged outside and that there was a need for a different way to be pedagogically present with his students.

What would cause a body – and in this particular instance, the teacher's body – to sense this displacement in a person's own world? Is the body the *res extensa* of the Cartesian definition of *corpus*? Therefore, it could be that for the teacher the bodily experience of leaving the inside world is a disturbance to the *cogito*. It could be possible for teachers, when stepping outside with their students, to be "no longer concerned with [their] body, nor with time, nor with the world, as I experience them in ante-predicative knowledge, in the inner communion that I have with them" (Merleau-Ponty, 1962, p. 71).

As humans, the world is around us and inside us. We are part of the infinite world. Merleau-Ponty (1962) explains, "The world is not what I think, but what [I] live through. I am open to the world, I have no doubt that I am in communication with it, but I do not possess it; it is inexhaustible" (p. xvii). The teacher who is comfortable outside the school can provide important insights into the lived experience of the corporeal encounter with the outside world. Important comparisons in this pedagogical experience can be found between the teacher who is at home outdoors and the teacher who hesitated at the door, the teacher who sensed a gulf separating the inside world from the outside world and the teacher who experienced a sense of displacement.

Gendlin (1988) explains, "we are always situated ... in the world, in a context, living in a certain way with others, trying to achieve ..." (p. 44). Polanyi (1969) offers interpretations of experience in general terms and a description of how the body can be seen in relationship with every physical experience:

> Our body is the only assembly of things known almost exclusively by relying on our awareness of them for attending to something else.... Every time we make sense of the world, we rely on our tacit knowledge of impacts made by the world on our body and the complex responses of our body to these impacts. (pp. 147–148)

This knowledge rests in making sense of the physical experience of *being* in the world. An important discovery would be the ability to distinguish the source of one's disassociation, displacement, and the feelings of not belonging. It is significant to note that Jody, in the end, remained outside and continued with the lesson of the early Canadian explorers, but he remained only as a trespasser.

To leave the classroom is to venture outside the bounds of what many teachers *know* to be familiar and consider inviolable about teaching. A teaching practice that can bridge these inside-outside worlds can allow for insight into what both worlds have to offer pedagogically. The following example (Olson & Craig, 2009) describes a teacher for whom the pedagogical relationship is not constrained by place:

> You should have seen this white teacher interacting with this group of African American boys – his basketball team, you know – at Chili's Restaurant in Dallas. While waiting for their lunch, the teacher posed this really tough mathematics problem and set two boys up to solve it: one student assisted by the teacher; the other student aided by the rest of the basketball team. What was going on was so dynamic and productive and contrary to common stereotypes held about minority youth and white teachers .... In fact, a crowd gathered around them ... other teams as well as parents and some police officers having coffee as well .... All of us were stunned. All of this teaching and learning going on at Chili's? Can you believe it? My wife [a principal] and I [a principal] decided to sign our son up for his team. Both of us agreed that we would hire this teacher in a minute if he were employed in our school district.

Because this teacher dwells pedagogically with children, every place is filled with pedagogical possibilities – even a restaurant can offer learning opportunities. When asked later, the teacher/coach described in the above anecdote, told his version of the story this way:

> When I teach my class number sense and mental math strategies, it is exactly the same as when I take my basketball team out of town .... I will share the following with you as a way to explain my approach .... My basketball team was waiting for dinner. I pulled one student aside and showed him how to do a strategy in his head. Then, I involved the rest of the team – through one player – but I don't teach them the strategy [although they desperately want to learn it]. Pretty soon, you know, parents are drawn in, you know .... They see their children motivated by mathematics as well as by basketball, and all the time, they are supposed to be goofing off with their friends.

The coach/teacher continued:

> And now we are in the middle of a restaurant, Chili's – I'll just use the example from Dallas two weeks ago. We're in the middle of Chili's and I've got one kid going up against another kid with the rest of the team involved .... Pretty soon, I have other basketball teams surrounding our table even though there is a game on television for

them to watch …. But instead these kids (along with their parents who also have gathered) are glued to my teaching my students number sense. Next thing you know, four policemen are surrounding our table, curious, perhaps even suspicious, about what is going on.

Outside the classroom lessons offer experiences that reach farther than classroom walls by informing educators about other ways to relate pedagogically to children. Therefore, we are attuned to emerging similarities and contradictions between the inside and outside worlds. We further this inquiry by considering what occurs relationally because of place.

BEING-IN-THE-WORLD

Inside and outside are co-constitutional, each helping to define the other. Heidegger (1962) explains this intricate balance between seeking experiences (*Erlebnis*) in the outside world, intensifying experiences (*Erfahrungen*) on the inside through reflection, and living through experiences (*Erleben*) (pp. 71–72). The ancient Greeks frequently used an expression, *ekstatikon*, to describe the experience of a person "stepping-outside-self." This term is affiliated with "existence [, which]…viewed ontologically, is the original unity of being-outside-self that comes-toward-self, [and] comes-back-to-self" (Heidegger, 1982, p. 267). This common ancient expression is applicable to the lived experience of a teacher (and her or his students) stepping outside her or his lifeworld (Husserl, 1970), and going inward, pedagogically, to understand the experience. Arendt (1978) captures, for us, the pedagogical importance of experience outside the classroom. Arendt posits that being outside the school is to be really inside the world and the classroom inside the school is a place that is outside the world. The classroom world, she argues, represents an abstraction of the real world. Lindsay and Ewert (1999) echo this sentiment:

> Teaching in … schools focus[es] on the facts as found in the textbooks and not … [on] applying knowledge …[;] textbooks are regarded as an efficient means of communicating information to students but, in reality, deny or restrict responsibility for learning as well as opportunities for active involvement in the learning process. (p. 16)

When Olson was teaching kindergarten, she was asked by a greatly puzzled teaching colleague, "How can you teach them anything when they can't read?" Taking textbooks as the sole or primary authority and repository of accurate information, of course, has considerable consequences. The following example describes an exchange between a student and Olson, and offers an illustration of a taken-for-granted privilege of textbook knowledge above other ways of knowing:

> I had taken my class on a field trip to the farm. While there, I found myself in a heated debate with one of my students. I had pointed out a cow grazing close by. "That's not a cow," said the young boy assertively. "It's too big." I tried hard to change the boy's misconception, but he adamantly insisted that this could not be a cow because it was too big. When I asked him why he was so sure that this was not a cow, he replied. "I

189

know what a cow looks like. I saw one in a book in our classroom. This is not a cow. It is too big." Realizing that I would make no progress here, I conceded the argument for the time being. Back in our classroom, I asked him to show me the book with the cow. Sure enough, he found it, saying "See. It's just little." There on the page was a picture of a pasture with a cow far in the background. The cow was indeed very small. Not having experienced cows, or possibly other animals moving, the young boy had not taken perspective into account yet, even at this young age, he was prepared to take the book as gospel over and above his own experience and anything I could tell him. It made me realize just how damaging books can be when they are seen as more authoritative than experience itself. (Olson, kindergarten teacher)

Arendt (1978) furthers understanding of pedagogical place by having teachers consider the following assertion: "Now school is by no means the world and must not pretend to be; it is an institution that we interpose between the private domain of home and the world in order to make the transition from the family to the world possible at all." (pp. 188-189)

Our concern is with *when* and *where* teaching is pedagogical – inside or outside! Arendt states that children grow into an "old world," gradually and the role for educators is to prepare them for their place in it (p. 177). Important here is for educators to preserve school as a transitional place. Arendt is clear when she states that teachers must know about the world and that their role is to "instruct others about it" (p. 189). In this context, the "function of the school is to teach children what the world is like and not to instruct them in the art of living" (p. 195). When does keeping children inside a classroom or taking them outside enable or disable the pedagogical relationship? This question is critical to ask because expectations are placed on children while they are in school. Teaching outside the classroom may very well be an attempt to bring students into closer contact with direct experience and thereby achieve a sound experiential pedagogy. This contact would seem to be contrary to more dominant methods and media of education delivery.

Inside and outside are dialectically related, dependent on one another for the experience of each, and this dialectic contributes to our sense of being in the world. The act of taking a class outside the building can create for teachers a unique inner-reflected experience that reveals the relational meaning of pedagogy. However, teachers may not be prepared pedagogically to undertake such a challenge. The potential lies in changing the notion of pedagogical place that can both compromise learning and enhance the educational experience of young people. Teaching outside is more than just covering a given subject outdoors; educators need to develop a pedagogical sense not only of the physical place but also of the relational place and what is pedagogically appropriate for particular students in particular places at particular times.

Visiting Richard's House

Richard's mother approached me excitedly to invite all Richard's kindergarten classmates and me as their teacher to their home for lunch. She explained that Richard had asked her if his friends could all come over for home cooked Chinese food. I assured her that she did not need to do that. "It would be a lot of work," I said. But she seemed as enthusiastic as Richard was and insisted that it would be a pleasure. She also wanted to teach the children how to make traditional Chinese egg rolls. She explained how she had thought about how to organize it so that each child would be able to make their own egg roll. I hesitantly agreed, feeling that she had no idea how much work she was creating for herself by inviting 27 five year olds to her home. She thanked me profusely, adding, "It won't be for a while. We are getting our basement refinished and when it is done the children can come."

The day finally arrived. Field trip permission slips had been signed and returned. I had gone over field trip rules with the children and we set off. We did not even need a bus! Richard proudly led the small parade headed off to his house with my teacher's aide Sharon and me bringing up the rear. On the way children pointed out places like "my house," "my friend's house," "the daycare," and "where we go to play." As we continued on our way the conversation subtly shifted from where children had been to where they were going. Some asked Richard questions about his house. Some began to talk of how they had "already been to Richard's house" and shared insider information. Neither Sharon nor I had previously been to Richard's house. My comment to students' questions was either: "I don't know. You will have to ask Richard." Or "We'll have to wait and see."

As the anticipation grew the little parade picked up momentum. A chant – "We're on our way to Richard's house" – began and soon spread though the group. Finally Richard stopped, pointed, and exclaimed: "There it is!" Suddenly children broke rank and scurried helter skelter up to Richard's front door. Richard's mom threw the door open and enthusiastically welcomed them in. After futilely attempting to regain some control by telling the children to get back in line and basically being ignored by the children and by Richard's mom, I too entered Richard's house as part of the bunch. The children were fine, Richard's mom was fine, Sharon was fine, and I was beside myself. I seemed to not know my place. This was not the way children entered our school as a class every day where they were expected to line up and wait for the bell to ring and be allowed in one-by-one.

We followed Richard's mom down stairs where, much to my relief, the children settled down, some more quickly than others! Sharon and I asked Richard's mom how we could help and soon everyone was arranged in groups in a very similar manner to what we would do together in our classroom with children busily engaged and adults assisting them in their learning. Some started eating while others went with Richard's mom to make their egg rolls and the groups rotated until everyone had made their own egg roll and eaten a variety of Chinese cuisine. Full and content, it was time to leave in order to get back to school at the time indicated on the field trip permission slips. Everyone thanked Richard and his mom for a very successful event. After trying to explain to some of the children why they could not just stay and play at Richard's house, we went on our way. (Olson, kindergarten teacher)

As teachers, our understanding of the term "outside the classroom," and our conception of teaching inside, often dictates our pedagogical practice. Yet, as the above anecdote exemplifies, the metaphorical, metaphysical, pedagogical relationship is as strong as any physical place in shaping pedagogical practice. We see similarities in the above anecdote in the story Jay told of being stopped at the door and wondering if he should or could go outside. While for Jay there appeared to be a distinct place where he seemed to believe his pedagogical relationship with students should occur, for Olson, this place seemed to stretch over space and time like a large rubber band until it reached the breaking point at Richard's front door. Olson had taken students on "field trips" many times to many different places and had not previously felt discomfort in taking students away from the school. How then was this particular field trip different? We look to the relational for clues. In this anecdote it was not so much the change in place as the change in relationship that occurred on Richard's front steps. For Olson, the pedagogical relationship had remained intact on other field trips, but in this case, Richard's mother was "at home" and Olson was not. This points to the pedagogical authority teachers are supposed to have, which was subsumed momentarily, under parental authority. Although teachers are legally supposed to behave in *loco parentus*, in this case, when a real parent appeared, the authority shifted and Olson needed to readjust. The children had no difficulty with this shift. As has been shown in the above example, what we think and believe on the inside influences our being in the world, the outside.

The experience of roaming the edge

> Crystal Cliffs is one of my favorite spots. It has the majesty of the trees of a typical Acadian forest. It has the wide-open fields, meadows that gradually rise to an exposed gypsum cliff. It has a little meandering river, a fresh water pond, a saltwater estuary, and the ocean. It offers everything needed for a biology field-trip designed to examine the insects that inhabit the edges of bordering habitats. To make the determination as to why certain species are present, the students collect bugs from various ecotones by pooting insects; sucking them up in a piece of rubber hose 4-5 inches long, with a piece of pantyhose tightly attached to one end that stops the insect. Then you can blow the bug into the collection jar. You have to go with the insects and I can't predict where or what will be along an edge at any given time. I have to be flexible allowing the kids to go between the zones. Students have to be able to roam, criss-crossing the ecotones; we were all over the place. It's hard at first, one would think it was teaching chaos, but it is not. There is a freedom in this lesson; we have to roam to learn. I still panic, at how disjointed the lesson appears, kids all over the place – the whole time I am feeling out-of-control. But it always comes together, the data linked to the bigger context: historical, geographical, and geological of the area, and why certain insects gravitate in certain zones. Crystal Cliffs is a convergence of curriculum; so many subjects come into play helping us make sense. Could you imagine trying to pull this off indoors? Everything is so interconnected out here and that includes us as well! (Bobby, Biology teacher)

Schools can be awkward places, for they distinctly segregate students' Being from the world, but their primary function is to prepare students for the world. The tension resides in how we as teachers prepare students through courses and how much of the real world we can use in this preparation. Bobby commented that when the teaching experience is extended to the outdoor world, there is *no want*; the outdoors offered all that was necessary for learning to occur. As Bobby stated emphatically on numerous occasions, "I had everything that I could ever want as a teacher when I went outdoors with my kids. All I have to do is roam and the outdoors will give me what I want!" The link with pedagogy is the experience of convergence: subject knowledge, student insect finds, the roaming between ecotones, and a teacher guiding the learning experience that presents itself; not a controlling force artificially predetermining what learning should occur.

Bobby comments several times that *other knowledge* was allowed to exist within the lesson plan; it was much more than just insects. Subject separation or segregation is hard or next to impossible to maintain when teaching outdoors. As Bobby states:

> How can I keep the world out of the lesson? When we are standing right in it, they see it, and I can't stop them from knowing it. As a teacher I am free to draw on what the outdoors offers at the time, and nature makes immediate sense for our learning. I cannot control everything out here. I have to go where the learning is best for my students.

This pedagogical freedom is not about Bobby breaking the teaching code, stepping outside the designated outcomes of the curriculum. Bobby allowed students to follow their learning interests and, pedagogically, gave them the freedom to roam the habitat edges to satisfy their inquiry. Pedagogically, we wonder if trust in the students is what allows Crystal Cliffs to stand out as a favorite learning place.

We see this as the simple connection that we, as humans, have to our world, which is primordial and existed before social conventions imposed their ways of being on our lives. The freedom for Bobby is in exploring, experiencing, and teaching his students without curricular restrictions; a manner of learning that existed long before schooling was institutionalized – learning by freely roaming and naturally making links. Does Bobby's outside pedagogical experience of allowing students to roam freely allow, in turn, for a fuller convergence of learning possibilities because the natural connections result in having an abundance of resources for the class? Bobby's statement – "I have everything that I could want" – reminds us that, for good learning to occur, a teacher needs to support students in their learning. Important to the relationship, naturally, is trust. Does going outdoors free Bobby from acquiring the needed resources to develop appropriate learning experiences, or does it provide him with the freedom to trust students as they roam edges to learn?

Gadamer (2001) clarifies the epistemological understanding of freedom: "Freedom is not a fact in nature but rather...a fact of reason, something we must think, because without thinking of ourselves as free we cannot understand ourselves at all" (p. 123). Gadamer (1986) asserts that freedom experienced as a conscious feeling is appropriate, because natural conditions allow for a being aware of choice and thus, being able to act freely. An explanation for Bobby's sense of freedom in his teaching lies in the understanding that in the outdoors it makes perfect sense to open up a lesson to the many ways of knowing the world.

Outside, Bobby could resist the artificial, over-rationalized, mechanistic, subject separation that has come to dominate Western curricular offerings. Bobby was able to teach out from underneath the tutelage of the classroom and allow a pedagogical bond to develop naturally between the learning opportunities and the needs of the students.

As Bobby's students roam in and connect with their environment, Bobby is able to connect to people and place – "everything is interconnected" – trusting students relationally by allowing them to roam outside. Bobby is able to become that link between the natural world, the learning, and the confidence in the student-teacher relationship outside the school. When possible, students can roam freely, and the teacher can become more of a guide in the experience who helps them make connections to the curriculum. In establishing our classrooms we inadvertently structure our version of the world. Leaving this inner world could become difficult, and the simple act of stepping outside of a school to teach may not be possible for some teachers.

SEEKING PLACE AND PEDAGOGY – A RELATIONAL ENCOUNTER

We can now situate this chapter as an examination of the tension between the inner and outer worlds. We are sure that pedagogy is neither exclusive to, nor restricted to, an inside classroom practice. For Aoki (1990), the pedagogical relationship becomes an opportunity in which the "educator and the educated are allowed to dwell in a present that embraces past experiences and is open to possibilities yet to be" (p. 114). Burkholder (2003) refers to *consilience* as the ability to see something in its wholeness: not as an abstraction, but as the thing itself and connected to you directly. Similarly, Dewey (1902) also advocated that education should start with a child's interest in concrete, everyday experiences and build on that understanding to connect children with more formal subject matter. To ensure connections are made to the intended learning, and that the curriculum has relevance, each student participates in experiences drawn from community life and occupations. The curriculum is constructed around exploratory themes, and the student progresses through exploration and discovery (Dewey, 1902).

Determinism or Indeterminism

Every year I teach a unit on Entrepreneurialism, and I do a field trip to one of our local-community businesses. That year was the Moon Sugar Shack. I will never forget this little girl had soot all over her face. At the beginning of the winter term she was so awkward; concerned about her presence, how she looked, what she said, she was stuck and struggling to be her natural self. She worked hard just like all the other kids. Her job was to manage the sugar shack: simply keep the sap flow measured and the fires stoked for boiling. I remember seeing this girl, as we were packing up. She was different: she was not fussing with herself, she did not care, she was on a high, and she was in that zone. She was having an experience that was so rich for her that she was not concerned about her hair or how she looked. During the closing statements, she mentioned that she loved the fact that she knew she could run her own business: she liked math, she was organized, but she loved the hands on. For the first time she felt in control of what she could do, felt awake out here in the woods. She said that school smothered her. She wanted to run her own business and could care less what it was. I was floored. What a difference a day can make. She had long, straight, blond hair and she was covered in charcoal and she smelled of smoke from the sugar-shack fire. This young girl was just captured by her experience. She flourished in the freedom, outside the school. She was alive. Education is all about change, but I realized that I could not measure or evaluate that day for her. That was beyond my control. (Jay, Career and Life Management teacher)

Jay aligns himself with a notion of pedagogy: leading students to their learning and allowing them the space to experience it, first hand, with little teacher interference. This *hands-off* approach is difficult to maintain as a teacher: instinctively and as a result of their education, teachers want to involve themselves in their students' learning. The outdoors provides space that allows for a distancing to happen naturally between students and teachers. Jay explained that when he watches children play, even role-play, he is witness to freedom in self-expression. A child at play is the embodiment of non-restraint. The student Jay describes was playing a role of entrepreneur. Jay observed that the outside experience allowed this child to learn that her future could be undefined:

Why does everything have to be cast in stone with kids? It seems that when they come into high school there is a pressure to determine their futures as some forgone conclusion; undefined can be good when you're a kid. The indeterminate world is living the possible.

Similarly, Gadamer (1986) refers to a beauty that is recognizable in freedom. The freedom of play is not "some substitute dream-world" where we lose ourselves; rather, it is a "mirror … in which we catch a sight of ourselves in a way that is often unexpected or unfamiliar: what we are, what we might be, and what we are about" (p. 30). Play, even a role-play for school, is a powerful and creative experience for people of all ages. Pedagogically, the out-of-doors for Jay became a pedagogical place where learning did not need to be confined to a measured-and-scored event that determines the future lives of students. The sugar shack showed a life that could be possible and that could not be determined by the conventions of scholastic performances. The teacher, away from the control of marking and evaluation, realized that not all learning could be measured.

Jay was also learning, or relearning, the pedagogical importance of freedom. Play is the power of spontaneous freedom. Play may very well be the human act that is without determinism. Jay's experience of freedom could very well be that of teaching the simple beauty of a role-play, and this witnessing of the educative change, by a teacher, would be liberating. The play here involved hands-on contact in the framework of the subject area – entrepreneurialism – and it approached maturity when what it hinted at became a serious possibility: the indeterminate freedom of possibility.

Freedom to learn: Swinging and singing, inside out

My principal, Mr. White, introduced me to Jason, his mother Mrs. Jones, and brother Anthony with the explanation that the family would be moving to our area in a couple of months. Jason would be entering my kindergarten classroom and Mrs. Jones wanted to ensure that we were aware of Jason's special needs. Anthony was in grade four and doing well in school. Jason, on the other hand was, according to Mrs. Jones, "not like his brother." Mrs. Jones went on to explain that Jason did not enjoy books the way Anthony and their preschool brother did. He did not know his alphabet the way his preschool brother already did and was behind in skills that other children in his kindergarten class had acquired. Jason had been assessed at his present school and a recommendation for special services had been made. Mrs. Jones was now concerned that with their move, all of these plans might become derailed. Mr. White assured Mrs. Jones that we would take good care of Jason when he arrived but he would need to settle in to this new place before decisions could be made about any special services.

Two months later, Mrs. Jones arrived with Jason duly in tow. While his mother reminded me of how much difficulty Jason had in school, he looked down at the floor and said nothing. Mrs. Jones then left and Jason came with me into what was his new classroom. I knew that one of my jobs over the next few weeks would be to take careful note of Jason's progress so we could determine what, if any, special needs he might have. Jason was extremely quiet, never speaking unless spoken to and asked a specific question, which usually elicited at most a yes or no response. He sat very still in his desk, attempting to do what he was asked, but often responding with "I can't do that." Or "I don't know how." Jason did indeed appear to have very limited vocabulary and few if any reading, writing, or math skills. The more I watched and listened, the more it appeared that Jason was indeed out of place in this classroom. We likely did need to have some reassessments made and special program services put in place.

About the time I had started to discuss my observations with Mr. White and arrange a meeting with Mrs. Jones, I was on regularly scheduled recess playground supervision. In the distance I happened to see a small boy on a swing going higher and higher. As I approached from behind to check on him and possibly suggest that he was likely going high enough now, I could see that it was Jason. I could also now hear him singing "The Alphabet Song" freely, fluently, and at the top of his lungs. I stopped, amazed. Could this be the same Jason who was so tentative, hesitant and quiet in the classroom? (Olson, kindergarten teacher)

We believe this is another example of freedom in action. Jason appeared to be experiencing a regularly scheduled daily recess not only as part of the imposed structure of schooling but also as a relief from the pressure he seemed to have learned would be a part of his time at school, a story he had been exposed to by his mother, likely at home and certainly in conversation with Olson. This story presupposed that Jason's introduction to schooling was to be fraught with difficulty and failure: school and Jason's natural ability would not be a good fit. It seemed as if Jason had absorbed this story of himself and was living it in the classroom space in ways that made his discomfort painfully apparent and confirmed the assumption that school was not the place for Jason. This taken-for-granted assumption had not included the playground. It was here that Jason was free to be himself, free to express his joy of learning without the pressure he had learned would be exerted on him to produce and perform in ways he already believed he was incapable of, free to behave naturally and be open to possibility. We believe that freedom to learn involves not only trust, but also faith in the child's natural ability and intuition to grow and develop, to move toward becoming a more mature, more educated individual. We also believe that it is incumbent upon teachers to ensure that students are able to feel this trust and faith and experience freedom to learn naturally in whatever physical places they find themselves together.

Pedagogy of place

Teaching has evolved greatly from the days of informal gatherings, prior to public school buildings, when education was a parental responsibility, a tutoring arrangement, an apprenticeship, or a provision made to a select few by a religious authority. School has developed into a formal institutional structure for educating children that is highly organized to include grade levels, outcomes to mark progression, established institutional modes of rational, subject-specific instruction, and credentialed teachers who are highly skilled and trained to work within school buildings. This evolution of educational development has tended to leave the outdoors outside the ways we teach our children. An important discovery from the shared anecdotes in this chapter is the existence of a phenomenological moment, when pedagogy is realized as a concrete experience between the teacher and students; it is a lived experience that supersedes the dominant indoor agenda. Places can become geographic centers in one's personal and professional lives that are "carved out of chaotic space ... [and] set apart from the rest of the world as a holy precinct" (Bollnow, 1961, p. 34). The importance a place can have in a person's Being can border on spiritual sanctity, evoking ardent feelings that remind one of what is most precious. This is a full-body experience, the intentional awareness of being-in-the-world that encourages the body, beyond the desk, the classroom, or the school.

How can the conditions of pedagogy change as a result of location, given that the experience of teaching is still involved? Pedagogical distinctiveness draws from the power of the place where teaching evolves, and learning activities are associated with the lesson. Dovey (1985) identifies place as "the interaction between people and a physical setting together with a set of meanings" (p. 94). Pedagogically, inside or outside, belonging was associated with a student's place in the world. The "outside the classroom" teaching experience underscored a convergence of the fundamental connections of three things: place, memory, and human identity. Tuan (1977) makes this observation: "Undifferentiated space becomes place as we get to know it better and endow it with value" (p. 6). Teaching away from the dominance of the classroom space enables learning away from the shrill bell, crowded halls, booming announcements, stacks of marking, and the confines of an institution. Outside learning is free to get caught up in the

197

power of doing – away from the desk, the text, and the chalkboard. For students and for the teacher outside the classroom, their excitement was the excitement of the unexplored and an uncharted way to experience learning.

After reflecting on the lived experiences of teachers outside the classroom, we have discovered that a few essential qualities of pedagogical place emerged: there are appropriate places for engaging in different kinds of pedagogical activities with students and that activities can be experienced as in place or out-of-place; dwelling pedagogically is being absorbed and being able to dwell authentically in a learning experience without interruption or distraction; nature is found in such areas as the natural ability and interests of the child, the relationship of the natural physical and social world, the nature of learning. Thus, because of place, pedagogy became something as *understood* for these teachers; they could *see* the significance of the relational qualities existing between teachers and students. Conversely, place became a shared experience between teachers and students and not just a geographical location that was walked over or through.

Pedagogy of place showed, that for these teachers, the place they were in became their world. The student in that place allowed the teacher to *see* the relational connection beyond contractual responsibility for a class list. The teachers experienced time not as a mechanistic division in the day, but as embodied and part of the learning process. Time was not something that governed them. Time was fluid between teaching and curriculum, students and learning, binding them to place. The pedagogical place allowed teachers to become attuned, not to the lesson as an abstraction, but to the student in a place as connected to a genuine process.

Tuan (1977) notes: "The designed environment serves an educational purpose. In some societies the building is the primary text for handing down a tradition, for presenting a view of reality" (p. 112). Clearly, then, place is important to pedagogy. Following Di Leo and Jacobs (2004) suggestion, research must begin to consider all places for teaching from the perspective of pedagogical theory (p. 10). Becker (2004) claims that being in a place allows a person to experience the world through the flesh. This is the educational move from the abstract to the tangible – from a concept to something palpable. Schooling is important in culturalization; assisting the social stability and continuation. The Industrial Revolution was the historical event that called the West indoors. As a people we turned away from one way of life to accept and embrace another way of existing that was disconnected from the natural world and this came to include learning from experience. Accordingly, we have come to accept a way of life that controlled our environment artificially. Gallagher (1993) states: "There are special things in the places all around us, but you may have to work hard to see them" (p. 23). Gallagher posits that the "interior worlds we create, from log cabins to airplane cabins, have climates that affect our well-being as surely as the climates outside" (p. 47). Considering Gallagher's insights, one should not take for granted indoor environments or outside places in how they could be impacting our relational capacity with children. And Gallagher posits: "When we enter 'behavior settings' – a school, restaurant, gas station, hospital – everything in that environment encourages us to maintain the status quo" (p. 128). Thus stepping outside allows pedagogy to develop as a way of being between the teacher and students that falls outside the behavioral expectations of the institution. Pedagogy could be experienced as uniquely as the place where students and teachers find themselves.

What do teachers and students learn about their world, their learning, and themselves every time they enter their school building? The dominance of school buildings for pedagogy can explain our need for schools as a means of structuring the world, giving teachers control to bring order and focus for learning and teaching. When teachers go outside, the simple change in learning engagement may allow people to exit their own egocentrism and connect, through vulnerability to other people, the environment, and the here and now. Simply put, going outside can enable curious and adventurous teachers to seek places for their students to learn best; a pedagogical seeking of appropriate places for better learning opportunities to meet the needs of learners. School as place thus should not be considered lightly, from an architectural standpoint or from the naturalist call that connects students to nature. Clearly, the places we learn in influence more than just the curricular outcomes in that they shape who we are and how we relate to one another.

REFERENCES

Aoki, T. (1990). Themes of teaching curriculum. In J.T. Sears & J.D. Marshall (Eds.), *Teaching and thinking about curriculum: Critical inquiries* (pp. 111-114). New York: Teachers College Press.
Arendt, H. (1978). *Between past and future: Eight exercises in political thought.* New York: Penguin Books.
Becker, C. (2004). Pilgrimage to My Lai. In J.R. Di Leo & W.R. Jacobs (Eds.), *If classrooms matter: Progressive visions of educational environments* (pp.115-131). New York: Routledge.
Bollnow, O.F. (1961). Lived-space. *Philosophy Today, 5,* 31-40.
Burkholder, R.E. (2003). To see things in their wholeness: Consilience, natural history, and teaching literature outdoor. In H. Crimmel (Ed.), *Teaching in the field: Working with students in the outdoor classroom* (pp. 17-32). Salt Lake City: The University of Utah Press.
Dahlberg, K., Drew, N. & Nyström, M. (2002). *Reflective lifeworld research.* Lund, Sweden: Studentlitteratur.
Dewey, J. (1902). *The child and the curriculum.* Chicago: The University of Chicago Press.
Di Leo, J.R., & Jacobs, W.R. (2004). *If classrooms matter: Progressive visions of educational environments.* New York: Routledge.
Dovey, K. (1985). An ecology of place and place making: Structures, processes, knots of meanings. In K. Dovey, P. Downton, & G. Missingham (Eds.), *Place and placemaking: Proceedings of the Paper 85 Conference* (pp. 93–110). Melbourne, Australia.
Foran, A. (2006). *Teaching outside the school: A phenomenological inquiry.* Unpublished Doctorial Thesis. University of Alberta: Edmonton, Alberta.
Gadamer, H.-G. (2001). *The beginning of knowledge.* New York: Continuum.
Gadamer, H.-G. (1986). *The relevance of the beautiful.* Cambridge: Cambridge University Press.
Gallager, W. (1993*). The power of place: How our surroundings shape our thoughts, and actions.* New York: Harper Perennial.
Gendlin, E. T. (1988). Befindlichkeit: Heidegger and the philosophy and psychology. In K. Hoeller (Ed.), Heidegger and psychology. *Review of Existential Psychology and Psychiatry,* Special Issue, 43–71.
Gröning, P. (Director). (2006). *Into great silence* [Motion picture video]. Germany: Mongrel Media.
Heidegger, M. (1962). *Being and time.* New York: Harper & Row.

Heidegger, M. (1982). *The basic problems of phenomenology*. Bloomington: Indiana University Press.

Hillier, B. & Hanson, J. (1984). *The social logic of space*. Cambridge: Cambridge University Press.

Husserl, E. (1970). *The crises of European sciences and transcendental phenomenology*. Evanston, IL: Northwestern University Press.

Husserl, E. (1989). *Ideas pertaining to a pure phenomenology and to a phenomenological philosophy* (2nd book) [Rojcewicz, R. & Schuwer, A., Trans.]. Dordrecht, The Netherlands: Kluwer Academic Publishers.

Lindsay, A. & Ewert, A. (1999). Learning at the edge: Can experiential education contribute to educational reform? *Journal of Experiential Education, 22*(1), 12-19.

Markus, T. (1993). *Buildings and power: Freedom and control in the origin of modern building types*. London: Routledge.

Merleau-Ponty, M. (1962). *Phenomenology of perception*. London: Routledge & Kegan Paul.

Olson, M. & Craig, C. (2009). "Small" stories and meganarratives: Accountability in balance. *Teachers College Record, 111*(2), 547-572.

Moran, D. (2001). *Introduction to phenomenology*. New York: Routledge.

Polanyi, M. (1969). *Knowing and being*. Chicago, IL: University of Chicago Press.

Relph, E. (1993). Modernity and the reclamation of place. In D. Seamon (Ed.), *Dwelling, seeing, and designing: Toward a phenomenological ecology*. Albany, NY: State University of New York Press.

Smits, H. (1997). Hermeneutically-inspired action research: Living with the difficulties of understanding. *Journal of Curriculum Theorizing, 13*(1), 15-22.

Sokolowski, R. (2000). *Introduction to phenomenology*. New York: Cambridge University Press.

Tuan, Y.-F. (1977). *Space and place: The perspective of experience*. Minnesota, MN: University of Minnesota Press.

van Manen, M. (1988). The relation between research and pedagogy. In W. Pinar (Ed.), *Contemporary curriculum discourses* (pp. 437–452). Scottsdale: AZ:Gorsuch Scarisbride.

van Manen, M. (1997). *Researching lived experience human science for an action sensitive pedagogy* (2nd ed.). London, Ontario: Althouse Press.

van Manen, M. (2002). *The tone of teaching*. London, Ontario: Althouse Press.

PATRICK HOWARD

11. HOW LITERATURE WORKS

Poetry and the Phenomenology of Reader Response

INTRODUCTION: THE PROMISE OF LITERATURE

Through symbol, sound, and the magic of meaning literature transports readers into imaginary realms and fosters complex reading behaviors that invite children to experience emotional and intellectual invocations far greater than the sum of the factual constituents on any given page. The Atlantic Canada Curriculum Guide (1997) for Language Arts states:

> Creating or responding to literary text is an aesthetic act involving complex interactions of emotion and intellect. Experiences centered on interpreting and creating literacy texts enable students to participate in other lives and worlds beyond their own. Students reflect on their own identities and on the ways in which social and cultural contexts define and shape those identities. (p. 117)

Nell Noddings (1991, 2002) argues for the use of literature and the "general recognition that stories have enormous power" (2002, p. 45) in the development of the moral imagination. Literature provides empathetic insights into the imagined experiences of others across time, space, gender, culture and species. Poetry, for instance, offers the opportunity to interrupt, to de-familiarize the familiar in ways that challenge the clichéd, the stereotypical, and the status quo (Howard, 2006). In poetry, life stands still for a moment, and we can take time to examine it, to have conversations about values, ideas, and insights. Mark Doty writes, "One of poetry's great powers is its preservative ability to take a moment in time and attempt to hold it .../ That's an extraordinary thing, that something as small as a poem extends our lives" (in Moyers, 1999, p. 59). Literature offers the reflective stance, inviting students to formulate moral and philosophical understanding of the meaning of life (Dewey, 1916; Green, 1973).

Reader response literary theory focuses on active readers and the literary text actually existing in the transaction between reader and text. It is the dominant theory guiding the literary response of student readers in schools. This transaction signals a mutualism in which reader and text act on each other. I position my interests and this inquiry within the scope of 'experiential' theories of reader response. It is my hope to elaborate on the work of theorists who concern themselves with the *experience* of literary engagement. At the center of this study is a primary interest in describing readers' experience of engagement with

N. Friesen et al. (eds.), Hermeneutic Phenomenology in Education, 201–216.

literature, specifically poetry, and their involvement in what Judith Langer (1992) has called their own "envisionments."

What is the experience of having powerful new feelings, ideas and insights aroused by what we read? What is the nature of this life-forwarding capacity of literature? How do stories and poems exercise the moral imagination? To fully understand the essential place of literature in the curriculum it is important to investigate phenomenologically the experiencing interaction between feelings and word-symbols and describe experientially the power of language to move our lives forward.

THE TRANSACTIVE SPACE

The grade 9 class is exploring a selection of poems by writers of the geographic region who have, as the teacher is fond of saying, "given voice to the essential fullness of life and landscape." The students are exploring their place through local and regional poetry. Rain runs in tiny rivulets and pools on the blackened sills. Heads turn toward the windows when the gusts slant forcefully, audibly washing clean an autumn's grime. The teacher reads a final stanza, his voice rhythmically invoking the pull of place as written by poet John S. Mitchell:

boats upside down

> on red wharf
> cliffs surround and close
> centuries of eyes
> in each eye
> whispers and whispers
> in me

The teacher's voice trails off quietly in diminuendo holding the last syllable. A hand goes up but not before a boy blurts out, "It's like he's being watched or something, it's a creepy feeling, isn't it?"

"Yes?" the teacher acknowledges a boy who has raised his hand.

"I think that the speaker feels there is a lot history in that place – there are people, but it seems to be a much longer history, centuries – or ... it's like geological time."

Katie, a girl near the window adds, "And it seems to be speaking to him, a feeling or, like, a spirit of the place whispering ... it's hard to explain."

Outside now, the bay and surrounding hills have become obscured – a thin skein of fog envelops all imperceptibly, as roads and houses fade; the light is forced, squeezed and burnishes roof lines and fence posts.

The teacher holds comment and chooses another poem *Watching My Grandmother Pick a Late Flower* by New Brunswick poet Allan Cooper. Once again his voice quickly adopts the cadence and flow of word and line as he begins to read. The poem tells of a memory, a longing for another place and time:

She wanted to pick the last fading iris

in a field
across the road,
she spoke of old homesteads,
now gone...

She walked out into the field.
She carried the past with her.
her presence stirred

the grass...

The last word seems to hang in the air. He closes the book and walks toward the window. "What I would like you to do is to write about what you were thinking when I read these poems? Did it remind you of something you experienced? Where were you? What was it like? Write quietly in your journals for the next ten minutes." The students are familiar with the journal writing activity; there is some rustling in desks, but most are busy already.

The girl by the window, Katie, twirls her yellow pencil, the poets' words still reverberating, "field," "homestead," "presence," "stirred" ... a felt-sense, a memory, an image arises and she begins to write in her journal:

I remember seeing my grandfather, sitting and rocking, his hands with their big blunt fingers resting in his lap like two old dogs. I remember thinking how he loved the water, his boat and how his hands tell the story of his life on the sea their creases, scars, deep lines are story lines. His hands were formed by hard work, always soaked by cold salt water (but not preserved!). Big and quick they knit twine, braid rope, haul nets filled with fish, countless cuts from fileting (sic) knives. Strong and gentle at the same time – hands to fix a doll and to build a boat. Wethered (sic), eroded like the cliffs, old like the drift wood ... tired now, trembling and turning the crinkled thin paper of his worn black Bible ... I can't help but think my grandfather belongs to the sea and the sea to him.

The bell rings to end the period. Outside a herring gull swoops on an empty potato chip bag skittering across the parking lot.

What is happening when Katie responds to the poems as an invocation of her relationship with her grandfather? There seems to be a dynamism, a meeting place between the child and the texts out of which arises the possibility to generate certain pools of experience, knowledge and feeling. It is a relational space, a Gadamerian "fusion of horizons," of sorts, in which, "the reader's world becomes re-woven, and it is this re-weaving of the reader's self that alters the reader's interactions with the world. "It is an infinite chain of significance" (Sumara, 1994, p. 49). At that moment, in that unique situation, Katie is part of the history of the text; she belongs to the poems, and the poems to her. We will return to Katie and her Grade 9 classroom later. But first a clear explication is required of the experiential, life forwarding dimension of the transactive space between reader and text as it is described by reader response theory.

EXPERIENTIAL READER RESPONSE THEORY

Rosenblatt (1995) introduced the term *transaction* to describe the reader-text relationship. The term is generative, inclusive and emerges out of Rosenblatt's idea of *mutualism,* the reader and the text act on each other, "each affecting and conditioning the other" (Karolides, 2000, p. 5):

> Through the medium of words, the text brings into the reader's consciousness certain concepts, certain sensuous experiences, certain images of things, people, actions, scenes. The special meanings, and more particularly, the submerged associations that the words and the images have for the individual reader will largely determine what the work communicates ... The reader brings to the work personality traits, memories of past events, present needs ... and a particular physical condition. These and many other elements in a never-to-be-duplicated combination enter into the reader's relationship with the text. (Rosenblatt 1978, pp. 30, 31)

Rosenblatt's theory, formulated in the 1920s and 30s, is considered today to have been far ahead of its time (Clifford, 1990), as it indicates a vital, dynamic relationship between reader and text. This unique relationship between reader and literary text and the existence of an imaginative, generative space is the central premise of reader response literary theory. Since Rosenblatt's initial theory was introduced other theorists have extended her ideas. Richard Beach (1993) imposes some structure to the loose collection of critics who may be considered to fall under the name "reader response." Beach outlines five theoretical perspectives on response according to how a theorist falls within one of the five primary theoretical orientations; the *textual, psychological, social, cultural* and *experiential.* Experiential theorists focus on the phenomenal nature of readers' engagement or experience with texts. Such theorists are particularly interested in the ways readers identify with characters, visualize images, or construct the world of the text.

Still other theorists have elaborated the notion of "transaction" picking up Rosenblatt's strands and weaving them still further. Sumara (1994, 2000, 2002) puts forward the idea of a complex, evolutionary, intertextual relationality of reader and text as represented by a "commonplace location" (2000, p. 33). This commonplace location does not exist "in" the reader, or "in" the text, but in the swirl and array of experiences, associations, and memories that arise before, during and after the interpretative activity. Sumara posits that engaging with literary texts can be considered a focal practice out of which may emerge deep meaning and personal insight. Engagement with texts results in "associational complexities" (Sumara, 2002, p. xv) that when attended to create transformative opportunities to re-create, re-imagine and re-interpret human identity.

Inquiring further into the transactive space and the experience of literary engagement, Sumara draws on recent research in cognitive science and evolutionary biology. The experience of engagement is viewed through recognition that human perception is inextricably linked to both body and mind. Sumara's theory is firmly grounded in the entwining of the human body "in other bodies; the social, the cultural, the epistemic" (Sumara, 2002, p. 137). In attempting to understand the implications of the science of human perception on the transactive space between reader and text, Sumara probes deeply into the potential of texts or "literary places" to interrupt the everyday, the mundane, and the familiar. Our everyday lives, our daily experiences are most often rendered invisible, precluding the learning of anything new from what is often closest to us. The space of literary engagement can serve to "de-familiarize" the familiar. The Russian critic Victor Shklovsky wrote of Tolstoy's novels as having just this ability to interrupt the everyday, the "invisible":

> After being perceived several times, objects acquire the status of 'recognition.' An object appears before us. We know it's there but we do not see it, and, for that reason, we can know nothing about it ... The achievement of art is the transformation of the object, describing it as though for the first time, communicating its particularities ... The purpose of the image is not to draw our understanding closer to what the image stands for , but rather to allow us to perceive the object in a special way, in short, to lead us to a 'vision' of this object rather than mere 'recognition' (in Masturzo, 2000, p. 132)

How is it possible for literary engagement to allow us to see uniquely, to challenge us in a process of *estrangement*?

THE ECOLOGY OF READER RESPONSE

It is in the lived, embodied dimension of reader response theory that I am most interested and on which, in this study, I will try to elaborate. It is *in* the transactive character of our relationship with a literary text, through the perceiving, emotional, imaginative, thinking, dreaming and embodied encounter that we experience, invent and discover the meanings by which we grow and make sense of the world in which we find ourselves "set down." In the transaction there is an embodied, participatory engagement – contact; ex-change, meeting, transmission, a fusion across difference, an encounter; a relational, interactive understanding that potentially disrupts the belief system of the culture allowing a more authentic self-understanding to arise. The transaction is the experiencing *in* the interaction, the inward sentience, as an internal relationship between symbols and feelings. It is our *being* potentially changed by the transaction with the different space of the text. In the science of ecology the term "ecotone" is used to describe a place where landscapes meet – a field with a forest, the ocean with the land. It is a place of great richness and diversity with a wealth of unique life forms existing as a result of the co-mingling of communities. It is a place where contact yields change. It is as in an intertidal zone where the land and sea merge and meld to create unique life; a fusion-across-difference that is never the same in the ebb and flow of endless flux. So too, I propose, is the space between reader and text and what happens when we live there. Sumara (1994) believes that reading does not only change the way we think and act:

> it affects, in every way, *who we are*. And if reading affects who we are, it necessarily affects what we *know* and what we do. We could say then, that the experience of reading has not only altered us *phenomenologically*, it has altered us *biologically*. (emphasis in original, p. 66)

205

There is a commitment in Sumara's words that meaning is grounded in the life process. The idea of "embodied realism" (Lakoff & Johnson, 1999), or an "intelligent body" (Fisher, 2002), the "felt sense" (Gendlin, 1992b), and the "situational body" (Gendlin, 1997a) all point to a precisely attuned intentional relationship with the world as we experience it from "within." The goal of this inquiry is to better understand literary engagement as nested in a larger web of relations that includes both the cognitive, the biological, even the spiritual. At this point, it is important to consider how reading may be placed within a broader process of a bodily living-in-the-world that includes language and participatory engagement.

THE PHENOMENOLOGY OF LITERARY ENGAGEMENT

Rosenblatt's transactive space is a meeting of the reader and the text; the text brings concepts, images, characters, scenes, emotions and feelings to the reader's consciousness. The reader brings to the text a unique personal history and personality. "These and many other elements in a never-to-be-duplicated combination enter into the reader's relationship with the text" (Rosenblatt, 1995, p. 37). Rosenblatt is aware of the bodily situatedness inherent in reading and response; however it is separated out from the conceptual or emotional. "The reading of any work of literature is of necessity, an individual and unique occurrence involving the mind and emotions of some particular reader" (Rosenblatt, 1995, p. 32). With these words Rosenblatt binds the experience of the reader and text in a dualistic, mind/body split:

> Because the literary work is organized and self-contained, it concentrates our attention and regulates what will enter our consciousness. Out of this arises a sense of an organized structure of *perception and feelings* which constitutes the esthetic experience." (emphasis added, Rosenblatt, 1995, p. 40)

Is it possible to inquire phenomenologically into the experience of the transactive space, into the lived meaning of literary engagement and the "esthetic experience?" In doing so, we must reflect deeply on the fact that we are biological, embodied beings. As such we are always already attuned to Being (Levin, 1985). This embodiment informs our perceptiveness and responsiveness to the world. How might it be possible to elaborate on this "structure of perception and feelings" that, according to Rosenblatt, characterizes the engagement with the literary text?

To help better understand the notion of perception as it relates to experience, I turn to the work of Eugene Gendlin (1981, 1987, 1988, 1991, 1992a, 1992b, 1996, 1997a, 1997b). Gendlin attempts to move beyond perception as a starting point, asserting that it is an ancient but incorrect taken-for-grantedness that experience starts with perception:

> Perception is never first, and never alone. It is not the way we are in our situations. Perception divides your perception of me from mine of you. But interaction is more than two perceptions. And interaction is not inherently divided ... We will move

beyond the subject/object distinction if we become able to speak from how we interact bodily in our situations. (1997a, p. 15)

Gendlin's philosophy, building on the work of Wittgenstein and Heidegger, describes phenomenologically our bodily sense of living in our situations and provides a language and a way of thinking from the implicit felt-sense inherent in our bodily living-in situations. We are challenged to think more creatively and in a fresh way about experiential theories of reader response. It promises to open new concepts and insights while deepening literacy educators understanding of literary engagement, of how literature "works" as a powerful relational, interactive agent of change in students' lives.

When Katie, in her Grade 9 Language Arts class, for instance, responds to the poem as an invocation of her relationship with her grandfather, her response, as Gendlin uses the phrase, "carries forward" an insight, a connection, something new that has never been said before. It is in this sense that literary engagement is at its most profound – in carrying our lives forward in meaningful ways. It is "a coming to understanding" (Gadamer, 1997, p. 446). On this Gadamer writes:

> This is not to be understood as if it were the purpose of language. Coming to understanding is not mere action, a purposeful activity, a setting up of signs through which I will transmit my will to others. Coming to understanding as such, rather, does not need any tools, in the proper sense of the word. It is a life process in which a community of life is lived out. (1997, p. 446)

The "life process" referred to by Gadamer includes the "sensuous experiences," the "physical condition," "the special kind of intense and ordered experience" alluded to by Rosenblatt and other experiential reader response theorists, but never fully described experientially. Gendlin's philosophy helps us think phenomenologically about the nature of the transactive space. His philosophy seeks a way to think about, with the bodily carrying forward, the felt meaning of the body, that which has been hidden, or concealed, by conceptual thought. Gendlin's sensitive phenomenological attention to the "mesh" among body, situation and language may provide a deeply meaningful account of how literature "works," something that is implicitly present in experiential reader response theory, but not clearly explicated. His writing opens up an understanding of how the dynamic, living space between reader and text can carry our lives forward in a process of change and continuity, affecting in every sense who we are. For the purposes of this chapter, it provides a clear and compelling means to think about the creative and generative power of literature to nurture the moral imagination. Understanding this power requires careful description.

LITERARY ENGAGEMENT AND IMPLICIT INTRICACY

Rosenblatt sees the literary text as concentrating our attention and regulating what will enter our consciousness. The text imposes concepts, images, characters and these work with and in "the submerged associations," "the personality traits," "memories of past events," "present needs and preoccupations," "a particular mood

207

of the moment and a particular physical condition" (1995, p. 37) of the reader. According to Rosenblatt, "Just as the personality and concerns of the reader are largely socially acquired and socially patterned, so the literary work, like language itself, is the result of the fact that man is a social being" (1995, p. 34). The idea that social patterns are an order imposed upon humans who are solely molded and made malleable by this imposition is a premise that Gendlin's philosophy sets out to challenge.

Gendlin posits that patterns, concepts, rules, and forms never work alone, but always within a wider more intricate order. Forms and social patterns are incapable of encompassing the intricacy of people and situations. In his thinking, this more intricate order includes social patterns. While the patterns and rules are always at work, they are at work *within* a wider, more intricate, bodily experiencing. Rules and social patterns function within a "wider saying" (Gendlin, 1991):

> Western philosophy ... by overstating the role of forms ... quite lost what is more than form. Everything is taken as ordered by imposed forms, patterns, rules. Most modern philosophers have utterly lost an order of nature, the person, the practice, the body. They deny that anything could have an order of its own. All order is assumed to be entirely imposed by a history, a culture, or a conceptual interpretation ... But what is this imposed order imposed upon? (pp. 24, 25)

Gendlin attempts to use language to describe the "more" than patterns, to elucidate what the intricacy of bodily-felt meaning can bring to theoretical thinking. He is not making an appeal for some "pure" realm of experiencing unaffected by specific social practices and cultural forms. While acknowledging that social patterns, rules, and forms do function even in our deepest and seemingly most private experience, he reminds us that these concepts, social forms, cultural expectations fall short of guiding what we do. These patterns do not work in a one-way determination; something "talks back" (Gendlin, 1991). Everyday we must improvise and create more intricate ways to act in many situations making these situations more intricate than identifiable concepts or patterns.

Experiential reader response theories may be elaborated by being read with a deeper sense of the intricacy of the "more than forms." What is imposed by the text functions in and with our deepest, pre-reflective experience. When I read a poem, the words, the structure, the images, the author's skill are at work ordering my experience. But there is something else at work – something implicit in the situation. It is an implying that is at once "vague and more precise" (Gendlin, 1991, p. 56) – a felt-sense. I have a sense what the poem is saying to me. But how does it say? I re-read the words, the lines, pause at certain phrases; there is a vague sense, something is there; yet the words won't come that will allow me to say it. I re-read; a line is puzzling, confusing; ideas arise, thoughts come. I reject these until the right fit is found. The implying demands, wants, and as Gendlin says, is "vague yet more precise" in its calling forth.

I know I cannot just attribute any meaning to a line from a poem. I may try on different possibilities. But how do I know when I have the possibility that is right? When it is accepted there is a sense, a felt-sense and a change occurs. The implying, the demanding, no longer implies or demands in the same way, but is "carried forward" (Gendlin, 1991, p. 66). The change has been described by Gendlin as becoming "unstuck" (1991, p. 63); the felt-sense carries life forward possibly into a deeper intricacy always leading further into itself.

Perhaps the poem, line, or word poses no puzzlement or confusion. I read, understand or simply dismiss any feeling or implying that may arise. Much of what I read during the day is this type of experience. It is straight-forward, boring, irrelevant, or read for information purposes. Most often it passes right by. But sometimes what I read unsettles, provokes, results in a gnawing, grasping, a vague, indefinable sense that I can choose to stay with, inquire into, or dismiss. However, Gendlin reminds us "a feeling is never there for nothing ... a feeling is an interaction in some situation ... it is a body-sense that is unclear in form but implicitly more precise than emotions" (1997a, p. 15). This body-sense adds intricacy to Rosenblatt's "structure of perception and feelings which constitutes for us the esthetic experience" (1995, p. 40). Gendlin reminds us that it is an old and false assumption that experience begins with perception. "Perception is never first, never alone" (Gendlin, 1997a, p. 15). It is not the primary way we are in our situations; we exist in terms of living and interacting. I sense my situation – my whole situation – and perception is part of a wider body-environment interaction. To illustrate this idea, Gendlin uses the example of seeing a person in the street, but you don't remember who it is. The person gives you a familiar feeling. You know that you know but the person's identity escapes you. You know by the gnawing feeling in your body. "That gnawing feeling does know. Your body knows who it is" (1997a, p. 16). That knowing is the implying, the felt-sense, a whole sense in your body. The body sense and the situation are not two separate things. We are in the situation; the situation is in us. Concepts and patterns are implicit in the situation that is always already more than any number of details.

If we read the word "text" in place of Gendlin's "situation" we may be led into a deeper sense of the experience of literary engagement. Texts are indeed "situations," not existing without readers who come to them; as Albert Borgmann (1997) said, "a text by itself is helpless" (p. 117). Our body-sense happens in, is part of, makes and re-makes the text. Body-sense and text carry each other forward. If we are willing to stay with the feeling, the body-sense, for it is never present before us, rather it requires us to "go into a murky sort of down and in" (Gendlin, 1997a, p. 16) perhaps something new can come from the body-sense. How can this description provide more to the transactive space of reader-response theory as it contributes the bodily-implying in and of that space? The feeling arising out of this space and so often referred to by Rosenblatt and other experiential reader response theorists is now fleshed out, so to speak. It is a felt-sense, the murky implying that is located spatially in the center of the body. This uneasiness, warmth, fluttery, or jumpy sense or quality "is not subjective, not just internal, not private, it is the implicit situation" (Gendlin, 1991, p. 82). The body has the situation implicit in it. We can access the felt-sense to inquire into it by quieting the conceptual mind.

The text demands, wants something, some sense, implying feelings that carry forward in the same direction. Possibilities arise, images, memories, connections, narratives, and thoughts move the sense forward, but not forward in a spatial direction. All my previous connections, possibilities, images that come out of the text are like steps that are not wrong, or incorrect, even as they are rejected by the strength of the implying. This is not to be understood as a linear or logical progression toward the "right" answer. The word "right" comes to mean something else. The steps, however, are life forwarding - forwarding in the direction of the implying. The implying evoked by the poem wants, demands, and I just cannot *will* a meaning; it must come, emerge, follow out of the progression and "make sense." When this happens I know it; I feel it; I become "unstuck" in a sense. The poem, line, or phrase seems true, right in some way, and there is a relief, an excitement, as meaning is carried forward. Of course this is not to say that the "change" will always come and that we will become unstuck. The implying is very precise and I may choose the next step and therefore go wrong or I can dismiss the implying altogether.

TEXTS AS 'SITUATIONS'

When we speak of *interpreting* stories, *analyzing* poems, *finding* meaning and themes in poems, plays or essays, our language may be concealing the intricate, embodied nature of the reader-text relationship. The matrix present in the relationship between the text, the reader and language can say something about how a response is evoked, how words come. A short story, for instance, is more than a series of words, sentences, paragraphs, details, or narrative techniques. When we read we enter the story on the level of general impression. The story happens, when we are involved, in much the same way as any situation happens. Our situations are far more intricately ordered than our conceptual patterns, or even as given to us by our five senses. When reading we may be aware of literary techniques and devices, but our experiencing is always much more. In the moment, as I read, I am taken up in the story, in a general impression. Later, I may reflect on the many different details. But these 'many details' were implicit in the impression before they were noticed.

Gendlin (1991) calls this a pre-separated multiplicity. Each situation is not one or many different details and most are never separate. They function implicitly – "pre-separatedly." I can reflect later to separate them out – but each detail, image, phrase, action can specify itself further and further. The most minute detail can evoke a further implying – a felt-sense that can carry forward into meaning, insight, into something new. Each little detail is a pre-separated multiplicity also.

The felt-sense, an implicitly intricate body-sense functions in every situation in a highly ordered way. In everything we do we are always bodily aware; there is an implicit sense of the whole intricacy of each situation. We can physically sense our body's implying the situation. "And we can make the transition from the unreflected to the reflected body-sense anytime" (Gendlin, 1991, p. 90). We can focus on this body-sense, stay with its implying to move toward a deeper self-understanding. This attunement can be taught as a means of contact and to feel in a body-sensible way the gift of our embodiment (Gendlin, 1981; Perl, 2004). When we focus on our own body of experience, it never leaves us unchanged. We reflect on this experience, this body-sense, as it is lived and felt and it moves our lives forward within the organic, self-ordering wisdom of the body.

When reading I am struck or touched in some way by a word, image or detail and stop to re-read, or ponder. My eyes come up from the page to stare out the window; they look without seeing. The stopping, the staring in space, implies what will happen. The felt-sense adjudicates my response to it. But to reiterate, this is not a sequence of steps to be followed, a logical progression, for each possibility that enters into my pondering potentially re-makes the "possibility system." My stopping is a demanding, but not an indeterminate one, because there is a precision or "truth" which must be met if I am to carry forward and meet the implying. I deliberate, further possibilities can be implied; I can stay with the implying or move on – and I can go wrong. But I can't "give" meaning, or simply add interpretation as if the text is mere Silly Putty out of which I can mold or stamp on whatever meaning I like. The implied intricacy of the text is "crossed" with the implied intricacy of my felt sense to create a demanding truth that can carry forward.

The transactive space of reader response may be seen as truly mutualistic, as Rosenblatt suggested when the processes of engagement and involvement are inclusive of the responsive order – a deepening sense of our biological nature as truly embodied beings.

LANGUAGE COMES IN THE BODY

It is important to see that this "crossed" sense-making occurs implicitly. As I read the poem many possibilities are implied, but their implying is also "the focal" implying of the next one. In life we do not usually stop to select from possibilities – we act, we do, we "decide" rather seamlessly or pre-reflectively. This is what Gendlin calls "focaled steps" (1991, p. 101). He uses the example of a common situation- smiling or saying hello to a passerby in the hallway. Without thinking, the tone of the hello and the nuanced quality of the smile is focaled from our history and recent interaction with that person. The focaled step forms out of the crossing – out of the implicit intricacy of the situation that the body knows. As the example illustrates most often the next step just comes and we are saying or doing it before we are even aware – we just "say" or "do."

But sometimes no next step comes. There may be confusion, puzzlement – and then a felt-sense forms out of the confusion. "The coming of a felt-sense is a large change from the confused condition. We feel relief. Now in a way we know what to do, but the words and actions have not actually formed yet" (Gendlin, 1991, p. 101). The felt-sense is a step, a crossing, a making sense; a decision comes. Having to decide means we don't know. We pay attention to the felt-sense and that will "imply further doable steps" (1991, p. 100). Gendlin warns that focaling can miss much and does not include all considerations of everything relevant.

211

When something we think, hear, or read makes sense, this sense-making is a fresh focaling that carries forward the implicit intricacy of the whole context. We cannot *will* something to make sense. The focaling has to come. It is in this coming that lies the bodily character of language, action, thought and images. They are not separated dimensions. All are "crossed" in the making of one next implied speech, action, thought or image. This is why Gendlin asserts we cannot begin with perception, but we must move away from the subject/object approach that comes from perception. He says, "Perception always divides what is seemingly over there from a perceiver here. Perception is never first and never alone. It is not the main way we are in situations" (Gendlin, 1991, p. 105). We are encouraged to move beyond the subject/object distinction by becoming able to speak from how we interact bodily in situations. His attention to experiential detail is the greatest strength of his work. It is this attention to experiential detail that provides a language by which we may describe phenomenologically the intricacy of the transactive space that is at the center of experiential reader response theory. Gendlin provides us with a language for how, ostensibly, the literary text "works." His theory and practice of language speaks to and can be applied to literary engagement and how it can be placed within a participative, bodily engagement. Gendlin's philosophy promises to deepen our phenomenological understanding of the nurturing the moral imagination in children by bringing this phenomenological understanding to bear on the process of literary engagement and by focusing our attention on the living responsiveness of the intelligent body precisely attuned for relationship with the world. Gendlin's work has profound implications for helping children experience their natural "intertwining" (Levin, 1982, p. 293), a deeply sensed interdependency and kinship with a larger living field that they can find within themselves. It promises to contribute to a revitalized understanding of experiential theories of reader response as it grounds language in the body and moves us toward a deeper sense of a "living literacy" – one that is embodied and honours our inherent need for relationship and belonging; one that is implicitly life-affirming.

And so I return, a last time, to Katie sitting by the window in the grade 9 language arts classroom. Outside the late November light hardens as the wind and tides obey the pull and tilt of the planet in an eternal rhythmic turn of the season, cycling as nearly every system does, from the human body to a galactic cluster.

> Today her body deepened
> As she picked a late flower
> And behind her
> The dust rose on the backroad
> Like a remembrance of her life.

The words, contained in Allan Cooper's poem call up, lift out, a memory, an association, a felt-sense. "I can't help thinking that my grandfather belongs to the sea and the sea to him," the girl writes. She describes her grandfather's hands as being "eroded like the cliffs" and "old like the driftwood." Does her language reveal a permeability of boundaries, a breaking down of perceived separateness, an identification with the greater rhythms of life? Her grandfather (and, presumably, she too) emerges as part of a greater community, a common ground or kinship. There is also a challenge in her words to a Sartrean existential isolation that becomes an unreality when we realize ourselves a part of larger life forces, when we discover the subtle organizing patterns of the universe and move toward a resonant relationship with them. The young writer chooses the image of her grandfather "turning the crinkled thin pages of his worn black Bible." Could this be a sense of her grandfather's life as an infusion into greater life processes that confront death? Katie's short piece is imbued with a completeness, a spirituality that touches on, and in some way, brings to the fore the interplay between birth and death in the larger stream of life.

It could be argued that the girl's response is not *about* the poem at all. There is no analysis of metaphor or personification in her response, or word choice, repetition, poetic style, form or structure. The response does reflect, however, the "lived–through" experience and the richness of the space between the young reader and the text as it emerges in the moment. Iser (1978) says of this experience, "The significance of the work, then, does not lie in the meaning sealed within the text, but in the fact that meaning brings out what had been previously sealed within us" (p. 157). The poem is generative; it serves to nurture and encourage understandings that lay within the student as she wrote "from" (Probst, 2000) the poem to call forth personal memories, associations, anecdotes and meanings.

When the teacher reads the lines from the second poem by John S. Mitchell, he is allowing for the voices of other presences, for a sentient landscape to emerge into a growing field of significant relations.

> boats upside down
> on red wharf
> cliffs surround and close
> centuries of eyes
> in each eye
> whispers and whispers
> in me

Katie responds with the beginnings of a beautiful piece of writing that nests her grandfather in an intimate interconnection with the life force of the ocean. The space of contact, of experience, between child, teacher and text is one of mediation, a place of exchange, a flow-through of the voices of the young and the old. The poet Gary Snyder (1990) writes, "In this huge old occidental culture our teaching elders are books. *Books are our grandparents*" (emphasis added, p. 61). Rachel Carson (1964), the pre-eminent marine biologist, who ushered in our contemporary environmental movement with the publication of her book *Silent Spring* in 1962, wrote in a short essay *The Sense of Wonder* (1964) of the pedagogical significance of the adult in the life of a child:

If a child is to keep alive his inborn sense of wonder he needs the companionship of at least one adult who can share it, re-discovering with him the joy, excitement, and mystery of the world we live in. (p. 7)

Perhaps, then, it is perfectly fitting that the young girl chose to respond to the poem by writing about her grandfather. It is a response that speaks to the intergenerational dynamic that renews the life process. It helps the child focus on what she has always already "known" and in its coming it is bound to carry the child's life forward, bound to educe and bound to eventuate a deeper self-understanding through the force of moral imagination. Simone Weil (1987) describes the imagination as, "a knot of action and reaction that attaches us to the world" (p. 50). Katie seems firmly anchored. Gendlin's theory of embodiment and felt-sense allows us to describe phenomenally the dynamic 'knots' of imagination, text and body that help us think about how literature 'works' and thereby articulate more fully and accurately its value and importance in the curriculum.

CONCLUSION

The prominent place of literature in the school curriculum has been justified by its capacity to foster articulation of, and reflection on, the complexities of life mediated through language. Literature creatively engages students in a *transaction* driven by their personal purposes and experiences that leads to the construction of new, alternative voices and perspectives. Children can envision different ways of being that move their lives forward. Literature is said to develop the moral imagination. Phenomenology can allow us to better understand the experiencing interaction of the transactive space created between reader and text.

Currently, reader response literary theory is central to guiding the literary experiences of children in schools. Reader response theories posit that the relationship between reader and text is dynamic. However, for decades, the study of literature and literary engagement has been understood as a passive act. The text lies before us inert, awaiting interpretation as the reader opens it up to discover what the author has hidden inside. Reader response theory positions the reading act as a co-mingling of reader and text. The literary engagement of children and texts can be better understood through the philosophy of Eugene Gendlin whose work allows us to think phenomenologically about the nature of the transactive space between reader and text providing a fresh and meaningful account of how literature 'works,' something that is implicit in reader response literary theory, but not clearly explicated. Phenomenology allows us to grasp this potentially transformative experience to open it up and describe how texts speak to us and how we in turn respond out of a space of bodily implying that moves our lives forward in an array of possibilities, images, memories, connections and insights. Phenomenology calls forth the intricate, embodied nature of the reader - text relationship allowing literacy educators a deeper understanding of how texts speak to children as it describes the lived, felt sense that orders the reading experience of children who respond as embodied beings precisely attuned for relationship with the world.

REFERENCES

Beach, R. (1993). *A teacher's introduction to reader response theories.* Urbana, Illinois: NCTE.

Borgmann, A. (1992). *Crossing the postmodern divide.* Chicago: University of Chicago Press.

Carson, R. (1964). *The sense of wonder.* New York: Harper Collins.

Clifford, J. (Ed.), (1990). *The experience of reading: Louise Rosenblatt and reader–response theory.* Portsmouth, NH: Boynton-Cook.

Cooper, A. (1983). Watching my grandmother pick a late flower. In B. Hatt (Ed.), *Easterly: 60 Atlantic writers* (p. 133). Don Mills: Academic Press.

Dewey, J. (1916). *Democracy and education.* New York: Macmillan.

Fisher, A. (2002). *Radical ecopsychology: Psychology in the service of life.* Albany, NY: SUNY Press.

Gadamer, H. (1997). *Truth and method* (2nd ed.). New York: Continuum.

Gendlin, E. (1981). *Focusing.* New York: Bantam.

Gendlin, E. (1987). A philosophical critique of the concept of narcissism: The significance of the awareness movement. In D. Levin (Ed.), *Pathologies of the modern self: Postmodern studies on narcissism, schizophrenia, and depression* (pp. 48-63). New York: New York University Press.

Gendlin, E. (1988). Dwelling. In H. Silverman, A. Mickunas, T. Kisiel & A. Lingis (Eds.), *The horizons of continental philosophy: Essays on Husserl, Heidegger, and Merleau-Ponty.* Boston: Kluwer Academic Publishers.

Gendlin, E. (1991). Thinking beyond patterns: Body, language, situation. In B. den Ouden & M. Moen (Eds.), *The presence of feeling in thought.* New York: Peter Lang.

Gendlin, E. (1992a). Befindlicheit: Heidegger and the philosophy of psychology. In K. Hoeller (Ed.), *Heidegger and psychology.* New York: Brill.

Gendlin, E. (1992b). The wider role of bodily sense in thought and language. In M. Sheets-Johnston (Eds.), *Giving the body its due* (pp. 192-207) Albany, NY: SUNY.

Gendlin, E. (1996). *Focusing-oriented psychotherapy.* New York: Guilford.

Gendlin, E. (1997a). How philosophy cannot appeal to experience, and how it can. In D. Levin (Ed.), *Language beyond postmodernism: Saying and thinking in Gendlin's philosophy.* Evanston, IL: Northwestern University Press.

Gendlin, E. (1997b). The responsive order: A new empiricism. *Man and World, 30,* 383-411.

Greene, M. (1973). *Teacher as stranger.* Belmont, CA: Wadsworth Publishing.

Howard, P. (2007). The pedagogy of place: Reinterpreting ecological education through the language arts. *Diaspora, Indigenous, and Minority Education: An International Journal, 1*(2).

Iser, W. (1978). *The act of reading: A theory of aesthetic response.* Baltimore: Johns Hopkins.

Karolides, N. (Ed.) (2002). *Reader response in secondary and college classrooms.* Mahwah, NJ: Lawrence Erlbaum Publishing.

Lakoff, G. & Johnson, M. (1999). *Philosophy in the flesh: The embodied mind and its challenge to western philosophy.* New York: Basic.

Langer, J. (1992). Discussion as exploration: Literature and the horizon of possibilities. In G. Newell & R. Durst (Eds.), *Exploring texts: The role of discussion and writing in teaching and learning literature* (pp. 23-44). Norwood, MA: Christopher Gordon.

Levin, D. (1982). Moral education: The body's felt sense of value. *Teachers College Record, 84*(2), 283-300.

Masturzo, H. (2000). With my artist's eye I see ... Encounters of estrangement with natural forms. In C. McEwan & M. Statman (Eds.), *The alphabet of the trees: A guide to nature writing* (pp. 132-137). New York: Teachers and Writers Collaborative.

Mitchell, J. (1983). Whispers. In E. Norman, J. Warr, & R. Goulding (Eds.), *Openings: Literature of Newfoundland and Labrador Book 1.* St. John's, NL: Breakwater.

Moyers, B. (1999). *Fooling with words: A celebration of poets and their craft.* New York: William Morrow.

Noddings, N. (1991). Stories in dialogue: caring and interpersonal reasoning. In. C. Witherall & N. Noddings (Eds.), *Stories lives tell: Narrative and dialogue in education* (pp. 157-170). New York: Teachers College Press.

Noddings, N. (2002). *Educating moral people: A caring alternative to character education.* New York: Teachers College Press.

Perl, S. (2004). *Felt sense: Writing with the body.* Portsmouth, NH: Boynton-Cook.

Probst, R. (2000.) Writing from, of, and about literature. In N. Karolides (Ed.), *Reader response in secondary and college classroom,* 2nd ed. (pp. 61-74) Mahwah, New Jersey: Lawrence Erlbaum Associates.

Rosenblatt, L. (1978). *The reader, the text, the poem: The transactional theory of literary work.* Carbondale: Southern Illinois University Press.

Rosenblatt, L. (1995). *Literature as exploration,* 5th ed. New York: Modern Association.

Snyder, G. (1990). *The practice of the wild.* New York: North Point Press.

Sumara, D. (1994). The literary imagination and the curriculum. Unpublished doctoral dissertation, University of Alberta, Edmonton, Alberta, Canada.

Sumara, D. (2002a). Challenging the "I" that we are: Creating liberating constraints with reader response practices. In M. Hunsberger & G. Labercane (Eds.), *Making meaning in the response-based classroom.* Boston: Allyn & Bacon.

Sumara, D. (2002b). *Why reading literature in school still matters: Imagination, interpretation, insight.* Mahwah, New Jersey: Lawrence Erlbaum Associates, Inc.

Weil, S. (1987). *Formative writings 1929-1941.* D. Tuck (Ed.) (D. McFarland trans.) London: Routledge.

ABOUT THE EDITORS

Norm Friesen is Canada Research Chair in Curriculum and New Media at Thompson Rivers University in Kamloops, British Columbia, Canada. Dr. Friesen is the author of the recent monograph, *The Place of the Classroom and the Space of the Screen: Relational Pedagogy and Internet Technology* (Peter Lang, 2011).

Carina Henriksson is a Senior Lecturer in Education at the Linnaeus University, Växjö, Sweden. Dr. Henriksson teaches and undertakes research in the areas of pedagogics and educational sciences, with a particular focus on the lived experience of school failure and methods of phenomenological writing.

Tone Saevi is a professor at the School of Education in the Norwegian Teachers' Academy. Dr. Saevi teaches pedagogy and philosophy of education, and her research focuses on phenomenological pedagogy, the phenomenology of disability, and pedagogy and film.